LABOR RELATIONS AND PUBLIC POLICY SERIES

REPORT NO. 10

THE DAVIS-BACON ACT

by

ARMAND J. THIEBLOT, JR.

with the assistance of

JAMES R. BELLUNE
GEORGE BUCKINGHAM

and

ROBERT G. LINEY

AF694141

LEGES SINE MORIBUS VANAE

Published by

INDUSTRIAL RESEARCH UNIT
The Wharton School
University of Pennsylvania

Distributed by

University of Pennsylvania Press
Philadelphia, Pennsylvania 19174

Copyright © 1975 by the Trustees of the University of Pennsylvania
Library of Congress Catalog Card Number 74-21729
MANUFACTURED IN THE UNITED STATES OF AMERICA
ISBN: 0-8122-9085-2

Foreword

In 1968, the Industrial Research Unit inaugurated its Labor Relations and Public Policy monographs as a means of examining issues and stimulating discussions in the complex and controversial areas of collective bargaining and the regulation of labor management disputes. The first four studies in the series dealt with aspects of the National Labor Relations Board and its administration. The fifth report contained papers read at the fiftieth anniversary conference of the Industrial Research Unit, at which many aspects of labor relations and public policy were discussed. The sixth monograph—*Welfare and Strikes*—was the first empirical analysis of the impact of government payments to strikers on the American collective bargaining system and on the settlement of disputes under that system. The seventh in the series, *Opening the Skilled Construction Trades to Blacks,* was the initial attempt to determine, by detailed field analysis, what actually occurs when the federal government insists that the skilled construction trades make a serious effort to increase the number and percentage of Negroes in their work force. The eighth and ninth in this series, *NLRB Regulation of Election Conduct,* and *The NLRB and Management Decision Making,* both published earlier this year, marked a return to the general subject matter of the first four monographs. Future monographs will also involve analyses of various NLRB policies and deal with other public policy issues as well.

This study, *The Davis-Bacon Act,* No. 10 in the series, again breaks new ground, for despite several shorter works, government reports, and congressional hearings, no recent thorough study of the act and its administration is available. The Davis-Bacon Act is a relatively obscure law, although it was enacted more than forty years ago. Its administration establishes minimum wages in the construction industry at levels deemed "prevailing." The impact of such wage determinations is felt throughout the construction industry even though the act applies only to federal funded construction. And, because of the size and pervasive nature of construction, it seems likely that Davis-

Bacon wage determinations affect wages paid in other industries as well.

The study reviews carefully the history of the act, the literature pertaining to it, and the various arguments pro and con; examines the act's administration and a number of case studies of wage determination; and analyzes the results of a questionnaire sent to 10,000 general and specialty contractors. The conclusion reached is that the Davis-Bacon Act adds fuel to the inflationary fires in the economy, that it benefits a few at the expense of the many, and that it should be either repealed or drastically amended.

These conclusions are hardly novel. Except for the construction labor unions, which are the prime groups supporting the act, nearly everyone who has examined the law has either reached similar conclusions or proposed substantial modifications in the act or in its administration. Academicians, businessmen and business organizations, contractors' groups, the Comptroller-General of the United States, and others, as the literature review contained herein clearly demonstrates, are among the act's critics. Perhaps the greatest contribution of this study is that it summarizes the findings regarding the act and points up their consistency.

* * *

This study grew out of a larger project which is examining manpower and public policy in open-shop construction, a virtually untouched field in which the majority of construction personnel are employed. Our first effort in this area, *Manpower in Homebuilding: A Preliminary Analysis,* by Howard G. Foster (Manpower and Human Resources Studies, No. 3), was recently published. The major volume on open-shop construction is scheduled for spring 1975. It was planned originally to devote a chapter in that book to the impact of the Davis-Bacon Act on open-shop construction. After that research commenced, however, the Chamber of Commerce of the United States offered to provide a grant to develop a full-scale study of the act. We were, of course, aware that the Chamber, like most business organizations, has gone on record in favor of repeal of the act, and therefore sought and received assurances that this grant (the first ever received by the Industrial Research Unit from the Chamber) would be made with the clear understanding that our only obligation to the Chamber would be to complete the study, and to provide the Chamber with 25 copies of the monograph. Our relations with the Chamber throughout the study have been no different from that which has prevailed with foundation and government grantors, and no attempt has been made by the Chamber to interfere with the authors or with the administration, the methodology, the procedures, or the conclusions of the study. As in all Industrial Research Unit projects, the responsibility for the research and writing is vested solely in the senior author; the views expressed are solely his and are not to be attributed to the grantor of funds, to the University of Pennsylvania, or to the organization with which the author is affiliated, in this case the University of Maryland.

In order further to assure that this study would meet the high research standards of the Industrial Research Unit, two prominent outside economists were requested to read and to comment upon the manuscript: Professor John P. Gould, Graduate School of Business, University of Chicago, who himself has authored a monograph dealing with the act, and Dr. George H. Hildebrand, Maxwell M. Upson Professor of Economics and Industrial Relations, Cornell University. Both made constructive suggestions to improve the study and strongly recommended publication.

The principal author of this study, Dr. Armand J. Thieblot, Jr., is Associate Professor of Management, University of Maryland. Dr. Thieblot is a graduate of Princeton University, received his M.B.A. from the Wharton Graduate Division, University of Pennsylvania, and his Ph.D. also from the University of Pennsylvania. He is co-author of *Negro Employment in Finance* and of *Welfare and Strikes,* both previously published by the Industrial Research Unit.

Those assisting Dr. Thieblot are all graduate students. James R. Bellune, a Ph.D. student at the University of Pennsylvania, drafted Appendix A dealing with the construction industry background, and the case studies involving Delta Engineering Company and Mountain Park Dam, and summarized the case studies originally prepared by the General Accounting Office. Robert G. Liney, an M.B.A. candidate in The Wharton School, handled the statistical and computer work involved in assembling and tabulating the results of the contractor questionnaire; and George Buckingham, a Ph.D. candidate at the University of Maryland, assisted in the writing of the chapter on administrative organization and in the analysis of bids received during the period of Davis-Bacon supervision. Others who assisted in the project include Mrs. Joan L. McGeorge, who typed the manuscript; Mrs. Jane W. Brown and Miss Sandra Dechert, who edited it; Miss Elsa Klemp, who checked the tables; and Mrs. Margaret E. Doyle, Office Manager, Industrial Research Unit, who handled numerous administrative details. In addition, many persons from government, industry, associations, and unions gave freely of their time for interviews. Since many consented to discuss the issues only if their participation remained confidential, no list of those whose assistance was indispensible can be presented.

HERBERT R. NORTHRUP, *Director*
Industrial Research Unit
The Wharton School
University of Pennsylvania

Philadelphia
January 1975

TABLE OF CONTENTS

LIST OF TABLES

LIST OF FIGURES

CHAPTER I

Introduction

It is fair to say that the Davis-Bacon Act is an obscure piece of legislation. But its obscurity does not detract from its significance. Under Davis-Bacon provisions, contractors doing work in which the federal government has certain financial interests must pay their employees, in each job category, wage rates and fringe benefits which are no less than those prescribed by the U.S. Department of Labor. Wage rates so prescribed are those found or determined by the Department of Labor to be prevailing for similar types of construction in the locality where the government work is to be done. Thus, the Davis-Bacon Act is a minimum wage law under which a different, specific minimum is set for each classification of workers in each locality for all types of construction for every job undertaken. Government-sponsored construction is currently going on at a rate of about $40 billion per year, so the task performed by the Davis-Bacon Act is a large one.

By American labor legislation standards, Davis-Bacon is an old law. It was passed in 1931, preceding the New Deal, when most of the laws which established the general framework within which labor relations are conducted came into being. Its purpose was to protect local construction wage standards from predatory, itinerant contractors who were taking advantage of the oversupply of labor (relative to the depressed business conditions of the period) by importing workers at very low wage rates to work on government jobs. They could underbid the local contractors for this kind of work because of their low wage rates. As business conditions worsened with the depression, the potential threat to local wage rates, and in particular to negotiated rates, intensified. Public clamor for Congress to take action increased, and the Davis-Bacon Act was the response. In passing it, Congress created the first federal law regulating the wages of nongovernment employees.[1]

---

[1] As we shall note in following chapters, the word "itinerant" is a pejorative one. There seems to be no reason why local contractors should be pro-

The functions of the Davis-Bacon Act were not pre-empted by the general minimum wage requirements of the Fair Labor Standards Act when that act was passed in 1938. There was no need for it to do so. Construction workers came under both, but because the Fair Labor Standards Act required a nationwide single minimum and Davis-Bacon a local prevailing wage, Davis-Bacon requirements could not be less stringent. So, within the segment of the construction industry to which it applies, the Davis-Bacon Act will always have precedence over the minimum wage laws, and its rates will always determine the job rates. To this extent, Davis-Bacon may be considered a "superminimum" wage law.[2]

The Davis-Bacon Act itself is misleadingly simple; it is less than three pages long, including the major amendments which were made to it in 1935, 1940, and 1964. Its over-all intent is clear enough (although some argue that its need died with the depression and its purpose was absorbed by the Fair Labor Standards Act), but it is immensely difficult to obtain any sort of consensus about the act's implementation among those responsible for administering it and those who must abide by its provisions. How should "prevailing wage" be defined? What is "similar construction"? Where is the "locality of the work"? What workmen are included in a particular job category? How should rates set by the Department of Labor be verified? How should its decisions be contested or appealed?

Almost from the day of its passage, questions similar to these have surrounded the Davis-Bacon Act with controversy. Considering the importance of the act to the construction industry and the nation's economy, one finds it somewhat remarkable that the controversy, although frequent and widespread, has been very low key. Seldom has the Davis-Bacon Act been brought to the attention of the general public. Perhaps this situation is understandable because the nature of the act does not excite crowds. But other factors, as well, are worth considering.

---

tected against competition any more than local manufacturers, local storekeepers, or local professors are.

[2] There are three superminimum wage laws besides Davis-Bacon. One, for airline pilots and co-pilots, is part of the Civil Aeronautics Act of 1938 (Section 401-L). The second is the Walsh-Healey Public Contracts Act of 1936. This act covers workmen on government contracts for the manufacture or furnishing of materials or supplies and as legislation, has had a checkered career. The third is the O'Hara-McNamara Services Act of 1965, covering workmen providing services under contract to the government.

Davis-Bacon applies only to contractors. And among contractors, it affects only those who are working on or who are interested in working on government-sponsored construction projects. Even among the members of this group, its impact falls mostly on the open-shop contractors. A moment's reflection reveals the reason. In most cases where differences exist between union or negotiated wage rates and those paid by open-shop contractors, the union rates are higher. If, for some particular job, Davis-Bacon prevailing rates are set at or below the lower open-shop rate, no effect on the competitive positions of union and open-shop firms results. Each may continue its established wage rates, and neither can complain of competitive changes, because no changes have been effected. But if, on the other hand, Davis-Bacon prevailing rates are set at the union scale or somewhere in between the open-shop scale and the union scale, then open-shop contractors will have to raise pay rates in order for their workmen to be employed on the project. Although this situation should create, for the open-shop firm, no problem with the immediate job involved (the government picks up the additional tab), it might well cause disruptions in the firm's relations with its employees—particularly if not all of them are assigned to the Davis-Bacon job—and affect its future work patterns. In addition, the competitive situation would be altered to the relative disadvantage of the open-shop firm.[3]

Only when the Davis-Bacon minimum rates are set higher than the union rates would both union and open-shop firms be affected. But this situation would require a very unusual circumstance, and it is not often seen. So, typically, with the exception of general problems of administrative cost, contractor complaints about the Davis-Bacon Act come from those open-shop contractors who are large enough and interested enough in government work to try to obtain it, but who find the predetermined wage rate schedules disruptive to their work relations. There are exceptions, but these typical characteristics require one further condition: the contractor complaining about, challenging, or protesting Davis-Bacon must be willing to bear the expense and effort of doing it from motives that border on the altruistic. He will derive no identifiable benefit from his activities. In the most common type of case—a protest of a rate

---

[3] Classification of employees and training patterns may also have to be changed by open-shop firms to accord with Davis-Bacon requirements. See Chapter V.

determination, for example—the administrative rules understandably require the protest to have been lodged some time before the bids are opened. But a particular contractor protesting the rate determination in a timely fashion, even if successful, will have no assurance of submitting the low bid or being awarded the job. This circumstance again is perfectly understandable, but it leaves the contractor little motivation to protest.

In this context, perhaps it is surprising that there is controversy about the Davis-Bacon Act at all, rather than surprising that there has not been more. But, in fact, here as elsewhere, some businessmen will fight an issue for the principle involved.

Of course, others besides the contractors themselves watch the operations of the act and raise questions about it. Contractors' trade associations, like the Associated Builders and Contractors, the Associated General Contractors, the National Association of Home Builders, or the American Road Builders Association; subcontractor associations for certain specialty trades; general organizations like the Chamber of Commerce of the United States and the Business Roundtable; and similar groups have members who are deeply involved with Davis-Bacon and who are affected as a class by the operations of the act. One or another of these associations has been involved with almost all Davis-Bacon appeals and with providing testimony to the various congressional hearings about the act which have been held every few years.

Individual unions or the AFL-CIO have also, from time to time, participated in the hearings or taken appeals. However, because the unions are generally content with the act, their involvement with it has been much less, and they seem content to keep a low profile.

Disinterested observers of the act and its operations include members of government agencies, other than the Department of Labor, and academicians who have evaluated the act for its economic and societal impact. A fair number of such studies have been undertaken during the act's history; references to the most important of these studies can be found in the footnotes. Those done by the General Accounting Office, and by Professors Damodar Gujarathi, John P. Gould, Ronald G. Ehrenberg, and David B. Johnson are the most recent. Indeed, although the contractors who are directly subject to the act have not often protested it, enough others have to have provided some guidance concerning the critical issues.

SCOPE AND ORGANIZATION

Under the guidance just mentioned, this study seeks to provide an over-all understanding of the Davis-Bacon Act, its operations, and its administration. The study is arranged in sequence following a logical progression of questions about the act. The questions are listed below, followed by the chapter number in which they are answered.

* What is the Davis-Bacon Act, and what is it supposed to do? (Chapters II and III)
* How is it administered? (Chapter IV)
* Are its administrative problems significant? (Chapter V)
* What costs are associated with the act, and what is its impact on the economy? (Chapter VI)
* In spite of its problems, does it do what it is supposed to do, and does it continue to serve a societally useful function? (Chapter VIII)
* How do contractors who are subject to the act feel about it? (Chapter IX)

In addition, Chapter VII provides several case examples of the situations found in Chapters V and VI, and Chapter X suggests conclusions and recommendations. A brief introduction to the nature of the construction industry is provided in Appendix A. Appendix B contains a copy of the Davis-Bacon Act. Appendix C lists the various federal statutes requiring the payment of prevailing wages under the auspices of the act. State wage provisions similar to the Davis-Bacon Act are listed in Appendix D. A sample survey questionnaire is contained in Appendix E, and an example of a Davis-Bacon Act wage determination is presented in Appendix F.

CHAPTER II

History of the Davis-Bacon Act

The Davis-Bacon Act, calling for payment of prevailing wage rates to laborers and mechanics engaged on construction projects for the United States government, was passed in 1931. Therefore, it preceded the New Deal and was an early example of federal involvement in social and labor legislation. It was the first federal wage law to apply to nongovernment workers.

BACKGROUND AND PHILOSOPHY

Early federal labor laws were almost always anticipated by state statutes, and this was also the case with the Davis-Bacon Act. The first state to enact a prevailing wage law for state construction, Kansas, passed it in 1891. The main purpose of this law was to close loopholes in the state's then-new eight-hour law by prohibiting contractors from scaling down wages, as well as hours, when the shorter workday was mandated. Similar laws followed in New York in 1897, Oklahoma in 1909, Idaho in 1911, Arizona in 1912, New Jersey in 1913, and Massachusetts in 1914.[4]

Following the earliest of these state actions, congressional hearings on maintaining local labor standards on construction were held beginning in 1898,[5] but neither from these nor from subsequent hearings in 1927, 1928, and 1930 did legislation result. As late as January 10, 1931, the comptroller general under the Hoover administration expressed his opinion that a prevailing wage rate law would conflict with the requirements for minimum bidding as follows:

---

[4] David B. Johnson, "Prevailing Wage Legislation in the States," *Monthly Labor Review* 84, No. 8 (August 1961): 840.

[5] W. S. Price, "A Review of the Application of the Davis-Bacon Act," *Labor Law Journal* 14 (July 1963): 614.

> However desirable the contrary may be, it seems clear that in the present state of law the proposal to fix by contract the minimum rate of wages the contractor must pay his employees in the doing of the contract work . . . clashes with the long recognized intent and purpose of section 3709, Revised Statutes, in that it removes from competitive bidding on the project an important element of cost and tends to defeat the purpose of the statute—that is, to obtain a need of the United States, authorized by law to be acquired, at a cost no greater than the amount of the bid of the low responsible bidder, after full and free competitive bidding.[6]

Nevertheless, by 1931, the country was in the throes of depression, and pressures on the administration and the Congress to "do something" were great. Work was scarce, thus creating an oversupply of labor which resulted in low wage rates. In construction, nonlocal contractors were said to be importing work crews willing to work for $2.00 a day or less—much lower than the already meager $3.50 to $4.00 a day then prevailing—consequently subjecting local rates to even greater pressure. Federal construction was very important to the local construction labor markets because the post offices and veterans' hospitals being built provided almost the only construction work then available.

For these reasons, scarcely two months after the comptroller general's opinion, a new bill for a prevailing wage statute was formulated and introduced simultaneously in both houses of Congress by Senator Davis and Congressman Bacon, thus precipitating another round of hearings. At the time of these hearings, in Congressman Bacon's home district in New York, a new veterans' hospital was being constructed. Local contractors had bid on the work, but wage rates prevailing in the local area prevented them from bidding effectively against a southern firm, which had undercut them by importing southern construction workers to do the job.[7]

Congressman Bacon thus set the tone of the new hearings:

---

[6] Cited in U.S., Congress, House, Committee on Education and Labor, *Legislative History of the Davis-Bacon Act*, 87th Cong., 2d sess. (1962), p. 2.

[7] Yale Brozen, "The Davis-Bacon Act: How to Load the Dice Against Yourself," cited in U.S., Senate, Committee on Banking, Housing, and Urban Affairs, *Improved Technology and Removal of Prevailing Wage Requirements in Federally Assisted Housing: Hearings Before the Subcommittee on Housing and Urban Affairs . . . on S.3373 . . . and S.3654 . . .*, 92d Cong., 2d sess., 20 June 1972, p. 398.

> A practice has been growing up in carrying out the building program where certain itinerant, irresponsible contractors, with itinerant, cheap, bootleg labor, have been going around throughout the country "picking" off a contract here and a contract there, and local labor and the local contractors have been standing on the side lines looking in. Bitterness has been caused in many communities because of this situation.
>
> This bill, my friends, is simply to give local labor and the local contractor a fair opportunity to participate in this building program.[8]

Given the depression and the tenor of the times, this was not a very controversial position, and it has been recognized as the philosophical underpinning of the act to this day. Nevertheless, some question whether it was the true reason for the act or simply the sort of rationalization and rallying cry that is often attached to a bill to allow easy passage. The one representative who spoke against it, Congressman Blanton of Texas, had this to say:

> Mr. Speaker, if this bill were not demanded by organized labor it would not have a chance of passage in this House under suspension of the rules. This is the most ridiculous proposition I have ever seen brought before a legislative body.[9]

As already reported, the historical evidence shows that the philosophy of the bill preceded by at least several years the depression itself and the massive government construction projects undertaken to stimulate the economy. Although their stated purposes were somewhat different, the Davis-Bacon Act and the Kansas prevailing wage act of 1891 are very similar in their wording. Also, the House Committee on Labor had entertained and favorably considered bills which were entered during a period of general prosperity in 1927 and 1928 and which were similar to the Davis-Bacon Act.

Another indication that the Davis-Bacon Act was a union oriented measure is that, under the Constitution, the federal government could not specify the use of union labor in connection with construction of public buildings; but under a prevailing wage law, union rates, at least in some areas, would be protected from nonunion wage competition. In the pre-New Deal period, the building trades were one of the strongest

[8] U.S., Congress, House, *Congressional Record,* 71st Cong., 3d sess., 1931, 74, pt. 7: 6510.

[9] *Ibid.*, pp. 6508-09.

groups in the labor movement. They had the political strength in the legislatures to secure passage of prevailing wage laws to protect the labor standards they had been able to negotiate.[10]

Third, the fear of "itinerant" laborers and contractors, although real from a local viewpoint, was overstated. On public construction (other than roadbuilding, which was excluded from Davis-Bacon coverage in the original act) as of September 29, 1930, the Treasury Department made a tabulation of the number of alien, local, and outside laborers. On the 26 projects, 1,724 men were employed—34 aliens, 1,356 locals, and 368 workers from outside the local community. More than one-half of these outside workers were employed on four projects: post offices in Boise, Idaho; Fargo, North Dakota; and Tucson, Arizona; and a federal building in Juneau, Alaska. No outsiders worked on projects in Brooklyn; Milwaukee; New Orleans; San Francisco; Pullman, Montana; Lowell, Massachusetts; or Seattle.[11] From this list one might conclude that the itinerant worker problem was not as severe as it was represented to be and that itinerant (outside) workers were employed principally in areas where the local labor force was of limited size but were not employed in areas where the local labor force was extensive.

Behind the fear of itinerant workers may have been some feelings colored by racial bigotry. This issue is mentioned explicitly only once during the House debate, but the allusions to it in other speeches—including Congressman Bacon's—are thinly veiled. Congressman Allgood raised it specifically:

> Reference has been made to a contractor from Alabama who went to New York with bootleg labor. That is a fact. That contractor has cheap colored labor that he transports, and he puts them in cabins, and it is labor of that sort that is in competition with white labor throughout the country.[12]

As for "itinerant" contractors, it should be noted that all contractors are mobile to some degree, moving about to find work. Much opposition to "outsiders" is expressed in all business fields by those who desire to monopolize local work.

Finally, refuting the contention that the Davis-Bacon Act was prompted by the depression wage conditions and problems

---

10 Johnson, *loc. cit.*

11 U.S., Congress, House, *Congressional Record, op. cit.*, p. 6506.

12 *Ibid.*, p. 6513.

of itinerant bootleg labor or contractors, Congress declined a suggestion that the bill be passed as special legislation or as a temporary measure to last only during the emergency of the depression. This suggestion was made by A. P. Greensfelder, President of the Associated General Contractors of America, Inc., in a letter to President Hoover. The suggestion was raised on the floor of the House by Congressman Blanton, but it was not given consideration.[13]

If one takes these factors into account, what is now believed to have been the motivating force behind the Davis-Bacon Act appears inaccurate. The true causes of its sponsorship and passage thus become somewhat more complex. There is little doubt, however, that the act was a creature of the depression to the extent that the mounting economic hardships of the depression created a climate in which legislation such as a national prevailing wage law could succeed. Although committees in both houses had reservations about the bill's effectiveness, amendments which might have delayed passage were rejected; it was passed under suspension of the rules as an emergency measure.

The original act was extremely brief. It provided:

> That every contract in excess of $5,000 in amount, to which the United States or the District of Columbia is a party, which requires or involves the employment of laborers or mechanics in the construction, alteration, and/or repair of any public buildings of the United States or the District of Columbia within the geographical limits of the States of the Union or the District of Columbia, shall contain a provision to the effect that the rate of wage for all laborers and mechanics employed by the contractor or any subcontractor on the public buildings covered by the contract shall be not less than the prevailing rate of wages for work of a similar nature in the city, town, village, or other civil division of the State in which the public buildings are located, or in the District of Columbia if the public buildings are located there, and a further provision that in case any dispute arises as to what are the prevailing rates of wages for work of a similar nature applicable to the contract which cannot be adjusted by the contracting officer, the matter shall be referred to the Secretary of Labor for determination and his decision thereon shall be conclusive on all parties to the contract: *Provided,* That in case of national emergency the President is authorized to suspend the provisions of this Act.[14]

[13] *Ibid.*, p. 6508.

[14] U.S., Congress, *The Davis-Bacon Act of 1931,* P.L. No. 798 (S.5904), 71st Cong. Also included is a second section which states that the "Act shall

Initial Reaction

Despite the recent opinions of his comptroller general, President Hoover signed the bill into law.[15] Shortly after it took effect, several serious shortcomings became readily apparent. A critical look at the original act yields some of the possible sources of discontent. First, the act lacked effective mechanisms for either policing or enforcing. Second, no provisions were made for informing laborers of the protection afforded them by the act. Third, definitions of the key terms were not provided (a condition which continues even today to cloud administration of the act). Fourth, the fact that the prevailing wage was determined after a contract was made caused an argument to ensue between contractors and the labor movement. Postdetermination of wages meant that a contractor could be forced to pay wages which, upon determination by the secretary of labor, were higher than the rate on which his bid was based. It was suggested by the comptroller general, in a memorandum on the act, that in order to keep contractors from inflating their bids to hedge against higher postdeterminations, predetermination was essential. However, labor organizations did not generally favor predetermination because they feared that this method was comparable to government wage-fixing, which at that time they opposed. Labor was also wary of adverse results from future administrations that might not be sympathetic to the unions.[16]

Criticism of the original act continued to increase; in 1932, following House Labor Committee hearings on proposed amendments, President Hoover issued an executive order aimed at strengthening the enforcement mechanism. The order set forth the following stipulations for all contracts subject to the act:

1. That wages be paid in full at least once a week;

2. That, despite any other contract between a laborer and an employer, persons performing the work of a laborer or mechanic should be regarded as such;

---

take effect thirty days after its passage." Cited in U.S., Congress, House, Committee on Education and Labor, *op. cit.*, p. 7.

15 40 U.S.C. 276(a)-77.

16 U.S., Congress, House, Committee on Education and Labor, *op. cit.*, p. 2.

3. That payrolls will be available for inspection by the contracting officer and that a schedule of prevailing wage rates should be displayed;

4. That if the wage provisions are violated, termination of contract might occur.[17]

Although the intentions of the order were to attack and to correct the problem of enforcement, the desire for amended legislation continued. It culminated in the spring of 1932, when Congress passed an amendment to the Davis-Bacon Act which: (1) called for the secretary of labor to predetermine prevailing wages; (2) provided for coverage of public works as well as buildings; and (3) made provisions for stronger enforcement, including fines.[18] President Hoover vetoed the bill on July 1, 1932, and returned it to the Senate with the following memorandum:

> The bill should not be approved. It is obscure and complex and would be impracticable of administration. It would stretch a new bureaucracy across the country. The bill is an amendatory substitute for the existing act of March 3, 1931, which is a clear and sufficient law. That law has been clarified and reinforced by an Executive order issued last January requiring certain stipulations in public contracts to make effective the manifest purpose of the statute. The law during its brief existence has worked with beneficial and generally satisfactory results and, without increase in personnel or appropriation, is being administered so as to accomplish substantially the ends sought by this legislation, without the many objectionable features which it would entail.[19]

Although President Hoover felt the provisions of this amendment unnecessary to the maintenance of an effective prevailing wage statute, many of the provisions it contained became the subject of renewed congressional hearings within the following few years. A 1933 investigation on racketeering by the Senate Committee on Commerce and hearings by a Senate subcommittee of the Committee on Education and Labor uncovered means

---

[17] Herbert Hoover, "Executive Order: Stipulation for the Payment of Prevailing Rate of Wages in Public Building Contracts," 19 January 1932. Cited in U.S., Congress, House, Committee on Education and Labor, *op. cit.*, p. 16.

[18] S.3847 (1932).

[19] Herbert Hoover, "Memorandum Upon Senate Bill 3847" (S. Doc. No. 134), 1 July 1932. Cited in U.S., Congress, House, Committee on Education and Labor, *op. cit.*, p. 13.

used by contractors to avoid paying the prevailing wage rates; these disclosures led to the Copeland (Anti-Kickback) and False Statement Acts of 1934, as well as to amendments to the Davis-Bacon Act passed in 1935.

AMENDMENTS

A number of new provisions were introduced with the 1935 amendment, which was a major modification of the Davis-Bacon Act.[20] One required unconditional payment of wages at least once each week without subsequent rebates or deductions. A second mandated prevailing wage payments to take place "regardless of any contractual relationship which may be alleged to exist between the contractor or subcontractor and such laborers and mechanics" (see Appendix B). This section was written to stop private agreements and partnerships which were formed so that wages below the prevailing level could be paid. Another provision found in the amended act is similar to one in President Hoover's executive order; it requires posting the scale of wages to be paid at an easily accessible place. This posting would also "provide for definite uniformity of wage rates to be paid all labor employed on the job." [21]

A fourth provision required that each contract stipulate that payments could be withheld from the contractor in sufficient amount (determined by the contracting officer) to reimburse workers who had received less than the wage to which they were entitled under the contract. The original act had no correction factor for underpayments.

The president had stipulated in his executive order that, if a contractor paid a wage less than that prevailing in the area or if rebating occurred, the government could terminate the contractor's role in the project and hold him liable for the excess costs which arose as the government had the work completed. The comptroller general, in a decision made in 1931, stated that there was no authority to withhold payments to contractors for the purpose of satisfying claims of workers who were paid less than the prevailing rate.[22] As a result, some unscrupulous

---

[20] P.L. No. 403 (S.3303), 74th Cong.

[21] U.S., Congress, House, Committee on Education and Labor, *op. cit.*, p. 74.

[22] Cited in U.S., Congress, House, *Congressional Record*, *op. cit.*, p. 6519.

contractors would rely on postdeterminations and would pay less than the prevailing wage, leaving their workers without protection. After four years of Davis-Bacon operation, the Senate found in its review for the amendment of 1935 that:

> As the right to cancel contracts was rarely exercised, and as the Davis-Bacon Law and Executive order relating thereto contain no other sanctions, the effect of the law was nullified in many instances by contractors who paid whatever wage they pleased regardless of the orders of the contracting officer.[23]

It should be noted, however, that in contrast with the proposal of 1932, the 1935 amendment sought only restitution of wages to covered employees and did not impose any fine on the violating contractor. Also retained was the right to terminate the contract in cases where the prevailing wage was not paid. Thus, in addition to the right to withhold payments to violating contractors, the comptroller general was also given specific authority to use the withheld funds to pay out "any wages found to be due laborers and mechanics pursuant to this act."

Another weak area clarified by the 1935 amendments was the ambiguity produced by the word "prevailing" in reference to area wage rates. The question of whether the act referred to wages for people in the same craft or on similar construction arose. Because classification of laborers was difficult, many contractors would hire mechanics as common laborers and pay them as such. The amendment made the wage rates in the contract's specifications conform to those "prevailing" for "the corresponding classes of laborers and mechanics employed on projects of a character similar to the contract work."[24] The adequacy of the new definition will be evaluated in Chapter III.

The basic provisions of the amended Davis-Bacon Act, the form in which it remains today, are:

1. Predetermination of wages—the secretary of labor determines the prevailing wage rate on contracts in excess of $2,000 for the "construction, alteration, and/or repair" of "public buildings or public works within the territorial United States." This determination is based on rates for "corresponding

[23] Senate Report No. 332, Part 2, pursuant to S. Res. 228 (May 13, 1935). Cited in U.S., Congress, House, Committee on Education and Labor, *op. cit.*, p. 78.

[24] 1935 House and Senate Reports (to accompany S.3303). Cited in U.S., Congress, House, Committee on Education and Labor, *op. cit.*, p. 63.

classes" of workers employed on projects whose character is similar "to the contract work in the city, town, village, or other civil subdivision" where the work is to be done.

2. Unconditional payment of wages—wages are paid in full at least once a week and conform to the prevailing wage rate. The contractor is supposed to post a schedule of wages on the site of the construction.

3. Enforcement—if a contractor is found in violation of wage payments, the government has the right to terminate the contract and proceed with the work at the expense of the contractor.

4. Sanctions—the comptroller general may:

(a) withhold from the contractors accrued payments, a sum deemed sufficient to reimburse workers for wages illegally withheld;

(b) disburse these sums to the workers with wage claims; and

(c) circulate a list to all government departments containing names of violators, thereby declaring these persons or firms ineligible for government contracts for a period of three years.

Amendments After 1935

The years which followed brought only minor additional amendments to the act. In 1940, it was extended to cover the territories of Alaska and Hawaii. (When these territories became states, the reference was removed.)[25] The act was further amended in 1941 to cover contracts awarded by means other than competitive bidding.[26] This action was taken because many contracts let on a cost-plus or other basis during the period of heavy defense contracting which preceded the entry of the United States into World War II were awarded without prior advertising for bids and proposals.

---

[25] Amendment (1940), P.L. No. 633 (S.3650), 76th Cong., 3d sess. See Appendix B.

[26] Amendment (1941), P.L. Nos. 22, 241 (H.R. 3325, 5312), 77th Cong., 1st sess. See Appendix B.

The act was once again amended in 1964 because of the changing pattern of wage payments.[27] At the time, proponents of the amendments argued successfully that fringe benefits had become so prevalent as to render meaningless any wage act which did not include them. They also contended that lack of inclusion of fringe benefit costs gave rise to unfair competition by contractors who did not pay them.

The resulting amendment expanded the meaning of "wage" to include the basic hourly rate of pay plus a number of allowable fringe benefits, such as: (1) medical or hospital care; (2) pensions on retirement or death; (3) compensation for occupational injury or illness; (4) unemployment benefits; (5) other bona fide fringe benefits, as long as these were not regulated by federal, state, or local law; (6) insurance for life, disability, sickness, or accident; (7) vacation and holiday pay; and (8) defraying costs of apprenticeship or other similar programs. The current Davis-Bacon Act is included in Appendix B.

Since its beginnings in the early 1930s, the Davis-Bacon Act has been extended to cover more than just the "public works" it mentions. Legislation subsequent to 1937 has produced over sixty statutes applying Davis-Bacon types of provisions to laws dealing with areas as varied as education, health, water pollution, drug addiction, and transportation. Projects which are federally assisted through loans, insurance, or direct financing are covered by these laws. A list of current legislation in which the Davis-Bacon stipulations are incorporated is included as Appendix C.

SIMILAR STATE LAWS

As already noted, several state prevailing wage laws preceded the Davis-Bacon Act. The first one, which Kansas passed in 1891, required payment of per diem wages at the prevailing rate:

> Provided further, that not less than the current rate of per diem wages in the locality where the work is performed shall be paid to laborers, workmen, mechanics, and other persons so employed by or on behalf of the State of Kansas, or any county, city, township, or other municipality of said State; and laborers, workmen, mechanics, and other persons employed by contractors or subcon-

[27] Act of July 2, 1964, PL 88-349, Sec. 1.78 Stat. 238, 88th Cong., 2d sess.

> tractors in the execution of any contract or contracts within the State of Kansas, or any county, city, township, or other municipality thereof, shall be deemed to be employed by or on behalf of the State of Kansas, or of such county, city, township, or other municipality thereof.[28]

If the purpose of this act was somewhat different from that of the Davis-Bacon Act, the form is remarkably similar. The six other state prevailing wage acts passed before 1931 were almost identical to the Kansas act.

Following enactment of Davis-Bacon in 1931, five states and one territory quickly passed similar laws; by 1935, 21 states and one territory had passed prevailing wage legislation covering state construction of buildings or public works. Thereafter, several of the state laws were successfully challenged in the courts and were declared unconstitutional. In the ensuing controversy, fewer states sought to pass new prevailing wage laws, and the pace of enactments slowed. By 1961, the total number of states enacting them had risen to 32, including Kansas, which had replaced its original law (declared unconstitutional) by new legislation. The pace of passage increased during the 1960s, the constitutional question having been settled, and again in the 1970s, particularly after President Nixon temporarily suspended the federal act. By 1973, only nine states had not enacted prevailing wage laws.

Although many of the state laws, often called "little Davis-Bacon laws," reflect the national act in its relevant provisions and definition, they vary greatly among themselves. The minimum contract amount that is covered ranges from $500 to $500,000. Some states cover highway work or maintenance; some do not. Some define "locality" for wage determinations in the same way as Davis-Bacon (i.e., city, town, village, or other civil subdivision); others include in the definition only county or only city or town; others include the entire state. In establishing prevailing rates, some states follow the 30 percent rule of the U.S. Department of Labor standards (to be discussed in the next chapter), and others understand collectively bargained rates as the prevailing wage; yet others specify collectively bargained rates should be "ascertained and considered" in the rate setting process, and several have no clearly expressed criteria. Similar degrees of variation occur in provisions for due process, enforcement, reporting requirements, and other

[28] Kansas L. 1891, C.114. Cited in Johnson, *op. cit.*, p. 840.

areas. Most state laws have provisions for central administration. Texas, however, provides that the governmental subdivision that is letting the contract must determine the prevailing rate and establish it.

Some of the state prevailing wage acts are voluminous. The Kentucky act is at least three times as long as Davis-Bacon, fully amended, and the New York act is more than five times as long. Therefore, it is very difficult to summarize their contents accurately and succinctly, except in extremely broad terms. Although, in Appendix D, we have summarized the coverage of the little Davis-Bacon acts and the wage standards followed by them, a complete understanding of the prevailing wage provisions of any particular state can be reached only by consulting the state's wage and hour laws. But for quick reference, Table D-1 shows the coverage provisions of the state prevailing wage laws, and Table D-2 outlines their wage standards provisions.

CHAPTER III

Definitions and Interpretations

The original wording of the Davis-Bacon Act is disarmingly simple, as previously mentioned. Its statement takes fewer than 300 words, but it provides little or no explanation of terms such as "prevailing rate of wages" or "work of a similar nature," which are critical to its understanding. In fact, the act made no effort at all to aid understanding of these key words or to delineate the rights and responsibilities of contractors, laborers and mechanics, contracting authorities, the secretary of labor, or other interested parties. Neither did it establish penalties for noncompliance or much in the way of redress of grievances. The vagueness more than the brevity of the act ensured that it would be surrounded by controversy soon after it was passed. This controversy continues today, especially in the area of definitions, despite the additional precision added to the act by the amendments of 1935 and 1964.

Stripped to its fundamentals, the Davis-Bacon Act requires the payment of prevailing wages to laborers and mechanics working on federal construction projects. The questions which must be answered by administrative and legislative determination are: (1) what are prevailing wages? (2) who are laborers and mechanics? and (3) what are federal construction projects? The answers, in part, depend on definitions or understandings sanctioned by administrative or judicial interpretations. Some of the key terms, as they are currently interpreted, follow. These definitions are meant to aid understanding of the Davis-Bacon Act and its administration rather than to provide decision-making guidelines by themselves, and so they are not exhaustive. They are taken from administrative interpretations for use by Department of Labor field personnel and from Departmental Regulations of the Secretary. These change or are modified from time to time, but they are not subject to judicial review because of the voluntary nature of government construction work; contractors are not required to bid on it.

WHAT ARE PREVAILING WAGES?

The current definition of prevailing wages used by the Department of Labor follows:

> The term "prevailing wage rate" for each classification of laborers and mechanics which the Administrator shall regard as prevailing in an area shall mean:
>
> (1) The rate of wages paid in the area in which the work is to be performed, to the *majority* of those employed in that classification in construction in the area similar to the proposed undertaking;
>
> (2) In the event that there is not a majority paid at the same rate, then the rate paid to the greatest number: Provided, such greater number constitutes *30 percent* of those employed; or
>
> (3) In the event that less than 30 percent of those so employed receive the same rate, then the *average rate.* [Emphasis added.] [29]

Even without considering any argument about the reasonableness or appropriateness of this definition, one can see that the work of defining "prevailing wage rate" is not finished by stating the above definition; it is filled with words of art which must, in turn, be defined.

For example, the definition first specializes the determination of prevailing wages to classifications of laborers and mechanics, classifications the administrator regards as prevailing. Thus, a particular job classification, such as carpenter, before a rate will be determined for it, must be held to be prevailing *as a classification.* Although this definition has not led to too many interpretive problems, it has created a few. Open-shop firms bidding on covered construction in predominantly union areas might find that some of their own classifications—notably helpers—would not be considered prevailing classifications as such; therefore, no prevailing wages would be determined for them. Consequently, those classifications could not be used on the contract work. Under such circumstances, the helpers would have to be reclassified as journeymen or laborers (journeymen, if they use the tools of the trade). Overlapping classifications can also be a problem for open-shop firms which might use a skilled man in several different tasks that would be different trades in the union classification; open-shop contractors would have to pay one man differently for each task under a Davis-Bacon contract. In addition,

[29] U.S., *Federal Register* 37, No. 194, Part 3 (5 October 1972): 21138.

many firms are using, or would like to use, semi-skilled labor for uncomplicated aspects of some tasks. Rough carpenters or forms carpenters are examples of such laborers. These would probably not be covered by Davis-Bacon rates. Such problems will be discussed in greater detail in a later chapter.

Once it is determined that a particular job classification itself is prevailing, the prevailing wage for that job is determined by the three-stage process previously described. In this type of sequential calculation, if a majority of workers in the job classification in the area where the work is to be performed are being paid a particular rate of wages for similar work, that rate becomes the prevailing rate. In the absence of a majority, if at least 30 percent are receiving a particular rate, then that rate prevails. If less than 30 percent receive the same rate, then a simple average (mean) rate is calculated, becoming the prevailing rate.

In the definition, four phrases require further attention—"rate of wages paid" in the "area where the work is to be performed" to the (appropriately calculated percentage) of "those employed in that classification in construction" in the area "similar to the proposed undertaking." Each will be discussed in turn.

1. "Rate of wages paid" includes, in addition to straight wages themselves, "bona fide" fringe benefits when payment of such fringe benefits is a prevailing practice. ("Prevailing" here is calculated by the previously outlined sequential percentage method, applied to wages.) "Bona fide" fringe benefits were mentioned in the last chapter, but include medical care; pensions; workmen's compensation; unemployment benefits; life, disability, sickness; or accident insurance; vacation and holiday pay; apportioned costs of apprenticeship programs; and others. They are not limited to cash payments actually received by workers, but if an employer wishes to, he may pay in cash or by enforceable covenants at an equal or higher cost to programs similar to those found to be prevailing.

2. "Area where the work is to be performed" refers, specifically, to the "city, town, village, or other civil subdivision of the state in which the work is to be performed." The objective of the act is to protect *local* wage rates, so the purpose of defining "area" is to establish the boundaries of the immediate locality in an operational way. This objective could be stated with equal force in a number of different ways, as the compendium of the

state prevailing wage laws in Appendix D shows. Current usage by the Department of Labor is said to put primary emphasis on the county as the appropriate area. However, if there has been no "similar construction" within the area in the past year, the department will consider wage rates paid on the nearest similar construction, even if it is across a state line. This practice raises other questions, not only involving what construction is to be considered "similar construction," but also involving determination of numerical adequacy. For example, if four plasterers had worked on a high-rise construction job near a proposed site six months ago, but seventy-five are currently employed a high-rise construction job of similar character fifty miles away in another county and state, which ones will be included in the sample to determine the prevailing rates? This problem will be discussed subsequently; but, in fact, no rule has been consistently applied; interpretation of the definition by the Department of Labor has varied.

3. "Those employed in that classification in construction" means other workers doing the same work or holding the same job titles. As indicated, problems arise when no workers or only one or two who hold similar job titles can be found in the area. Other problems arise when the tools of the trade or the character of the work differs significantly (among carpenters on home-building job, carpenters on commercial buildings, and carpenters on highway jobs or bridges, for example), when workers are performing in various classifications, or for other reasons. Here, too, definitional experience has shown flexibility.

4. The definition of work "similar to the proposed undertaking" presents no problems as a definition, but it is subject to varying interpretations. Davis-Bacon rates for messboys on dredges are set by comparison to the prevailing rates for construction laborers, for example, despite the obvious dissimilarities of their tasks. And on the other hand, the rate set for a backhoe operator may be quite different from that set for another operating the same equipment in the same way, because the job of which the operation is a part may be classified as a building job instead of a highway job or some other category.

WHO ARE LABORERS AND MECHANICS?

The general definition of who is or is not a laborer or mechanic is no less complex than other definitions involved in Davis-Bacon. Specific cases seem to be handled by example rather than by definition as such. No distinction is made between "laborers" and "mechanics" for Davis-Bacon purposes, but the combined classifications are distinguished by their requiring manual or physical duties rather than mental or managerial ones.

Apprentices, as learners of a craft or trade, are recognized as such only when they are participating in a bona fide apprenticeship program registered with a certified state apprenticeship agency or with the federal Bureau of Apprenticeship and Training. If they are not formally participating in this type of program, they must be considered, for pay purposes, journeymen of the trade to which they are apprenticed.[30]

Helpers who assist journeymen were mentioned previously. They will be recognized for Davis-Bacon rate purposes only in those geographic areas where the practice of employing them is prevalent enough that their classification becomes a prevailing one. This recognition will only apply in areas where open-shop firms predominate, because unions rarely recognize the helper category. In the words of the Department of Labor;

> The use of helpers who use tools in assisting journeymen and who are paid below the minimum rates for journeymen is ordinarily not proper, since the apprentice is recognized as the individual who is to perform the less skilled craft work of his training period level.[31]

Demolition workers, landscape contractors, installers of equipment, survey crews, and a number of others in fringe categories are sometimes covered by Davis-Bacon, depending on whether the work they are doing is intimately connected with or merely incidental to construction or repair. Guards and watchmen, flagmen and timekeepers, supervisors, and certain other types are

---

[30] One of the state prevailing wage acts (Nevada) specifically excludes even registered apprentices. Because there is no supremacy clause in prevailing wage laws, this contradiction of definitions might pose a considerable interpretative problem for a contractor in the state working on a job with federal-state funding.

[31] U.S., Department of Labor, "Davis-Bacon and Related Acts and Contract Work Hours and Safety Standards Act," in "Field Operations Handbook," internal document, entry no. 15b11 (9/26/69).

covered, depending on whether they use any tools or do any work in the craft areas.

Force account construction—that is, construction performed by "in-house" employees of nonconstruction firms—is not covered, even when, in the case of loans or grants, the lender or grantor specifies as a condition of construction that it is to be performed in accord with Davis-Bacon stipulations.

Owner-operators of trucks have proved a coverage problem, although it would appear to the layman that bona fide owner-operators could not be appropriately termed either laborers or mechanics. Nevertheless, such operators were deemed covered by the Department of Labor until 1961. Then, at the request of the Corps of Engineers, the department gave heed to the practical, if not the legal, problems involved.

> Corps of Engineers representatives charged with assuring contract labor standards compliance have encountered serious problems in their efforts to determine whether these owner-operators have been properly paid in accordance with the computation procedures previously explained in rulings and interpretations issued by this Department. Despite preconstruction conferences and on-site interviews and investigations, serious doubts have arisen as to compliance, especially since it has been established that generally the owner-operators seek and usually work under payment arrangements rooted in a unit price basis, for example, so much per cubic yard of material hauled, rather than on the basis of an actual truck or equipment rental rate plus the appropriate driver's (or operator's) rate. Moreover, although weekly certified payrolls may be submitted pursuant to contract requirements, substantial difficulties have arisen with respect to securing adequate data on rental arrangements in order to determine whether the contract minimum rates have been in fact paid.[32]

Accordingly, the Department of Labor

> reached the conclusion that, as a matter of administrative policy, the provisions of the Davis-Bacon and related Acts will not be applied to bona fide owner-operators of trucks or other similar construction equipment who are independent contractors, until such time as it may appear to be practical to devise workable and easily enforceable procedures for obtaining compliance with respect to such owner-operators.[33]

Then, without notice beforehand to other affected parties, Secretary of Labor Brennan wrote Frank E. Fitzsimmons, General

---

[32] Letter from Charles Donahue, Solicitor, U.S. Department of Labor, to Labor Relations Branch, Office of Chief of Engineers, Department of the Army, September 13, 1961.

[33] *Ibid.*

President of the Teamsters, on July 10, 1974, that "no practical solution" to the owner-operator problem had been found and that therefore he was "rescinding the policy enunciated in 1961." That same day, the department issued Memorandum No. 117, attaching a copy of the secretary's letter. This policy about-face is now being protested, both as to procedure and content, by contractor groups.

Site of Work

The Davis-Bacon Act provides that prevailing wages will be paid to laborers and mechanics "employed directly upon the site of the work," but does not define "site of the work." Since more and more parts of buildings, such as windows, are factory prefabricated, this lack of definition has created problems over the years. Under current interpretations, this sort of work would not be taking place "upon the site of the work," and so would not be covered. If the laborers or mechanics of the manufacturer are required to go to the place designated as the site of the work to perform activities on the contract there, such as maintenance or installation, however, their time so spent is covered by the prevailing wage decisions. On the other hand, the site is not limited to the building itself and the ground on which it stands. Fabrication plants, batch plants, barrow pits, job headquarters, tool yards, quarries, etc., are part of the site—even if they are miles from it—provided they are dedicated exclusively or nearly so to the performance of the contract and are so located that it would be reasonable to include them. For example, in the case of highway construction, gravel pits or cement plants are often opened and used exclusively for a particular job. Workers in these pits or plants are covered—usually in the laborer category—although classifying these fringe workers who are doing jobs not normally contemplated by construction trades is difficult.

One of the trickiest areas involving job site determinations and Davis-Bacon rates is that of teamsters and drivers. Contracts with bona fide suppliers or manufacturers to produce, supply, or deliver items to the site of the work for use in construction activities are not subject to Davis-Bacon rates, nor is transportation by common carrier over regular routes. However, anyone on a covered work site who temporarily leaves the site to transport materials and equipment used in the course of contract operations is covered, as are teamster or driver employees of a construction contractor or subcontractor.

WHAT ARE FEDERAL CONSTRUCTION CONTRACTS?

The last of the three basic questions about interpretations of the Davis-Bacon Act is: what are federal construction contracts? In 1931, when the act was first passed, federal construction contracts were fairly straightforward, almost entirely involving post offices, veterans' hospitals, custom houses, immigrant stations, federal office buildings, and the like, of a cost of greater than $5,000 and to which the federal government was a party. In 1935, under the major amendments to the act at that time, the minimum covered contract amount was reduced to $2,000, and public works as well as building construction or repair were included.

Since that time, a number of federal acts have included Davis-Bacon wage requirements by reference. Many of these, such as the Federal Aid Highway Act or the National Housing Act, are more or less expected, but some are quite surprising. Here are some of the surprising ones:

- Federal Civil Defense Act of 1950
- Cooperative Research Act of 1966
- National Foundation on the Arts and Humanities Act of 1965
- Federal Water Pollution Control Act (1965)
- Heart Disease, Cancer and Stroke Amendments of 1965
- Medical Library Assistance Act of 1965
- Alaska Purchase Centennial
- Allied Health Professions Personnel Training Act of 1966
- Vocational Rehabilitation Amendments of 1967
- Juvenile Delinquency Prevention and Control Act of 1968
- Alcoholic and Narcotic Addict Rehabilitation Amendments of 1968

(The complete list is included as Appendix C.)

Under the provisions of all of these acts or the $2,000 minimum of the Davis-Bacon Act itself, it is not necessary for the federal government to be undertaking construction which will be used by the government itself; highways, for example, are covered. Nor is it necessary that the federal government pay for the construction; it might only be guaranteeing commercial bank loans for construction, for instance. In some cases, the construction need not even be construction, for destruction (demolition) is sometimes covered. It is probably safe to say that any bid contract involving building or buildings, or earthmoving above or below water, in which the federal government has an interest through ownership, ownership participation, funds guaranty, or second-level funding (where the government is funding a program which is in turn involved in building, for example) will probably be covered by Davis-Bacon provisions.

SUMMARY

The Davis-Bacon Act itself does not define the terms that are used in the act. Many of these are vague and subject to various interpretations. Thus, as an administrative matter, the Department of Labor has discretion over three very important variables in official wage determinations: (1) the scope of the market area; (2) the classification of the project; and (3) the designation of the job classifications and job structure.

Definitional vagueness encourages interpretive flexibility, administrative inconsistency, and abuse, all of which are relatively insulated from court challenge. Before these problems are examined in Chapter V, the machinery and organization created to administer the Davis-Bacon Act will be discussed.

CHAPTER IV

Administrative Organization

Over the years, the Davis-Bacon Act has required the development of an extensive organization to search out, calculate, determine, and promulgate prevailing wage rates, handle inquiries and protests, and in other ways involve itself with the act's administration. Those who have duties associated with the operations of the act extend outside the ranks of government to include contractors, employers' associations, and labor organizations.

PARTICIPANTS IN ADMINISTRATION

Briefly, those involved in Davis-Bacon administration include the following:

1. Department of Labor—The Department of Labor has the major administrative responsibility for the act. Its interpretations establish the definitions and operating patterns which the act will follow. The regulations and procedures which it establishes are then carried out in large measure by the Department of Labor personnel charged with determining the prevailing rates and distributing them as necessary. The government agencies which are interested in contracting for federal construction or public works cannot let contracts unless they are supplied by the Department of Labor with prevailing rate information. Finally, any reviews of procedures or appeals of rates are handled within the Department of Labor by other personnel assigned those duties. Because there is no appeal of Davis-Bacon rates or procedures to the court system, everything is handled internally.

2. Contractors—In addition to paying the rates which the Department of Labor establishes for covered work, contractors must also file detailed reports on wages paid to avoid putting the enforcement machinery of the act into effect. Further con-

tractor involvement stems from a desire to influence the rate determination process or secure modifications of rates or classifications associated with a contract award. Contractors, as interested parties, may initiate review or appeal procedures.

3. Federal agencies—Federal agencies desiring to have buildings or public works constructed, or repairs or maintenance performed, whose value is greater than $2,000 must have a schedule of predetermined prevailing minimum rates attached to any contracts before they can be let. Contracting officers of the agencies are also responsible for auditing employer conformity to the act. To facilitate or ensure greater accuracy in their rate determinations, some agencies have begun supplying the Department of Labor with rate survey information covering the type of construction which that agency usually conducts. The agencies may also, as interested parties, take appeals and request reviews of Davis-Bacon determinations. The General Accounting Office has special duties for overseeing administration of the Davis-Bacon Act, but it cannot compel performance or change by the Department of Labor.

4. Employers' associations and labor organizations—Employers' associations and labor organizations are also interested parties in Davis-Bacon areas, and they may initiate or participate in reviews and appeals of the rates determined. They may also contribute input to the Department of Labor's determination process by supplying it with rate schedules or survey information. For a number of years, craft and industrial unions have routinely supplied the rate determination branch of the Department of Labor with new contract agreements in construction and have examined the resulting decisions. Some employers' associations have also supplied contract or survey information about wages. Information so supplied by either contractors' associations or labor organizations is relied on very heavily by the Department of Labor, which does not have sufficient staff to secure the information independently.

RESPONSIBILITY FOR ADMINISTRATION

Under the original terms of the Davis-Bacon Act, the various contracting agencies were responsible for determining if contractors were paying the prevailing wage. The 1935 amendments affixed the responsibility for predetermining the prevailing wage on the secretary of labor.[34] Between 1931 and 1950, however, the major responsibility for enforcement rested with the individual government agencies for whom the work was being performed.[35]

1950-1969

Reorganization Plan #14 became effective on May 24, 1950. It authorized the secretary of labor:

> to prescribe appropriate standards, regulations and procedures and to make such investigations with respect to the enforcement of the labor standards under the Davis-Bacon and other statutes covered by the Plan, as he deems desirable.[36]

The secretary of labor was thus given major responsibility for the administration of the act; this he delegated to the solicitor of labor, who further delegated the tasks to an associate administrator responsible for the Branch of Wage Determinations and the Branch of Coordination and Enforcement. After this change, the Department of Labor's internal machinery responsible for the administration of the act remained essentially unchanged until mid-1969.

1969-1973

In mid-1969, administration of Davis-Bacon was transferred to the Wage and Labor Standards Administration pursuant to Secretary's Order 24-69, effective July 1, 1969. On August 24, 1970, by authority of Secretary's Order 19-70, the name of the Wage and Labor Standards Administration was changed to the Workplace Standards Administration. Then, by virtue of Secretary's Order 13-71, effective April 28, 1971, the Workplace Standards Administration became known as the Employment Standards Administration. Thus, at the present time, determination of the prevailing wage and administration of the act is vested in the Employment Standards Administration, Wage and Hour Division, Office of Special Wage Standards, Division of Wage Determinations, Branch of Construction Wage Determina-

---

[34] Damodar Gujarathi, "The Economics of the Davis-Bacon Act" (Ph.D. diss., University of Chicago, 1965), p. 21.

[35] *Statutes on Labor Standards in Construction Field* (Washington, D.C.: United Association of Journeymen and Apprentices of the Plumbing and Pipefitting Industry of the United States and Canada, 1954), p. 1.

[36] Gujarathi, *loc. cit.*

tions. (The relationship of the Employment Standards Administration to other functions of the Department of Labor can be seen in Figure 1.)

The early months of 1971 saw, in addition to the name changes, several changes affecting the Employment Standards Administration (ESA) and the Branch of Construction Wage Determinations (BCWD), where the rate determinations are made. In February, President Nixon suspended the Davis-Bacon Act in an effort to curb inflation generally and construction wage escalation in particular. The Department of Labor, acting as though the suspension were to be permanent, disbanded the branch responsible for prevailing wage determination. When Davis-Bacon was reinstated shortly thereafter, most of the approximately sixty branch employees had been placed in other civil service positions or had left government service altogether.

At the time of reinstatement, perhaps to facilitate return of service, the branch was given field administration authority. Thus, existing ESA regional offices were given some responsibility for Davis-Bacon surveys in their areas in addition to their existing duties. About a year later, in March, 1972, the ten regional offices (see Figure 1) were given, in a decentralization move throughout ESA, additional authority and responsibility in determining the prevailing wage. Nevertheless, the BCWD retained final decision authority over the regional offices' determination of the prevailing wage and continued to make almost all of the regional or other large-scale rate determinations. As of September, 1973, the Branch of Construction Wage Determinations consisted of a total of thirty employees, twenty-one of them classified as professional.

SECURING THE RATE

As a contemplated project to be done under Davis-Bacon related statutes nears the bidding stage, the federal agency responsible for the project determines the applicability of Davis-Bacon provisions. If coverage is indicated, the agency, through the contracting officer, must secure an appropriate prevailing wage for the project. Thus, the federal agency responsible for the construction is the ignition point for operating the Davis-Bacon machinery. At the present time, these agencies have two distinct methods for securing the necessary prevailing wage rate schedule from the Department of Labor.

FIGURE 1. *Organization of the U.S. Department of Labor 1973*

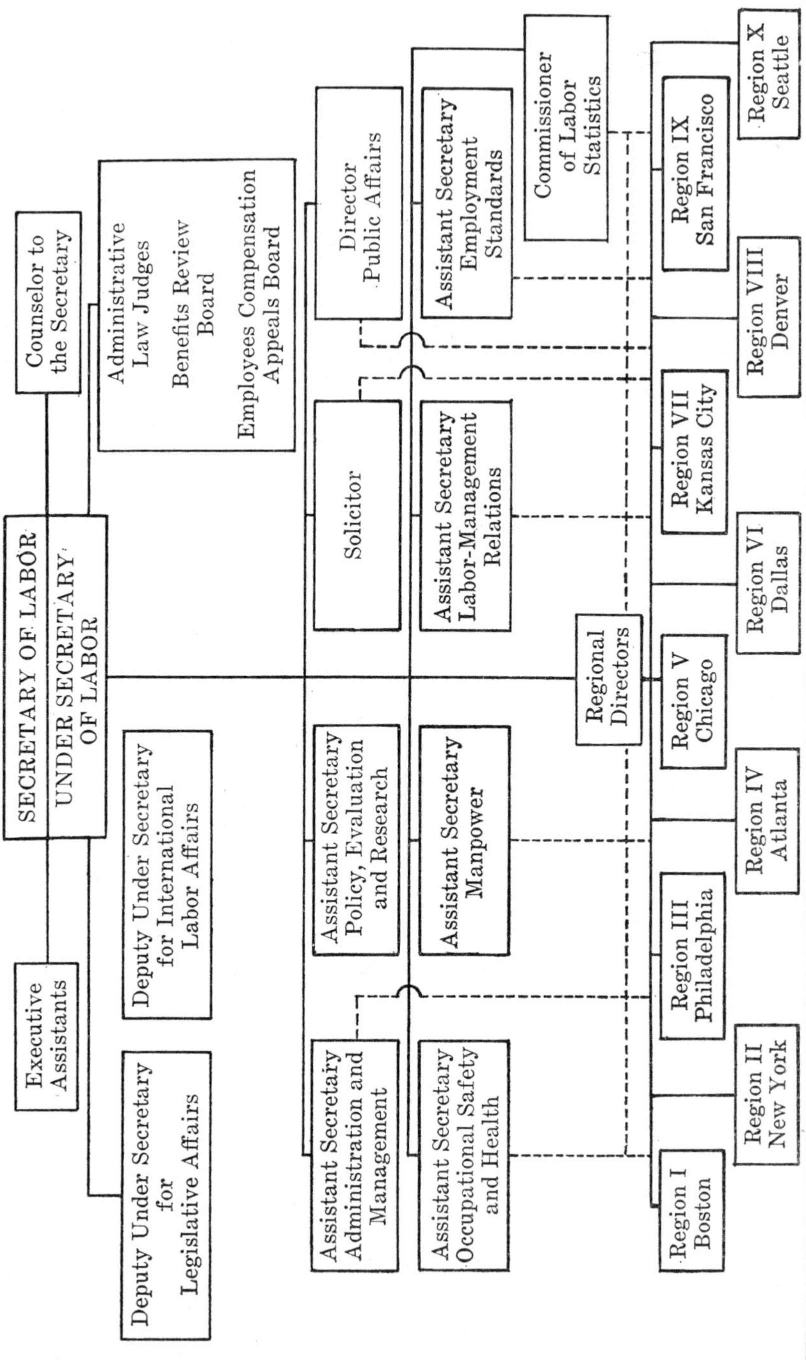

Area Rates

To increase efficiency in handling an expanding workload with proportionally fewer staff members, the Branch of Construction Wage Determinations, in August 1971, began publishing general or "area" wage determinations in the Friday issue of the *Federal Register.* These area decisions are used for localities that have a rather steady flow of construction in a particular category and where there is some assurance that the rates are likely to remain fairly stable. (Usually, this means areas which are prevailingly union rate.) The area rates have no expiration date. They remain in effect until they are either superseded in a subsequent *Federal Register* or until they are withdrawn. At the present time, approximately 527 area decisions are in force. A very large proportion of certain types of construction work is now covered by the published area decisions. The General Services Administration, for example, estimates that from 90 to 95 percent of all prevailing wage rate schedules for its work are obtained from the published area rates.[37]

The first step of the contracting officer to secure a rate schedule is to check the current area decisions in the *Federal Register.* If he finds the appropriate rates, he attaches them to the requests for bids sent to various contractors along with the necessary plans and specifications. However, the contracting officer must continue to monitor the *Federal Register* in case the rates are updated prior to ten days before opening the bids.

Project-Type Decisions

If the contracting officer cannot find a rate for the type of work contemplated in the locality under consideration, he must request a special or project-type determination from the appropriate regional office of the Employment Standards Administration. The regional office receiving the request for a project decision first checks to determine if there is a prevailing area determination. If there is, the request is returned to the requesting agency, advising it to use the appropriate area decision. If the regional office cannot find an area determination, a project decision will be rendered after obtaining the appropriate information on which to base a determination. Normally, thirty

---

[37] Interview with General Services Administration personnel, October 15, 1973.

days' lead time is required to make a project decision. These relationships are shown in Figure 2.

Because the bidding period on most projects averages to 30 days also, the contracting officer must make his request early enough to be able to transmit rate schedules to the bidding contractors for their use in making a bid. A request made too early can also cause problems, however. Normally, the period between the opening of bids and the awarding of a contract is 30 to 40 days. Project decisions are valid only for a period of 120 days, unless an extension is granted. Therefore, if a contracting officer requests a project decision too early, he may find the rate expired before the contract is awarded. But if he requests it too late, the bid opening may have to be postponed. The contracting officer appears to have a maximum of 20 to 25 days leeway.

Changes to the Initial Rate

Once the contracting officer has obtained the rate schedule and attached it to the requests for bids (or forwarded it to the bidding contractors if the requests went out before the rate decision was made), the cycle has been completed unless: (1) a subsequent modification is issued; (2) an "interested party" makes a protest; or (3) a clerical error is found in the determined rate.

If the Branch of Construction Wage Determinations modifies a decision on a project-type determination, its action must occur no later than ten days prior to the scheduled bid opening date in order to become automatically effective. If it occurs between ten days prior to the bid opening and the bid opening date, use of the changed rate is at the agency's option. Between bid opening and contract award, no modifications are possible. If serious errors are found then, the rate schedule must be withdrawn completely. This possibility negates the contract bid-awarding process and forces a completely new round of bids after revised rates are secured. This time-consuming and painful process is thus avoided whenever possible. Rate schedules have been withdrawn only two or three times in the past two years. Once the contract has been awarded, only changes resulting from clerical errors may be made. (See Figure 3 for a time-based diagram.)

If the rate schedule resulted from an area decision found in the *Federal Register* rather than from a project-type decision, only changes published at least fifteen days prior to the sched-

FIGURE 2. *Method of Securing Rate Determinations For Work Covered by Davis-Bacon Act Provisions*

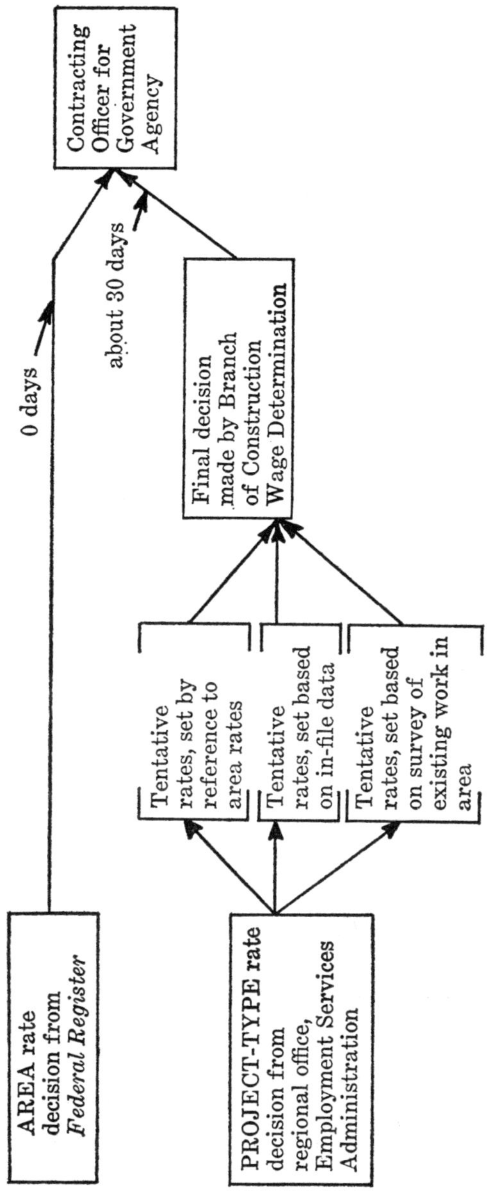

FIGURE 3. *Time Frame for Contract Awards and Rate Modifications for Project-Type Rate Determinations*

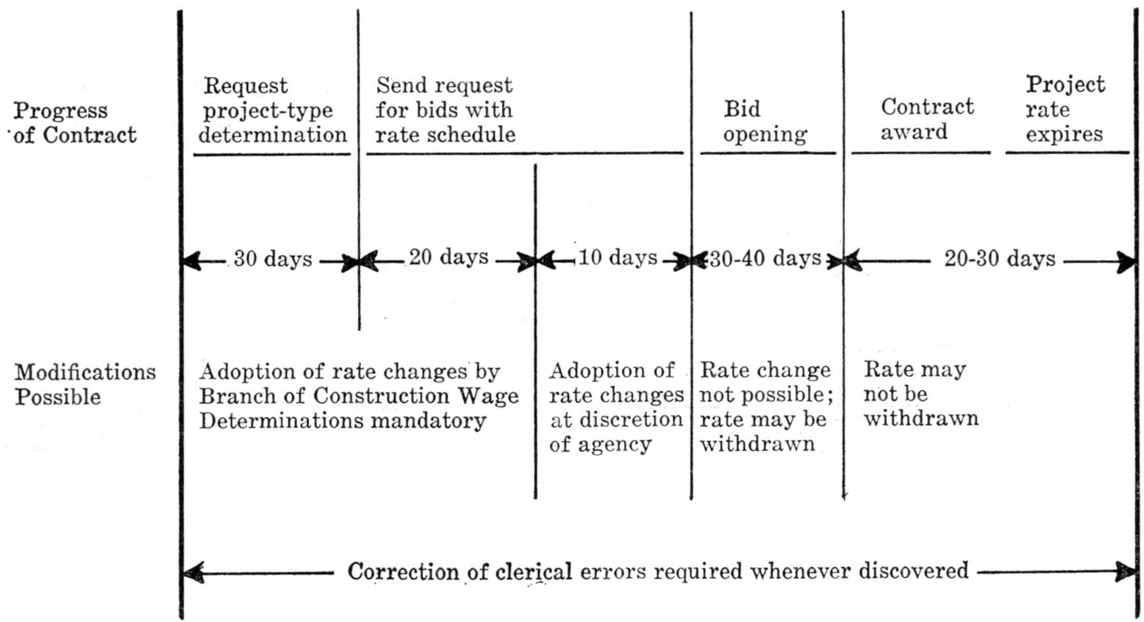

uled bid opening will be automatically effective. If they are published within the period between fifteen days prior to the bid opening and bid opening date, the agency has the option of using the existing rate or the modified rate, depending on whether it believes it can make timely notification to all bidding contractors. Beyond this, the pattern is the same as for the project-type determination (see Figure 4).

Within the ten- or fifteen-day discretionary periods for project-type and area decisions, respectively, the agency's action about revised rates will depend on its judgment of the magnitude of the change and its expectation of repercussions from organized labor, employers, employers' associations, or others, if the change is not incorporated.

The other two possible exceptions to the normal cycle previously discussed are protests and clerical errors. If an "interested party" protests, it is necessary for BCWD to make an evaluation of the protest and possibly a modification of the previous rate. Any modifications so made are governed by the ten- and fifteen-day rules already mentioned. If a clerical error is found, the rate schedule can be amended, regardless of the state of the project. That is, the amended rate may be mandatory even after the contract has been awarded. In such cases, the contracting agency can increase the price of the job by the amount of the difference, if the difference is in that direction.

DETERMINATION OF THE RATE

Sole responsibility for determining prevailing wage rates is in the hands of the secretary of labor. The Davis-Bacon Act reads, in part, that the rate "shall be based upon the wages that will be determined by the Secretary of Labor to be prevailing." Because Congress did not provide a definition of "prevailing," the interpretation was left to the secretary of labor. His definition, which is not subject to judicial review, is the 30 percent rule discussed in the previous chapter.

The operation of the 30 percent rule is in terms of the "same rate" to the very cent. By this definition, the rates of $7.35 and $7.36 would not be the same for purposes of the 30 percent rule. Thus, in any area where unions have organized one-third or more of the workers, the union rate has an excellent prospect of being declared the prevailing wage, because it would be highly improbable to find the nonunion sector paying any significant

FIGURE 4. ***Time Frame for Contract Awards and Rate Modifications for Area Rate Determinations***

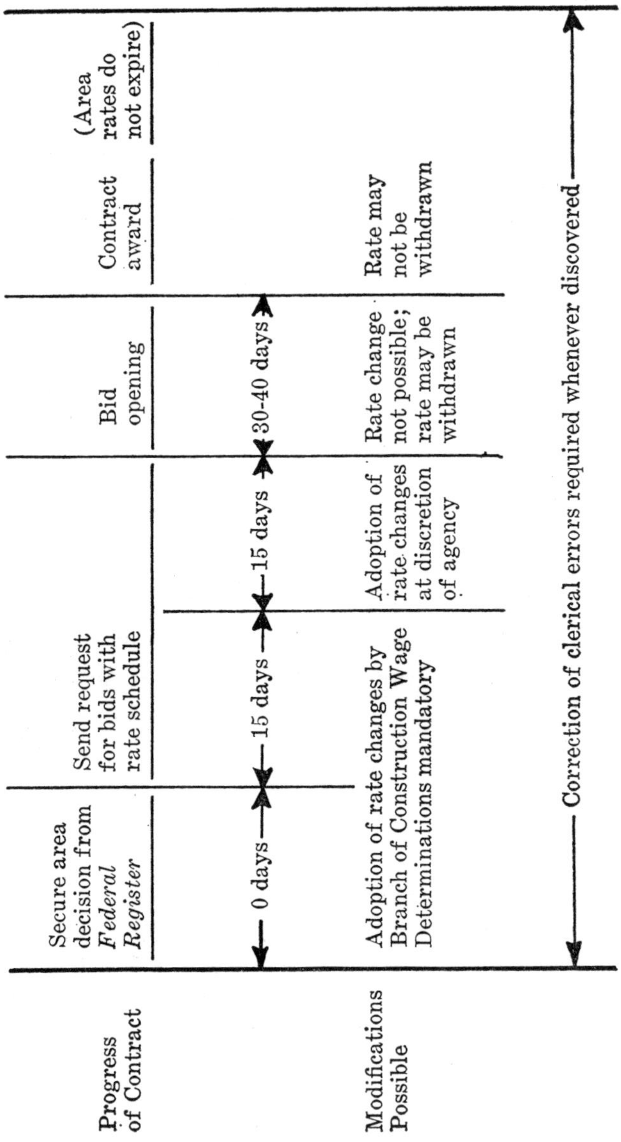

proportion of its work force a wage exact to the cent. The application of the 30 percent rule and the contract inputs, which organized labor makes to the wage determination process, grants organized labor great influence and allows the Department of Labor latitude in assuming that union rates prevail in areas where actual surveys are not conducted. The Department of Labor has examined this definition of "prevailing" within the past two years and has decided not to make any change, despite many requests to do so. One source in the department forecasts continued adherence to the current definition into the foreseeable future.[38]

Economic Controls Machinery

At approximately the same time that the Davis-Bacon Act was reinstated after its suspension in 1971, a twelve-person committee, the Construction Industry Stabilization Committee, was established to oversee wages in the construction industry. For about three years, this committee, responsible to the Cost of Living Council, was a factor in determining the prevailing wage.[39] Without the committee's approval, increased rates could not be paid in construction and therefore could not become prevailing. This committee may have exerted a constraining influence on increases in the prevailing wage in unionized sectors, but its influence on Davis-Bacon administration or procedures was small.

Inputs

Although the Branch of Construction Wage Determinations has the task of determining the prevailing wage rate, the opportunity for other parties to influence it by submitting inputs of various types does exist. Contractors, employers' associations, labor organizations, or other interested parties may submit:

1. Statements showing wage rates on projects.
2. Signed collective bargaining agreements.
3. Wage rates determined for public construction by state and local officials pursuant to prevailing wage legislation.

---

[38] Interview with U.S. Department of Labor personnel, September 26, 1973.

[39] "New Controls Get Their Opening Test," *Business Week* 2171 (April 10, 1971): 35.

4. Information furnished by federal and state agencies.
5. Any other information deemed pertinent.

In addition, the Branch of Construction Wage Determinations is authorized to supplement such voluntary information in any manner deemed necessary, including hearings.

The Determination Process

When a contracting officer requests a project decision from the regional office of the Employment Standards Administration, the regional office checks its file to see if it has the required inputs to make a determination. If not, the regional office may make a survey. Following either case, a preliminary determination is made and submitted along with the input data to the Branch of Construction Wage Determinations, which holds veto power over the regional office. Once the final determination is made in Washington, D.C., the results are transmitted to the regional office which, in turn, sends it on to the requesting federal agency.

The process for data determination follows much the same sequence. If an area rate becomes outdated, the regional office may be called upon to conduct whatever information-gathering is necessary, although this task could also be conducted directly from Washington. If the task is conducted by a regional office, the office makes a tentative decision which it submits along with the input data to Washington for final approval. There the input data are examined for sufficiency, and the decision is examined for validity. Approval of the tentative decision may follow, or a change in the rate schedule may be made. The Branch of Construction Wage Determinations may also direct the regional office to gather more information.

To aid BCWD in planning its workload, every agency using wage determinations is requested to provide, at the beginning of each fiscal year, a schedule of proposed construction projects for the year and then to notify the various regional offices of any proposed changes.[40]

PROTEST OF RATE DETERMINATION DECISIONS

During the early 1960s, hearings were held in Congress concerning judicial review of Davis-Bacon decisions, among other

[40] 29 CFR, 1, Sec. 1.4.

matters.[41] The general feeling held judicial review to be inappropriate because of the time delay involved. Nevertheless, as a result of the criticism, the secretary of labor established an appeals procedure within the Department of Labor. On December 30, 1963 (filed on January 3, 1964), Secretary of Labor Willard Wirtz established the Wage Appeals Board as a three-man group to review and hear appeals of:

> (1) Wage determinations issued under the Davis-Bacon Act and its related minimum wage statutes;
>
> (2) debarment cases . . . ;
>
> (3) controversies concerning the payment of prevailing wage rates or proper wage classifications which involve significant sums of money, large groups of employees, or novel or unusual situations; and
>
> (4) recommendations of a Federal agency for appropriate adjustment of liquidated damages which are assessed under the Contract Work Hours Standards Act.[42]

In the formative years, the Wage Appeals Board heard few appeals. Many who could have utilized the procedure, had they known of its existence, were unaware of the appeal procedure. In addition, may were skeptical of the board's ability to render a just verdict, because it was a creature of the secretary of labor and charged with interpreting the rules of the secretary of labor and their application by persons within the Department of Labor responsible to the secretary. For example, organized labor shunned use of the board until very recently. However, as experience with the board has grown, its use has accelerated to a current average of approximately fifteen appeals heard per year.

Protest and Appeals Procedure

In order to utilize the Wage Appeals Board, an interested party must first protest the established rate determination. "Interested party" is broadly defined to include contractors likely to seek work involving the protest, contractors' associations, workers likely to be employed under the rate, labor organiza-

---

[41] U.S., Congress, House, Committee on Education and Labor, *Administration of the Davis-Bacon Act: Hearings Before the Special Subcommittee on Labor . . . , A General Investigation of the Davis-Bacon Act and its Administration,* Part 2, 87th Cong., 2d sess. (1962).

[42] Secretary of Labor, Order No. 32-63. Cited in 29 CFR, 7, Sec. 7.1(b).

tions, or any federal, state, or local agency likely to be involved in administration of a contract under the rate. In protesting, the petitioner must raise a sufficient question about the determination to force review of it by the Department of Labor. In his efforts to secure a modification, the petitioner has the right of access to the working papers leading to the determination. It may be necessary for him to conduct a detailed wage survey in order to convince the Branch of Construction Wage Determinations that an error exists. On project decision rates, to point out that the field investigation failed to include a key project or made some other obvious error may be sufficient. Rejection of the petitioner's request gives him standing before the Wage Appeals Board.

The contesting person or group may then file a petition before the board to request a review. The petition should:

(1) Be in writing and signed by the petitioner or his counsel (or other authorized representative);

(2) be described as a petition for review by the Wage Appeals Board;

(3) identify clearly the wage determination, location of the project or projects in question, and the agency concerned;

(4) state that the petitioner has requested [reconsideration of] the wage determination in question, and describe briefly the action taken [in response to the request];

(5) contain a short and plain statement of the grounds for review; and

(6) be accompanied by supporting data, views, or arguments.[43]

The Wage Appeals Board

The operation of the board is somewhat less formal than a courtroom proceeding. In addition to documented evidence from the petitioner and the Branch of Construction Wage Determinations, the board may allow oral suasion or the intervention of other interested parties. The board may dispose of the case in any of the following ways:

1. The Board may decline review of any case whenever in its judgment a review would be inappropriate or because of lack of timeliness, the nature of the relief sought, or other reasons.

---

[43] 29 CFR, 7, Sec. 7.5.

2. The Board shall decide the case upon the basis of all relevant matter contained in the entire record before it. The Board shall notify all interested persons participating in the proceeding of its decision.

3. Decisions of the Board shall be by majority vote. A case will be reviewed upon the affirmative vote of one member.[44]

A key to successful review is the timeliness of the petition. Once the contract is awarded, the Wage Appeals Board will decline review. Furthermore, it will not request the agency involved to change its bid-award process. Therefore, given the one or two weeks a review may require, early appeal seems necessary. Equally important to successful appeal is the substance of proof presented before the board to offset Department of Labor data. The board does no investigative work; rather, it renders decisions on the basis of the matters laid before it.

SUMMARY

Considering the magnitude of the task involved in establishing prevailing rates for each of the dozens of job categories required for each of the thousands of rate determinations made each year, the administrative superstructure of the Davis-Bacon Act is not overly extensive. In the next several chapters, the effectiveness with which this administrative organization carries out the duties assigned to it will be examined.

---

[44] Stuart Rothman, "The Work of the Wage Appeals Board With Respect to the Davis-Bacon Act and Related Federal Construction Laws," *Constructor* 46 (September 1964): 34-37. See also 29 CFR, 7, Sec. 7.8.

CHAPTER V

Experience and Problems

The problems which contractors and others have experienced with the Davis-Bacon Act and its administration have been reflected in congressional hearings and a fair number of dissertations, studies, and independent analyses during the past decade. Many of the problems raised continue today, and most of the arguments propounded by the studies remain uncontroverted. All together, they make a strong case against the act, as the following material will make clear. Responses of the Department of Labor, counter arguments by the Building Trades Division of the AFL-CIO and other unionists, and independent studies supporting the Davis-Bacon Act are included where available. Case histories and similar illustrations, however, are generally left for Chapter VII.

For convenience in presentation, problems associated with Davis-Bacon and its administration are divided, somewhat arbitrarily, into several categories. Classical and empirical problems associated with the administration of the act are covered in this chapter. Those associated with costs are in Chapter VI. Case examples are in Chapter VII, and philosophical and miscellaneous problems are covered in Chapter VIII.

ADMINISTRATION OF THE ACT: EMPIRICAL ARGUMENTS

In the hearings, studies, and reports dealing with the Davis-Bacon Act during the past twelve years, certain themes have recurred. These have often been documented by case studies or empirical research and deal mostly with administration, with the increased cost of federally financed construction, and with the effects of the act—even properly administered—on the construction industry and on the economy.

Davis-Bacon's intent is to prevent government construction and public works contracts from upsetting local wage standards. When 30 percent or more of all new construction is covered by the federal prevailing wage determinations, involving every year the establishing of perhaps more than one million separate hourly rates and fringe benefits, it is easy to see that the degree to which Davis-Bacon's intent is carried out depends on the quality and consistency of the act's administration. Unfortunately, ample evidence exists that wage determinations are less than completely accurate, thus having in many cases a serious impact on local construction wage conditions, frustrating the intent of the act. This unfortunate effect happens in a number of ways, some unavoidable because of the very magnitude and complexity of the task, but others are apparently the result of conscious or unconscious bias by the administrators.

Classification of Workers

Both the Davis-Bacon Act itself and the Department of Labor's implementing regulations require the determination of prevailing wages for laborer and mechanic classifications found to be prevailing in the locality. One of the findings in the several studies conducted by the General Accounting Office, however, was that in some cases the Department of Labor applied the wage rates of one classification to another without investigating the rates paid to each classification or the work practices in the area for which the determination was being made.[45]

One might suppose this problem would arise only in a limited number of cases, such as on very small jobs by firms of limited resources or on unusual jobs requiring nonstandard skills. Actually, because of the difference in operating patterns and employee training methods between union and open-shop firms, the problem acquires significance both in terms of flexibility and in the case of helpers and trainees. The National Association of Home Builders presented testimony to a congressional hearing in 1972 that:

---

[45] This section relies heavily on the final GAO report of this series: U.S., Comptroller General, *Report to the Congress: Need for Improved Administration of the Davis-Bacon Act Noted Over a Decade of General Accounting Office Reviews*, B-146842 (Washington, D.C.: General Accounting Office, 1971).

> The job classifications prescribed by the Department of Labor frequently do not coincide with the job responsibilities of workmen in the residential construction industry. As is true with wages, these classifications are usually derived from job assignments in commercial and industrial construction.[46]

In our companion study, *Manpower in Homebuilding,* recently published by the Industrial Research Unit, it was shown that various homebuilders regularly utilize personnel in two or more trades—e.g., framing carpenters and cement finishers—and usually hire several grades of on-the-job trainees and helpers, their training frequently informal.[47] Other open-shop contractors, as the Unit's forthcoming study on open-shop construction will demonstrate, likewise utilize workers over craft boundaries. Within crafts, they also hire helpers and various levels of trainees and journeymen. Such builders must reorient their labor supply, organization, and methods of using and compensating employees in order to conform to Davis-Bacon union-oriented job classifications.

A subsidiary aspect of this problem applicable to the small firm is that an employee must be paid for the day at the highest level at which he does any work at all. Thus, if a laborer picks up a hammer to nail up a temporary barricade, for example, he automatically becomes a carpenter and must be paid as such.[48]

Generally speaking, the Department of Labor prescribes rates for the classifications of workers recognized by the building trades unions. This means that, with the exception of three or four crafts, no rates for helper classifications are determined or set for trainees (other than apprentices in certified programs). This situation seems to be true even in those areas where open-shop contractors predominate, and it is their practice to pay differential rates within classifications according to skill.[49]

The Department of Labor's general failure to recognize helper, trainee, or other learner rates (again with the exception of

---

[46] Statement of Stanley Waranch, President, National Association of Home Builders, in U.S., Congress, Senate, Subcommittee on Housing and Urban Affairs, *op. cit.,* p. 169.

[47] Howard G. Foster, *Manpower in Homebuilding: A Preliminary Analysis,* Manpower and Human Resources Studies, No. 3 (Philadelphia: Industrial Research Unit, The Wharton School, University of Pennsylvania, 1974).

[48] Statement of Stanley Waranch, in U.S., Congress, Senate, Subcommittee on Housing and Urban Affairs, *loc. cit.*

[49] David B. Johnson, "Prevailing Wage Law," in *Labor Management and Social Policy,* ed. Gerald G. Somers (Madison, Wisconsin: University of Wisconsin Press, 1963), p. 250.

certified apprentices) causes several effects. Faced with the choice of paying a learner, not yet fully productive, at the journeyman rate or not using him on the job, most contractors are forced, in the interests of productivity, to replace the learner with a journeyman. Not only do costs increase, but the development of new journeymen is also inhibited. This problem has been particularly noticeable for minority group members:

> In Alabama, we have been an open-shop contractor for a number of years, and there are no certified apprenticeship training programs in that State except those that are union oriented and union dominated, and they are not open to . . . open-shop members.
>
> As a result, in Alabama, on Davis-Bacon projects, we have not been able to use any apprentices whatsoever. We can't use helpers unless we pay helpers the prevailing standard for the journeyman. . . .
>
> It just happens that I favor strongly upgrading the minorities in our company. We work at it actively and with some success. But if we bid a job that comes under Davis-Bacon, that upgrading is stopped in that work.[50]

The administration of Davis-Bacon in this area thus tends to hold back minority development in nonunion construction and has served to institutionalize the building trade's craft designations and demarcations. It has also limited flexibility and increased costs for open-shop firms and has helped to prevent development of more realistic training patterns to compete with the industry's often inappropriate apprenticeship programs.

Importation of Wage Rates

In the 1972 Senate hearing, Senator John Tower noted that the problem of wage scales determined in larger, municipal areas but applied to rural counties was one of the three most often heard complaints from builders and sponsors.[51] This procedure, referred to as "importation of wages," is intimately connected with other problems involved in setting the boundaries on areas for the purpose of administering the Davis-Bacon Act.

DETERMINATION OF AREA. As noted previously, the Act and its implementing regulations provide that the area to be con-

---

50 Statements of Thomas Hails, general contractor, on behalf of Associated Builders and Contractors, in U.S., Congress, Senate, Subcommittee on Housing and Urban Affairs, *op. cit.*, pp. 49, 50.

51 U.S., Congress, Senate, Subcommittee on Housing and Urban Affairs, *op. cit.*, p. 4.

sidered in determining prevailing wage rates is the "city, town, village, or other civil subdivision of the State in which the work is to be performed."[52] This is perhaps the most specific language which can be found in the act and the closest that it comes to an operational definition of any term or specification. The Department of Labor has chosen to honor it largely by ignoring it and using instead informal guidelines not sanctioned by either law or regulation. The under secretary of labor at the same 1972 hearings, for example, responded to a question on this point as follows:

> In determining whether wage rates from urban centers are regularly "imported" into nearby rural areas, two kinds of situations need to be considered;
>
> (1) where the city and the rural area are in the same county; and
>
> (2) where the urban center and the rural area are in separate counties.
>
> In the first situation, wage rate surveys normally encompass the entire county. As a result of the larger number of projects being located in the urban center, the wage rates being paid there would normally be found prevailing throughout the entire county.
>
> In the second situation, urban rates are not issued for adjoining rural counties unless information establishes that these rates do, in fact, prevail in the rural area.[53]

Even at its best, this response indicates that "city, town, or village" have given way to "county" as the standard civil subdivision of the state which the Department of Labor follows. But considerable evidence exists that even this demarcation is not consistently followed and that the department often fails to establish what rates do, in fact, prevail in nonurban areas. Further extensions are made under the shield of the departmental regulations which provide that, if no similar construction projects have been undertaken within the area (presumably county) in the past year, wage rates paid on the nearest similar construction may be considered.

TIME HORIZON. Flexibility in determining the time horizon for wage surveys opens up a number of possibilities to the department. First, the department has flexibility in determining whether to include rates on similar work in the area during the

---

[52] 40 USC 276(a) (1969) and 29 CFR 1, Sec. 2(b) (1968).

[53] Cited by L. H. Silberman, Under Secretary of Labor, in U.S., Congress, Senate, Subcommittee on Housing and Urban Affairs, *op. cit.*, p. 37.

entirety of the past year. In an interview with the author, personnel from the Division of Wage Determinations indicated that, in at least some cases, only current work is included in wage surveys:

> It would take too long to find all those who completed work within the past year. Contractors come in here from all over: New York, Chicago, etc. It might take a year to do it. The firms which did the work a year ago might now be out of business. So we use only current work.[54]

In other cases, at the discretion of the department, such an effort is apparently undertaken. This can be quite important in cases in which terminal, bonus wages are paid employees during the final weeks before completion of work, and in other situations where going back over a year yields far different wages to survey and results in different rates found to be prevailing for new work.

SIZE OF DATA BASE. The department also exercises flexibility concerning how many jobs or how many rates are sufficient to form a data base for the purposes of determination. Surprisingly, this judgmental flexibility has seldom been questioned. But in those cases for which the department feels there is insufficient local (however defined) similar construction to form a data base and goes outside the area to seek other similar projects, it apparently exercises its own judgment in how far to extend the search. In one case—the Mountain Park Dam—to be subsequently discussed, the department went 225 miles from the site of a proposed dam, thus leapfrogging over a number of similar projects—including another dam, only one-third the distance away.

For building construction in nonurban areas, the typical search is extended to the nearest metropolitan area, where negotiated rates are presumed to prevail in sufficient number to overpower any other rates found in the locality.[55]

SIMILAR NATURE. The department likewise exercises judgmental flexibility in determining what construction work is of a "similar nature" for inclusion in the survey data base. This situation will be discussed in a subsequent section, but it might be advantageously noted here that a tight definition of similar-

---

[54] Interview with Division of Wage Determinations personnel, U.S. Department of Labor, September 26, 1973.

[55] Johnson, "Prevailing Wage Law," *op. cit.*, p. 249.

natured work, e.g., public utilities construction, could easily require extending the survey search by many miles.

Administrative Burden

It is doubtful that the impetus behind the Labor Department's importation of rates is anything more than an administrative accommodation to the magnitude of the task involved in determining what rates actually prevail in the vast number of determinations required annually. One former Division of Wage Determinations employee interviewed by the author said:

> In general, the rate determination procedure was automatic. Except for a few states in the South and Midwest and in a few specific suburban areas, signed collective bargaining agreements served as the prevailing wage rate.
>
> The administrative problem was a compound one, not at all helped by the niggardly level of support provided by Congress and Administration to support fact-finding activities. In many cases, halfhearted mail surveys were the only thing attempted, and then the union rate was fallen back on when the response was too low.[56]

Each year the department makes a staggering number of wage determinations. By the early 1960s, the department was issuing almost 50,000 wage decisions annually, involving a total of perhaps 3,000,000 individual wage rates. The burden was rapidly becoming overwhelming, and beginning in fiscal year 1965, the Department of Labor began issuing determinations for entire areas, to govern all projects of the type specified within the area and to last until modified or updated.

AREA DETERMINATIONS. The new system of area determinations successfully reduced the number of wage rate determinations to approximately 25,500 in the year it was instituted—a level at which it has approximately remained.[57] Although this new procedure may be administratively simpler, in many cases it imports the metropolitan wage rates to the suburban and rural localities intermixed in the areas covered, and it institutionalizes the previous pattern rather than freeing administrative resources for conducting actual surveys. Some of these area determinations take in entire states. The result is an escalation of con-

---

[56] Interview with former employee of Division of Wage Determinations, U.S. Department of Labor, May 14, 1974 (in the files of the author).

[57] U.S., Comptroller General, *Report* (B-146842), 1971, *op. cit.*, p. 8.

struction costs and a disruption of local wage standards—precisely the opposite effect from the act's intended purpose.

Beginning in 1972, the area determinations issued by the department have been published in the *Federal Register*. The issue for September 7, 1973, reveals the extent of area determinations coverage at that time. These are summarized in Table 1, which shows the number of statewide decisions in effect, and in Table 2, which shows the locations of the only counties in the country which had not effected any sort of area determination.

For all other parts of the country, some form of area decision existed, and a great many of these had jurisdiction over several counties simultaneously. Illustrating the situation, Table 3 shows the area determinations in effect in Maryland (chosen for its convenient size). Here one can see, for example, that the metropolitan Baltimore residential construction rates apply in the generally rural Cecil and Harford Counties and in the suburban Howard County as well.

It is something of a mystery why the dredging rate for Baltimore County should be the same as that determined to prevail in Worcester County, the southernmost Maryland county on the Delmarva peninsula, at least 75 miles from Baltimore, and separated from it by five intervening counties by the most direct land route. Somerset and Wicomico counties, the two contiguous to Worcester, pinning it against the Atlantic Ocean—and separating it from the general direction of Baltimore—carry a different determination.

The degree to which urban rates spread into suburban and rural areas as a result of increasing reliance on area determinations varies from state to state. Certainly, the wider the area covered, the smaller the chance that local contractors in the less populated regions will be able to obtain local work of a federal or federally supported nature and employ local workers at the local wage.

EMPIRICAL EXAMPLE. One of the lengthiest and best documented studies of the Davis-Bacon Act devoted considerable attention to the problem of imported wage rates. This study was the doctoral dissertation of Damodar Gujarathi. It provides extensive empirical analysis of regular (or non-"area") rate determinations.[58]

---

[58] Gujarathi, *op. cit.*

TABLE 1.
The Davis-Bacon Act
Statewide Area Wage Determinations in Effect
September 7, 1973

State	Type of Contract						
	B	D	F	H	Hw	R	S
Alabama		1					
Alaska	1	1		1	1	2	
Arizona				1	1		
Arkansas		1			2		
Colorado					1		
Delaware	1	2		1	1		
District of Columbia	1			1			1
Hawaii	1			1	1		
Louisiana		1					
Mississippi			1		2		
Montana				1	1		
Nevada				1	1		
New Mexico	1			1	2		
North Carolina					1		2
North Dakota					1		
Oregon	1	1		1	1		
Puerto Rico	1			1	1		
Rhode Island		1					
South Carolina					1		2
South Dakota					1		
Tennessee			1		2		
Utah	1			1	1		
Washington	1	1		1	1		
West Virginia				1	1		
Wyoming					1		

Source: *Federal Register*, September 7, 1973.

Notes: B = building, D = dredging, F = flood control, H = heavy, Hw = highway, R = residential, S = sewer

Different numbers appearing in the rows indicate different decisions. The same number appearing under several column headings indicates that rates for these headings were set by the same decision.

TABLE 2.
The Davis-Bacon Act
Location of Counties for Which No Area Determination Existed
September 7, 1973

State	Number of Counties
Florida	24
Illinois	8
Iowa	75
Maine	8
Maryland	6
Minnesota	59
Missouri	95
New Hampshire	8
New York	32
Ohio	49
Vermont	1
Total	365
Total counties in country	3,141
Percent of counties for which no area determinations in effect	11.6

Source: *Federal Register,* September 7, 1973.

Gujarathi found that 25 to 38 percent of building construction and 46 to 73 percent of heavy and highway work carried union wage rates from noncontiguous counties or statewide union wage rates. (The slightly separate problem of overemphasis on negotiated rates will be examined later in this chapter.) The study notes:

> The practice of "leap frogging" in search of prevailing wage rates does not conform to the Act . . . All the noncontiguous counties that were reached to obtain prevailing wage rates, were either metropolitan areas or areas of 50,000 and more population.[59]

[59] *Ibid.,* pp. 48-51.

TABLE 3.
The Davis-Bacon Act
Types of Area Determinations in Effect
Maryland Counties
September 7, 1973

County	Type of Contract					
	B	D	H	Hw	R	None
1. Allegheny						X
2. Anne Arundel	2B	2A		2B		
3. Baltimore	3A	3C	3A	3A	3B	
4. Calvert		2				
5. Caroline						X
6. Carroll						X
7. Cecil					3	
8. Charles		2				
9. Dorchester		2				
10. Frederick						X
11. Garrett						X
12. Harford		2			3	
13. Howard					3	
14. Kent		2				
15. Montgomery	15A				15B	
16. Prince Georges	15	2			15	
17. Queen Annes		2				
18. St. Marys		2				
19. Somerset		2				
20. Talbot		2				
21. Washington						X
22. Wicomico		2				
23. Worcester		3				

Source: *Federal Register*, September 7, 1973.

Notes: B = building, H = heavy, R = residential, D = dredging, Hw = highway

Baltimore City is an independent city, not part of Baltimore County. Baltimore City and County determinations are identical, however.

Numbers in the rows refer to the number assigned the counties. Thus, beside Worcester County the 3 in the dredging column indicates that the determination for this county is the same as that for Baltimore County.

The suffixes A, B, or C associated with some of the numbers indicated different determinations for different types of contract. Thus, the dredging determination for Anne Arundel County is different from that for building or highway construction in that county.

Table 4 shows the frequency distribution of noncontiguous county determinations by distance. This table covers wage determinations for nine crafts: bricklayers, carpenters, plasterers, electricians, painters, plumbers, power equipment operators, laborers, and cement masons. The average distance between the place of construction and the area from which the rates were taken ranged from a low of 72 miles to a high of 84 miles.[60] The standard deviation ranged from 10.5 to 26.5 miles. The highest average distance for the craft was 84.1 miles for power equipment operators, and the lowest average distance was 72.0 miles for bricklayers.[61] This table gives strong evidence for the department's tendency to import wage rates by expanding the area to be included in making surveys for prevailing wage purposes.

An example of expanding the area of consideration for a wage determination is the 450-unit Capehart housing project at the Marine Corps School in the vicinity of Quantico, Virginia.[62] Without going into detail about this case, which has been extensively reviewed since it was documented by the General Accounting Office in 1962, the conclusions were that wage rates established as prevailing for the job in Quantico, Prince William County, Virginia, had been imported from Washington, D.C., an entirely different polity not even contiguous across a state line but separated across an intervening county by a distance of 35 miles. The wage determination so imported necessitated additional labor costs of more than $1 million, required deletions of some planned facilities, such as sidewalks and carports, and considerable substitution of inferior materials, such as plywood siding for brick, to meet the limited funds appropriated; as a result, the project was of considerably lower over-all quality than originally contemplated.

In interviews, the author asked General Accounting Office personnel, who had been involved with review or rate determinations over a number of years, whether there had been any recent change in administration in this area. The answer was that determination of area for survey still largely follows union local

---

60 *Ibid.*, p. 61.

61 *Ibid.*, p. 62.

62 U.S., Comptroller General, *Report to the Congress of the United States: Review of Wage Rate Determinations for Construction of Capehart Housing at the Marine Corps Schools, Quantico, Virginia,* B-145200 (Washington, D.C.: General Accounting Office, 1962).

TABLE 4.
The Davis-Bacon Act
Frequency Distribution of Noncontiguous County Determinations By Distance in Miles

Distance (Miles) (1)	Bricklayer (2)	Carpenter (3)	Plasterer (4)	Electrician (5)	Painter (6)	Plumber (7)	P.E.O. (8)	Laborer (9)	Cement Mason (10)
45-60	16	14	6	9	12	11	10	11	10
60-75	15	10	12	20	12	12	10	13	10
75-90	13	11	14	13	14	12	10	14	14
90-105	5	4	5	11	3	5	8	6	8
105-150[a]	2	5	5	8	6	5	9	3	8
N	51	44	42	61	47	45	47	52[b]	50
X	72.0	76.4	81.1	81.8	77.9	77.8	84.1	81.5	83.1
σ	10.5	19.2	21.3	26.5	22.5	22.5	24.0	24.0	24.2

Source: Damodar Gujarathi, "The Economics of the Davis-Bacon Act" (Ph.D. diss., University of Chicago, 1965), p. 62.

[a] Because of the smallness of the number, the class interval was taken as 45 miles. A very few determinations went beyond 150 miles.

[b] Total is inconsistent because of error in mileage figures.

jurisdictional lines rather than geographic or political subdivisions, "except in those places where the contractors have been putting on pressure."[63] This aspect of the act's administration does not, however, seem quite as acute a problem currently as it was a few years ago.

Emphasis on Negotiated Wages

In the views of many researchers, extension of the area for wage survey purposes is related to union organizational strength and the easy availability of negotiated rates in the larger metropolitan areas. They feel that, by establishing out-of-county union wage rates, the Department of Labor extends de facto union organization and boosts union organizational power at the expense of higher construction costs for the government. Here is Gujarathi's opinion:

> there is a pronounced tendency to establish union wage rates regardless of the area of construction. The establishment of large county rates in small counties, the establishment of metropolitan county rates in nonmetropolitan areas, and the distance which the Labor Department traverses [average: 75 miles] in search of prevailing wage rates all point out to the preponderence [*sic*] of union rates.[64]

This opinion was reached on the basis of extensive sampling of wage rates used in Davis-Bacon determinations. Gujarathi found that an overwhelming majority of wage rates—for 9 common crafts in a sample from 48 states plus the District of Columbia—of 372 wage determinations were union rates. The lowest percentage was 84 percent for common laborers; the highest was 98 percent for plasterers in building construction. Highway and heavy construction were somewhat lower, the range from 62 percent for laborers to 100 percent for plasterers.[65]

In selecting a representative sample for the 372 wage determinations studied, one must make certain assumptions about the extent of union and open-shop construction in the country. For the study here discussed, Gujarathi assumed that the level of union activity in a county is directly proportional to the county's population: the larger the county population, the greater the degree of organization. Thus, counties with a population of 200 people up to 50,000 people were assumed to have a low degree

---

63 Interview with General Accounting Office personnel, June 13, 1973.

64 Gujarathi, *op. cit.*, p. 63.

65 *Ibid.*, p. 47.

of union organization, counties of population 50,000 to 250,000 a medium degree of organization, and counties with populations over 250,000 a high degree of organization.

Under the not unrealistic assumption stated,[66] one would expect prevailing rates set for the smallest counties to reflect open-shop or mixed rates consisting of partially open-shop and partially union rates. In fact, the opposite was found to be true. Of the 259 wage determinations studied for this grouping, 174 (67 percent) have out-of-county union wage rates.[67] Table 5 gives the results for prevailing wage determinations in counties of various sizes. The table makes it apparent that the influence of union, or negotiated, wage rates is immense and very definitely reflected in the prevailing wage determinations issued by the Department of Labor. The author of the study noted:

> It would . . . be a fair generalization to say that the Davis-Bacon wage rate determinations follow union jurisdictional boundaries regardless of the area of Federal construction.[68]

Or, as Senator Tower put it:

> A . . . perversion of Davis-Bacon is reflected in the instances where a union scale or the product of a collective bargaining agreement have been adopted as the prevailing wage in the area, despite the fact that but a small percentage of the labor force within the jurisdiction is organized.[69]

Another study, generally favorable to the Davis-Bacon Act, puts it in these words:

> The staff [of the Department of Labor] depends largely upon ascertaining the negotiated rate for the area. And this certainly is the only realistic view for them to take.[70]

Interviews by the author with contractors, officials of contractors' associations, government officials outside the Department of Labor, and former employees of the Department of Labor all indicated dissatisfaction with the degree to which the department has relied on negotiated wages in establishing, setting, and

---

[66] A major study of the extent and nature of open-shop construction is scheduled for publication by the Industrial Research Unit in the spring of 1975.

[67] Gujarathi, *op. cit.*, p. 54.

[68] *Ibid.*

[69] Statement of Senator John Tower, in U.S., Congress, Senate, Subcommittee on Housing and Urban Affairs, *op. cit.*, p. 4.

[70] Johnson, *loc. cit.*

TABLE 5.
The Davis-Bacon Act
Davis-Bacon Determinations by County Population

Population	Total	Union Wage Rates: Entirely or Mostly Local	Union Wage Rates: Out of County	Mixed Rates	Non-Union
200-50,000	259	25(9.6)	174(67.2)	28(10.8)	32(12.4)
50,000-250,000	76	35(46.1)	27(35.5)	5(6.6)	9(11.8)
250,000 and over	37	23(62.2)	10(27.0)	3(8.1)	1(2.7)

Source: Derived from Damodar Gujarathi, "The Economics of the Davis-Bacon Act" (Ph.D. diss., University of Chicago, 1965), pp. 53, 54.

Note: Figures in parentheses are percents.

leaving the Davis-Bacon rates until and unless protested. Although this problem is represented as less severe at the present time than it was a few years ago, it is difficult to determine if the difference results from changes in policies or procedures of the department (such as the decentralization of 1971), or from more active and better organized protests by contractors and their associations in some areas of the country. As long as the haphazard survey procedures, characteristic of the act since 1931 (and including those followed since decentralization in 1971), continue to be followed, problems will persist in this area.

Determination of Similar Construction

One question which administrators of Davis-Bacon must answer properly and consistently in making surveys for rate purposes is: what is similar construction? Is building a two-story frame house "similar" to building a seventeen-story hospital? Is building a levee more similar to building a superhighway than to building the seventeen-story hospital? Is building an atomic power plant sufficiently different from building a fossil power plant to require rates of its own? Here again is an area where the Department of Labor is allowed considerable latitude in interpretation and one where a great many problems and apparent inequities have arisen.

Department of Labor regulations classify construction into the three general categories of building construction, heavy construction, and highway construction[71]—both too many and too few categories. In its 1971 report on the administration of the Davis-Bacon Act, the General Accounting Office concluded that the broad spectrum of federal construction projects made these three classifications too wide, especially in the area of building construction; but it also concluded that in many cases the department did not make proper distinctions among the categories which it had set forth.[72]

The two most common areas of weakness are in building construction, where the distinction between commercial building and residential construction of a homebuilding nature is not clearly delineated, and in heavy construction, which is determined sometimes at building trades rates and sometimes at highway rates. The concern in this area arises because not all segments of the construction industry share the same level of union organization. Again, very little trustworthy statistical information establishing precise levels of union organization has been available. But generally speaking, commercial construction in urban areas is highly organized, whereas residential construction and highway work are much less so. Thus, if a housing project is classified as a project similar in nature to commercial construction, and if commercial construction rates form the basis for its wage predetermination, the rates for the job will most likely be much higher than if homebuilding rates formed the basis. The same relationship between commercial construction rates and highway rates is pertinent; one or the other of these rates will probably form the basis for heavy construction.

Until fairly recently, the biggest problem area here was residential construction for which commercial rates were assigned. The General Accounting Office found that this situation affected such projects as single houses, garden apartments, and barracks.[73] The Department of Housing and Urban Development (HUD) was also concerned about commercial rates prescribed for low-rise residential construction, high-rise rates prescribed for garden apartments or town houses, and residential construction rates applied to housing rehabilitation.[74]

---

[71] 29 CFR 5, Sec. 3(a) (2) (i) (1968).

[72] U.S., Comptroller General, *Report* (B-146842), 1971, pp. 16, 17.

[73] *Ibid.*, p. 17.

[74] Statement of Richard Van Dusen, Under Secretary of the Department of Housing and Urban Development, in U.S., Congress, Senate, Subcommittee on Housing and Urban Affairs, *op. cit.*, p. 76.

Consternation over misapplication of rates on residential construction reached such proportions that an agreement was made in 1972 between the Department of Housing and Urban Development and the Department of Labor; the former would conduct wage surveys of its own and submit the evidence to the latter along with any requests for wage determinations. Although this procedure has helped immensely in the housing area (where HUD is the typical contracting agency), it has been neither cheap nor flawless.[75] The Department of Housing and Urban Development has found it necessary to train a special staff at considerable cost for handling this sort of work which, by the terms of the Davis-Bacon Act, should be done by the Department of Labor. The procedure also seems to establish a rather bad precedent; it leaves the impression that if the Department of Labor does a poor enough job on rate determinations for some segment of the construction industry, another government agency will perhaps assume its workload and responsibilities.

To the degree to which the similar work problem has ameliorated in residential construction, it has worsened for heavy construction. As Table 6 shows, heavy construction categories vary considerably. These projects have little in common beyond their large scale. One thing which they definitely do not share is a need for or reliance on the standard classifications of carpenters, glaziers, plumbers, electricians, roofers, tile setters, etc., of which the AFL-CIO building trades are composed—although, to be sure, some of these trades would be necessary to most of the projects listed.

A large proportion of the jobs require extensive earthmoving, however, much of which is done by machinery similar to that employed in large scale roadbuilding. Perhaps it is for this reason that traditionally heavy construction has been more closely associated with highway work than with building construction.

Where rates are negotiated, they have traditionally been negotiated for "building" rates on one hand and "heavy and highway" on the other. Within the last few years, however, a greater incidence of "building and heavy" rates has been negotiated, and the trend in this direction appears well established in some part of the country. For instance, negotiated wage rates for dump truck drivers under "building and heavy" rates could be substantially

---

[75] See Portage Realty case in Chapter 7.

TABLE 6.
The Davis-Bacon Act
Classifications of Heavy Construction Work

railroads	viaducts	pipe lines
large sewers	dams	water power projects
heavy foundations	reservoirs	transmission lines
abutments	drainage projects	telephone lines
tunnels	sanitation projects	radio towers
subways	gas mains	mining tipples
elevated highways	hydroelectric projects	mining washeries
ovens	dredging	breakwaters
furnaces	underwater rock	channels
kilns	removal	cofferdams
silos	pile driving	dikes
docks	jetties	levees
locks	piers	watermarks
wharves	land reclamation	water mains

Source: U.S., Executive Office of the President, Bureau of the Budget, Office of Statistical Standards, *Standard Industrial Classification Manual* (Washington, D.C.: U.S. Government Printing Office, 1967).

higher than under "heavy and highway" rates, principally because of the greater competitive pressures exerted by nonunion road builders on that segment of the industry.

The significance of these considerations is that, for a heavy construction project situated near a major metropolitan area which has a "building and heavy" rate, the chances are quite good that the Department of Labor will follow the administratively easy procedure of assuming that the rate will prevail.[76]

Another significant problem related to this one is overspecification of similarity. The department will sometimes specify a particular type of heavy construction as the only type it will include in surveys for rate purposes. In interviews, personnel of the Wage Determination Division informed the author that sewer rates were different from heavy construction rates, as were dams, levee work, and other work along rivers.[77] This situation is also reflected in Table 1, where it was shown that area rates were established for building, dredging, flood control, heavy, highway,

[76] See Washington Metro Extension case in Chapter 7.

[77] Interview with Wage Determination Division personnel, U.S. Department of Labor, September 26, 1973.

residential, and sewer contracts in some instances. Where area rates do not exist, it is quite possible that only work of the tightly defined similar nature would be considered for surveys. This method usually has the effect, as previously noted, of importing wage rates from a considerable distance and imposing them on a local community.

A number of cases taken to the Wage Appeals Board have concerned this question of similarity. Although the decisions of the board have not been inconsistent among themselves, their nature has made generalizations difficult. Here are some samples from a series of decisions involving the construction of levees in Jefferson County, Texas:

> Because of available evidence concerning such heavy construction work in Jefferson County, Texas, the Solicitor did not err in excluding highway construction projects altogether in his wage determination respecting certain levee construction in that County. . . . [P]etitioner did not sustain its burden of showing that the comparisons here were not made with projects of a character similar in the appropriate subdivision. (WAB Case No. 67-7, May 5, 1967.)

> Where there was a substantial likeness between the proposed levees and the highway projects described to the Board, i.e., those resembling the proposed levees but differing as to ultimate use, the Solicitor was directed to consider projects of this type in the county as projects similar to the levees. (WAB Case No. 67-11, April 18, 1968.)

> In this case the Solicitor, in applying the statutory test, should have considered as a factual matter in determining this wage decision all projects in Jefferson County, Texas, which are of a character similar to the contract work (construction of levees), which include the timely highway projects and the listed heavy projects. (Petition for clarification of WAB Case No. 68-1, August 15, 1968.)[78]

Here, as in other matters involving the Davis-Bacon Act, the burden of documentation is on the petitioner. The decisions of the Department of Labor about similarity of work will stand unless challenged. If such a decision is challenged, it will become a matter of evidence in the individual case to determine what work is similar to that proposed and should be included in predetermination surveys. Broad precedents are not set by the Wage Appeals Board.

---

[78] *Decisions of the Wage Appeals Board: Index-Digest, 1964-1968* (Washington, D.C.: U.S. Department of Labor, n.d.), pp. 28-30.

Mixed Contracts and Incidental Work

The problem of what to do administratively about mixed jobs—that is, those which have construction requirements in several different categories—is also important. Several different types of mixed contracts might be considered. First, the contract which is "mixed" because it requires work which is partially building and partially heavy construction should be considered. This might be the case of a school for which extensive playing fields, parking lots, and roadways might be constructed in addition to buildings; or alternatively, a tunnel project for which pumphouses or air shaft caps might be needed. In these cases, the Department of Labor has taken the view that, if the work is done under a single contract, the over-all nature of the work determines the rate structure under which the job will be done. This position is complicated only because situations occasionally arise in which rates for the heavy construction portion of a building job (or the building portion of a heavy job) are not included in the predetermination because the appropriate job titles were not used on the "similar" work included in the survey.

A more difficult situation arises when the mixed rates are for contracts involving some construction and some other sort of work, such as supply, research and development, maintenance, or services. Procurement regulations of the government prescribe different sets of contract clauses for these different categories. The Davis-Bacon Act, the Walsh-Healey Act, and the Service Contract Act each might apply, and all have different contract provisions for wages.

For a long time, the comptroller general and the secretary of labor have disagreed over the applicability of the Davis-Bacon Act to mixed contracts. The secretary of labor has taken the position that the Davis-Bacon Act applies to the installation portion of a combined supply and installation contract (and the Walsh-Healey Act to the other portion), if the installation requires more than an "incidental" amount of construction work:

> If such a [supply] contract involves more than an incidental amount of erection or installation work it may also be subject to the Davis-Bacon Act with respect to such work if the site of such work is known at the time the invitation to bid is issued. Examples of such contracts are those for the manufacturing or furnishing and installation of elevators or of generators requiring prepared foundations or housing.[79]

[79] *Rulings and Interpretations No. 3, Under Walsh-Healey Public Contracts Act* (Washington, D.C.: U.S. Department of Labor, 1963), 6(b), p. 2.

The comptroller general, on the other hand, feels that the Davis-Bacon Act holds only if the over-all contract is "essentially" or "substantially" for construction, and is not otherwise applicable.[80] Resolution of this conflict seems to be left up to the individual contracting agencies (such as the Air Force) which, under the Davis-Bacon Act, are responsible for deciding whether to include the act's provisions and for seeing that they are carried out if assigned. Under Reorganization Plan No. 14 of 1950, the contracting agencies must follow "appropriate standards, regulations, and procedures" prescribed by the secretary of labor.[81]

The individual agencies must be responsive to the guidance of the Department of Labor for establishing coverage and to the General Accounting Office, in turn, for enforcement procedures. As long as the conflict exists between the secretary of labor and the comptroller general, the contracting agency could conceivably prescribe Davis-Bacon rates, the contractor could conceivably resist paying them, and the comptroller general could conceivably refuse to pursue enforcement. Needless to say, this resistance would involve great risk to the contractor, and the procedure has seldom been followed.[82]

Nevertheless, on at least three occasions, contracting agencies have pursued this issue and contested the decision of the solicitor of labor to cover work by Davis-Bacon rates. These occasions involved assembly of a mobile nuclear reactor experimental system, assembly of 40-foot waveguide modules for subsequent installation into a linear accelerator, and assembly of the crawler-transporter used at the Kennedy Space Center for lifting and transporting a launch vehicle and spacecraft to its launch site.[83] In two of these cases, the agencies' position against the solicitor was upheld by the comptroller general,[84] and in the third, the

---

[80] Louis A. Cox, "The Davis-Bacon Act and Defense Construction—Problems of Statutory Coverage," in *Proceedings of New York University Fifteenth Annual Conference on Labor*, ed. Emanuel Stein (New York: Matthew Bender & Co., 1962), p. 159.

[81] Reorganization Plan No. 14 follows 5 USC 133 z-15.

[82] Cox, *op. cit.*, p. 165.

[83] U.S., Commission on Government Procurement, *Report of the Commission on Government Procurement*, vol. 3, part E (Washington, D.C.: Government Printing Office, 1972), p. 138.

[84] U.S., Comptroller General, opinion B-150828, February 18, 1965, and opinion B-161858, October 11, 1967.

Wage Appeals Board reversed the solicitor's decision to cover the work.[85]

Given the complexity and size of these projects and the usual considerable difference between industrial union rates and heavy construction worker rates, it is not difficult to understand the agencies' concern. Here again, however, are cases in which the Department of Labor's decisions will stand unless challenged, the burden being placed on the challenger and the challenge on the basis of the individual project. The department's regulations and procedures do not change simply because they were challenged successfully in one instance.

The regulations as they exist and are interpreted by the department call for including Davis-Bacon provisions on any government contract if more than an "incidental" amount of construction activity is involved. "Incidental" involves aspects of both quality and quantity. In terms of quantity, incidental activity is interpreted as more than $2,000 of work (the amount which would be covered were the construction job bid separately). In terms of quality, the work contemplated must be complex rather than simple, at least to the point of requiring some building trades skills. In addition, the act does not cover all construction, but only that of a "public building" or a "public work." [86]

From the contracting agency's standpoint, to include or not to include a job under these provisions is a matter of deciding on the basis of the department's somewhat vague criteria. The greater uncertainty involves deciding exactly how much of the contract work is covered and how much is not. When the act applies, presumably all "laborers and mechanics employed on the site of the work" are covered.

In the past, some strange situations have been covered by the Davis-Bacon Act:

> The Department of Labor has held that the construction under an AEC contract of a full-scale operating prototype of a reactor compartment and associated components and systems for a submarine is covered; but—at least in practice—the construction of naval vessels is not covered. In 1936, the Acting Attorney General took the position that a contract for the repair of a damaged aircraft was covered.[87]

---

[85] Wage Appeals Board, Case No. 65-2, April 12, 1965.

[86] Cox, *op. cit.*, pp. 157-163.

[87] *Ibid.*, p. 166.

Also covered in 1936 were contracts for remaking cotton mattresses owned by the government and for manufacturing uniforms from cloth owned by the government. As recently as 1962, the Department of Labor determined prevailing wage requirements for repair of an aircraft for the Department of Agriculture.[88]

That prevailing rates are no longer predetermined for work of this type is interesting, but it is only a partial answer. The department has not been prohibited from including such work and presumably could do so again without needing legislative approval. As new technologies evolved, particularly in the nuclear power plant and missile site areas, a considerable period of sorting out was required before accords were reached among all of the interested parties, the contracting agencies, and the Department of Labor concerning what was and was not covered. Undoubtedly, a similar period of confusion will surround the development of any new technologies which may be required—for instance, in unusual power generation requirements, offshore drilling rigs, or other consequences of the energy crisis.

Site of Work

The Davis-Bacon Act provides that every covered contract will stipulate that laborers and mechanics will be paid at rates not less than those stated in the advertised specifications when they are employed directly upon the "site of the work." As is the case with a number of other provisions of the act, controversies have arisen because of the lack of definition given the key phrase. Operating decisions based on opinions of the solicitor have been issued for use by Department of Labor field personnel. Here, as for mixed contracts and incidental work, the comptroller general has expressed opinions more narrowly defining the scope of application; however, such action has not often been taken, and the conflict is not resolved.[89]

As the definition is currently construed, the site of the work includes the construction project itself, the grounds on which it stands, and other nearby land or structures that the contractor uses in the course of performing the particular job. The site also includes fabrication plants, "mobile factories," batch plants, borrow pits, job headquarters, tool yards, etc., provided they are

[88] *Ibid.*, pp. 166-168; statement of Solicitor of Labor Charles Donahue.

[89] U.S., Commission on Government Procurement, *op. cit.*, pp. 137, 138.

dedicated exclusively or nearly so to the performance of the contract and are so located in proximity to the actual construction location "that it would be reasonable to include them."[90] Once the limits of the site are defined, all laborers and mechanics employed on it are covered, including drivers who temporarily leave it to transport materials and equipment used in the course of contract operations and, for the time so spent, laborers and mechanics who come onto the site to install factory-made items, to perform maintenance on owned or leased equipment, or to become involved in other ways.

Even under these operating guidelines, considerable latitude is given the department to include or to exclude workplaces and individual workers. This attitude has been particularly troublesome to the road builders, many of whom feel that Davis-Bacon rates are spread to suppliers and others who are not really in the construction business. In that segment of the industry, it is common on a large job to subcontract for special asphalt plants, gravel pits, quarries, concrete plants, and other supply operations. These are often set up especially for the job.[91] These suppliers and their truckers can and do fall within jurisdiction of Davis-Bacon.

In one Wage Appeals Board case, a road building contractor who leased his equipment from an equipment rental dealer found that the repairmen and servicing employees of the rental dealer maintaining the equipment were covered by the act.[92] As on-site construction costs continue to increase, and as more and more items are prefabricated in factories in order to take advantage of the generally lower labor rates found in industrial work, one may feel reasonably certain that the determination of job site and coverage will create additional controversies in the future.

The 30 Percent Rule

Of all the aspects of the Davis-Bacon Act, none except the existence of the act itself seems to trouble contractors and contracting associations more than the 30 percent rule. After making all of the preliminary determinations about the area and type

---

[90] U.S., Department of Labor, *Field Operations Handbook, op. cit.*, entry no. 15b18 (1/16/70), FOH insert no. 1090.

[91] Interview with American Road Builders Association personnel, March 15, 1974.

[92] Wage Appeals Board, Case No. 64.3, July 2, 1965.

of work to be surveyed, establishing whether only current jobs or jobs for the past year will be included, and evaluating jobs for their similarity to the proposed job, the Department of Labor then lists (by hand) the number of persons paid at each rate (to the penny) found in each category of workmen and makes notes of the fringe benefits they received. The prevailing rate for each category is, as already noted, then determined as: (1) the rate received by a majority of workers; (2) the rate received by at least 30 percent of the workers, if a majority do not receive the same rate; or (3) the weighted average of all rates, if fewer than 30 percent of the workers receive the same rate. (The same procedures are presumed for fringe benefits; however, because these tend to vary even more than wage rates, the method actually used seems to be to determine the prevailing wage and attach to it the associated fringe benefits. This method becomes judgmental in the event of "average" rates.)

The method for selecting or determining the prevailing rate is always stated as a three-step process. It is difficult to understand why such a method is used, because the second step inevitably overrides the first. Any rate paid to a majority of workers will, of necessity, also be paid to at least 30 percent. Thus, there is no reason to mention rates paid to a majority of workers at all. The rule is really 30 percent, or the average.

An interesting aspect of this calculation is that it is quite possible for more than one rate to "prevail" under the 30 percent rule. In a wage rate survey made for South Carolina in 1972, for example, three utility tractor operators were found.[93] One was paid at $2.50 per hour, one at $2.75, and one at $3.25. Each of these rates qualifies as the prevailing rate, since each is paid to more than 30 percent of the workers in the category. Perhaps in such circumstances the Department of Labor would simply use the average rate. But if the department did so, the average rate of $2.83 which would be found to be prevailing is higher than that paid to two-thirds of the workmen employed in this category.

In the major empirical study of Davis-Bacon by Gujarathi, a representative sample of wage rate determinations was analyzed. Gujarathi found that only 8 of his sample determinations were based on actual surveys, the balance (364) based on qualitative assessments of the extent of unionization in various areas by the

[93] S.C., Public Utility Commission, "Summary of Wage Rate Survey for South Carolina," August 18, 1972 (from the files of the Carolina Branch of the Associated General Contractors of America).

department. Of the 8 surveys actually made, survey data were available in the files of the department for only one. That one is very instructive about the 30 percent rule and its attendant problems, so it is included in detail here.[94]

The case involved construction of an addition to Beebe Hospital, Sussex County, Virginia, in 1960–1961. An initial wage determination for this project reflected entirely union rates. On protest by interested parties, a wage survey was actually conducted, resulting in a new determination. The wage survey data on which this revised determination was based are shown in Table 7. Table 8 then summarizes the determination and survey data of the case.

Examined together, these tables present a number of commentaries on the 30 percent rule and rate determinations in general. First, out of eight crafts, only three rates—those for carpenters, electricians, and common laborers—accurately reflect the department's rules for calculating prevailing rates. For cement masons, the rate should have been $3.75 in place of $3.55—the union rate. In Gujarathi's words, "Apparently the Department did not want to establish a rate higher than the union rate even though the payment evidence warranted it." [95] The rate for plumbers should have been $2.00, $3.00, $2.50, or $2.84, depending on what interpretation might be given within the rules to this specialized situation of multiple rates paid to the same number of persons over the 30 percent rule. It was actually determined to be $3.95, the union rate, and a rate at which only three of thirty-nine workmen within the craft were paid. The rate for plasterers was determined to be the lowest and bears no relationship to either the union rate or any others; it simply appears to be a mistake. The same reason is probably true for bricklayers as well, although the bricklayer rate could have possibly resulted from an arithmetic error in thinking that the eighteen persons who were paid the $2.85 rate constituted 30 percent of the employment in that craft. The rate for painters is also hard to understand. It was actually set higher than the union rate.

Indeed, this case does not present a very attractive picture of Davis-Bacon rate administration. Perhaps it has improved since the time of this example. That is very hard to say, however, because no routine audits of the accuracy of these determinations

[94] Gujarathi, *op. cit.*, p. 67.

[95] *Ibid.*, pp. 67-69.

TABLE 7.
The Davis-Bacon Act
Wage Survey Data for Beebe Hospital Addition
1960-1961

Trade	Rate Paid	Number Employed	Total Employed	30% of Total Employed (A)	Method Required by Rules for Calculation of Rates	Rate Calculated by Rules
Bricklayer	$2.85	18				
	3.00	12				
	3.375	14				
	3.50	3				
	3.75	2				
	3.925	15				
	4.05	4	68	21	average	$3.49
Plumber	1.65	2				
	2.00	13				
	3.00	13				
	3.825	8				
	3.95	3	39	12	(B)	$2.50
Painter	1.85	2				
	2.00	14				
	2.60	21				
	3.20	1				
	3.30	17	55	17	30% rule	$2.60
Common Laborer	1.00	1				
	1.15	10				
	1.25	20				
	1.30	6				
	1.35	2				
	1.375	29				
	1.50	5				
	1.95	12				
	2.00	4				
	2.05	93				
	2.50	5	187	57	30% rule	$2.05

TABLE 7 (Continued)

Trade	Rate Paid	Number Employed	Total Employed	30% of Total Employed (A)	Method Required by Rules for Calculation of Rates	Rate Calculated by Rules
Carpenter	$1.75	1				
	1.90	1				
	2.00	23				
	2.60	20				
	3.50	2				
	3.575	121				
	3.75	6	174	53	majority	$3.575
Plasterer	2.75	8				
	3.125	16				
	3.70	5				
	3.80	8				
	3.90	—	37	12	30% rule	$3.125
Electrician	2.00	10				
	2.25	11				
	3.15	27				
	3.975	2				
	4.125	38	88	27	(C)	$4.125
Cement Mason	2.825	10				
	3.00	6				
	3.55	9				
	3.75	12				
	4.80	1	38	12	30% rule	$3.75

Source: Developed from Damodar Gujarathi, "The Economics of the Davis-Bacon Act" (Ph.D. diss., University of Chicago, 1965), p. 69 (in turn from the files of the U.S. Department of Labor).

Notes: Union rates are underlined.
(A) Rounded to next largest integer number.
(B) Not covered by regulations. Perhaps average, but probably average of rates above 30% rule (taken as such).
(C) Not covered by regulations, but probably model rate above 30% rule (taken as such).

TABLE 8.
The Davis-Bacon Act
Summary of Determinations and Survey Data
Beebe Hospital Addition
1960-1961

Craft	Original Determination (Y-5, 908) (also union rate)	Survey Rate Calculated per Rules	Final Determination (Y-13,926)	Weighted Average of Survey Rates
Bricklayer	$3.925	$3.26	$2.85	$3.35
Carpenter	3.575	3.575	3.575	3.24
Plasterer	3.90	3.125	2.75	3.27
Electrician	4.125	4.125	4.125	3.35
Painter	3.20	2.60	3.30	2.65
Plumber	n.a.	2.50	3.95	2.84
Common Laborer	2.05	2.05	2.05	1.76
Cement Mason	3.55	3.75	3.55	3.37
Simple average of rates	3.475	3.123	3.269	2.98

Source: Developed from Damodar Gujarathi, "The Economics of the Davis-Bacon Act" (Ph.D. diss., University of Chicago, 1965), p. 69.

are made outside of the division establishing them, and the methods followed here have not changed materially.

The 30 percent rule is a very important aspect of wage rate administration. It determined six of the eight rates, or at least is the process which would have determined them, if the rules had been followed. Even if properly applied, the 30 percent rule is responsible for setting rates higher than they would be under an averaging concept in the typical case where the union rate is higher than the nonunion rate. In the example here, the average of the rates which should have been set following the 30 percent rule is $3.123, as shown in Table 8. If a weighted average rate were used instead, for each of the crafts, then the average of the rates would have been $2.98, about 15 percent less.

The General Accounting Office has presented examples drawn from actual rate surveys where the application of the 30 percent rule, based on 102 carpenters, resulted in determined wage rates

27.7 percent higher than the weighted average rate for the same group; in another example, the rate determined by the 30 percent rule, based on a survey of 16 electricians, was 22 percent less than the weighted average rate.[96] In the words of the comptroller general:

> The Department's application of the so-called 30-percent rule . . . as a method of determining the prevailing wage rates in an area has led to some unrealistic wage determinations and to inequities among the contractors and workers affected thereby. We believe that these cases show a need for a more equitable rule.[97]

SUMMARY

At the Roosevelt hearings in 1962, Secretary of Labor Arthur J. Goldberg was quite emphatic that the Davis-Bacon Act was being fairly administered with due regard for the rights and equities of individual employees and employers.[98] But the hearings brought out the need for a number of administrative changes, and a number of these have been made by the Department of Labor. Area surveys were begun in 1965. Some of the responsibilities for surveys and determinations were decentralized in 1971, when existing Employment Standards Administration regional offices were given responsibility for Davis-Bacon work in their areas. Publishing area determinations in the *Federal Register* may have helped disseminate information, and certainly the establishment of the Wage Appeals Board in 1964 helped immensely. In 1970, the Department of Housing and Urban Development began making its own wage surveys for determinations for federally assisted housing projects; after conducting these surveys it makes the information available to the Department of Labor.

Some of the specific administrative problems of greatest concern during the 1960s are no longer of as great concern today: residential housing construction rates are under much better control; problems at the missile sites decreased even before the missile sites were phased out; and less is now heard of rates following local craft union jurisdictional boundaries. On the other hand, the question of what rates are to be included in wage sur-

[96] Comptroller General, *Report* (B-146842), 1971, *op. cit.*, p. 23.

[97] *Ibid.*, p. 22.

[98] U.S., Congress, House, *Administration of the Davis-Bacon Act, op. cit.*, Part 1, 87th Cong., 2d sess. (1962), p. 49 (Roosevelt Hearings).

veys is still a concern, and some specific administrative problems have intensified. Building rates spreading into heavy construction, projects of a similar character receiving identification under a tight construction of "similar work," metropolitan rates becoming institutionalized through area determinations, and several other problems are in this last category. Moreover, still other problems have remained the same or show no clear indication of a trend. Thus, despite administrative changes and shifts of emphasis, many problems have certainly remained in the years since the Roosevelt hearings.

During this time, a number of extensive and well-documented studies have been produced which have investigated various aspects of Davis-Bacon administration. Among them have been eight published reviews and a summary by the General Accounting Office, a report of the Commission on Government Procurement, a Ph.D. dissertation from the University of Chicago, a special analysis of the American Enterprise Institute, and numerous journal articles, as well as considerable high-level analyses by interested parties such as the Chamber of Commerce of the United States, various contractors' associations, and labor unions. As was noted from the excerpts in the preceding sections drawn from these studies, they have not often reflected favorably on the procedures and policies of the Department of Labor in administering the act.

By 1972, in hearings before the Senate, then Under Secretary of Labor L. H. Silberman agreed that the Davis-Bacon Act had not always been administered in the most efficacious manner but stated that corrective action had been taken to eliminate the shortcomings.[99]

This type of action would probably please the General Accounting Office were it actually to come to pass, for GAO's concern is mainly with improving administration of the act.[100] Housing and Urban Development would also be satisfied:

> The problems which the Department of Housing and Urban Development has had in the past with the Davis-Bacon Act have related to the way in which the act was administered. We have no problem when actually prevailing wages are appropriately applied within similar classes of construction.[101]

---

99 U.S., Congress, Senate, Subcommittee on Housing and Urban Affairs, *op. cit.*, p. 23.

100 U.S., Comptroller General, *Report* (B-146842), 1971, *op. cit.*, p. 2.

101 Statement of Richard C. Van Dusen, Under Secretary of Housing and Urban Development, in U.S., Congress, Senate, Subcommittee on Housing and Urban Affairs, *op. cit.*, p. 76.

Others are less sanguine. The executive vice-president of one contractors' association feels that because of the volume of work, if for no other reason, the Davis-Bacon Act cannot possibly be administered equitably.[102] But administrative problems are not the only ones which beset the Davis-Bacon Act. As one study put it:

> The GAO classified wage determinations as "inappropriate" if they were clearly higher than would have been the case if the secretary of labor's directive on the appropriate procedures for making wage determinations had been followed. . . . Thus, it is important to emphasize that the determinations deemed "appropriate" by the General Accounting Office are themselves likely to be well above rates that would obtain under competitive bidding.[103]

---

102 Interview, September 10, 1973.

103 John P. Gould, *Davis-Bacon Act: The Economics of Prevailing Wage Laws*, Special Analysis No. 15 (Washington, D.C.: American Enterprise Institute, 1971), p. 27.

CHAPTER VI

Costs and Inflationary Impact

Whether well or poorly administered, the Davis-Bacon Act is a costly piece of legislation. This cost occurs in several forms. First are direct administrative costs of maintaining the federal Davis-Bacon machinery, which involves expenditures by the Department of Labor, by governmental contracting agencies such as the Department of Housing and Urban Development, and by contractors. Second are indirect costs forced on a portion of the construction industry by the institutionalization of job titles, training techniques, and other aspects influenced by the act's requirements. Third are increased direct costs to the government in higher construction prices which, given the likely absence of offsetting productivity gains, are highly inflationary.

ADMINISTRATIVE COSTS

Of the three major cost categories, perhaps the least significant in amount is the cost to the government of administering the act. The Department of Labor budget for wage determinations, the records maintenance, the Wage Appeals Board, and other Davis-Bacon machinery cost less than $1 million in fiscal year 1970 and about $1.4 million in 1971. Although it is probably somewhat higher now, this amount is several orders of magnitude less than others associated with the act. Actually, if anything, it is probably lower than it should be, considering the size of the task. Too many "inadvertancies," as mechanical errors in determinations are known, result from the cumbersome and haphazard techniques followed by the department. That the department lacks computers and other sophisticated data collection and reduction may be at least partially caused by insufficient funding, and the same cause may underlie their inability to conduct many actual surveys and their subsequent reliance on negotiated and other supplied rates. Very few governmental or other agencies face so extensive a task as determining more than a million wage rates and fringe benefits a year for 60,000 federally supported contracts without an automatically updated data base or computer equipment. On the other hand, perhaps the department feels it has greater flexibility without these aids.

Coverage Threshold

One alternative to increasing the support level for administration is to cut down the size of the task and the amount of administration required. One way which has often been suggested is to change the dollar threshold from the $2,000 level established in 1935 to some more reasonable amount, such as $25,000 or $100,000, as the minimum contract size subject to coverage. The Department of the Interior, suggesting such a course in December 1971, recommended a $25,000 minimum.[104] The General Services Administration, the Department of Housing and Urban Development, the General Accounting Office, and others have all made similar recommendations, with amounts ranging from $10,000 to $100,000.

Two arguments support such a change. In the first place, $2,000 in 1935 represented a considerably larger sum in terms of the amount of construction or repair work which it could then buy than it does today. On a straight construction price index calculation, it cost $10,200 in 1972 to buy as much as $2,000 in 1935, and the rampant price increases since 1972 have certainly pushed this figure even higher.[105] Second, lower cost projects are usually alteration, maintenance, or repair jobs. They are small jobs and have little or no impact on wage levels in the area.[106] The General Accounting Office studied 600 wage determinations covering $663 million of construction in four states in fiscal years 1965 and 1969. It found that 191 of them were issued for contracts of less than $25,000. This 32 percent of the 600 determinations represented about two-tenths of one percent of the total construction dollar volume.[107] The number of persons employed on a job is directly related to the cost of the job. Thus,

---

104 Memorandum from the Department of the Interior to the Office of Management and Budget, December 3, 1971, cited in U.S., Commission on Government Procurement, *op. cit.*, p. 135.

105 U.S., Commission on Government Procurement, *loc. cit.*

106 U.S., Comptroller General, *Report* (B-146842), 1971, *op. cit.*, p. 37.

107 *Ibid.*, pp. 36, 37.

it seems that considerable administrative savings could be made without substantially affecting the number of persons covered by the act's umbrella.

The Department of Labor's position is that increasing the minimum cut-off point would ease the department's workload, but that the amount of savings is not quantifiable.[108] It further contends that the workload would not ease greatly, because most of the small jobs are in areas already covered by area determinations or are homebuilding jobs for which Housing and Urban Development personnel are making the wage surveys.[109] It is difficult to ascertain the validity of these positions, but on the surface they seem weak arguments to be raised by an agency which complains of being chronically understaffed and which might save at least one-third or more of its workload. It is possible that there is a relationship between this position and promises by the AFL-CIO to oppose strongly any legislation calling for an increase in the $2,000 threshold, which, it feels, would reduce the level of protection for workers on small repair and painting contracts, the type said to need it most.[110]

Contracting Agency Costs

Even less is precisely known about the cost of Davis-Bacon administration incurred by the various government departments and agencies which actually contract for construction work. As mentioned previously, the Department of Housing and Urban Development has recently set up its own independent survey administration, which is not much smaller than that of the Department of Labor. Every agency, as well as the General Accounting Office, has personnel assigned full- or part-time to contract administration and enforcement required by Davis-Bacon. The total costs involved are indeterminate, but are very likely about $1 million per year or more.

Contractor Costs

The administrative costs to the government are high, but they are insignificant compared with the costs to contractors of complying with the reporting requirements of the act. Contractors

---

108 U.S., Commission on Government Procurement, *loc. cit.*

109 Interview with Department of Labor personnel, September 26, 1973.

110 U.S., Commission on Government Procurement, *op. cit.*, p. 136.

under Davis-Bacon are required to be familiar with and maintain an extensive list of forms and records. These will vary somewhat, depending on the agency for which the contract is performed. Table 9 summarizes those required for contractors in homebuilding or other activities contracted for by the Department of Housing and Urban Development.

The question of how much it costs to fill in and maintain the forms in Table 9 is a significant one. With about 60,000 federal construction contracts per year—totaling as much as $40 billion or more—a very small cost on each project or a very small percentage of contract costs for administration magnifies itself with alarming rapidity.

At the request of the Commission on Government Procurement, the Associated General Contractors of America (AGC) sampled its membership in the fall of 1972 to obtain some feel for the extent of the costs involved. An AGC internal memorandum summarizing the sample results notes the sense of futility contractors feel in preparing the required reports, which many believed added considerably to their cost of doing business without providing information that was ever used by the contracting agencies.[111] The following comments were taken from the sample:

> Payroll records must be kept open for review by the Federal Government at any given time. Why submit a separate report when they have this right at any time?
>
> We feel that in many cases, the reports are filed and not even reviewed. We have purposely made errors on reports to check this out, and they have never been brought to our attention.
>
> When bidding a job that requires certified payrolls we add approximately 1% to our bidding price for the extra paperwork.[112]

Based on the statistical information provided by its sample, the Associated General Contractors estimated that one-half of one percent of overall contract costs ($5,000 per million of contract) was required for Davis-Bacon report requirements alone. The total annual expense for this purpose is $190,000,000.[113]

---

[111] Associated General Contractors of America, internal memorandum from John Shipper to Arthur Hintze, September 27, 1972 (in the files of the author).

[112] *Ibid.*

[113] Letter from Associated General Contractors of America to the Honorable John H. Dent, Chairman, Committee on Education and Labor, U.S. House of Representatives, November 9, 1972 (in the files of the author).

TABLE 9.
The Davis-Bacon Act
Required Homebuilding Forms
For the Department of Housing and Urban Development
And the Department of Labor

---

1. *Explanation of Labor-Standard Procedures and Prevailing Wage Requirements* (HUD-196921-1)

   This form explains requirements which must be met by the contractor. It does not have to be filled out by the contractor, but he must be familiar with it.

2. *Statement of Compliance* (WH-348)

   This is a certification which must be filed weekly by the contractor that all persons employed on the project have been paid the full weekly wages earned, that no rebates have been or will be made either directly or indirectly to or on behalf of the contractor from the full weekly wages earned by any person, and that no deductions have been made either directly or indirectly from the full wages earned by any person, other than permissible deductions as defined in regulations (specified). It requires further certification that payrolls required to be submitted are complete, that the wage rates for laborers or mechanics contained in them are in keeping with the Davis-Bacon requirements, that apprentices employed are duly registered in a recognized state or federal program registered with the Bureau of Apprenticeship and Training, and that fringe benefits have been paid, either to approved plans or in cash. (There is a full page of instructions for this form.)

3. *Supplementary Conditions of the Contract for Construction* (Article 1—Labor Standards) (FHA-2554)

   Two and one-half pages of instructions on how to handle payrolls, what to do about workers assigned to more than one job category, what records must be maintained, and the like.

4. *Contractor's Certification Concerning Labor Standards and Prevailing Wage Requirements* (FHA-2482)

   A two-page form, which must be filed for each contract, that the contractor is not ineligible because of the Davis-Bacon Act (or other acts) from undertaking the contract.

5. *Subcontractor's Certification Concerning Labor Standards and Prevailing Wage Requirements* (FHA-2482-A)

   The same regulations as for subcontractors.

6. *Contractor's Supplemental Prevailing Wage Certificate* (FHA-2482-B)

   A deposition, which must be notarized, that the contractor is familiar with Section 212 of the National Housing Act, that he has delivered a written copy of applicable prevailing wage determinations to all subcontractors and has required them to pay wages as so determined, etc.

7. *Wage Letter* (HUD)

   Letter of transmittal, required weekly, for the submission of payroll information.

8. *Instructions for Completing Payroll Form WH-347*

TABLE 9 (Continued)

9. *Payroll Report Form* (WH-347)
Required weekly. Contains:

name of contractor
address
project and location
project or contract number
payroll number
week of filing
for each employee:

name, address, social security number, number of withholding exemptions, number of hours worked each day of the week, total straight time hours and overtime hours worked each week, rate of pay, gross eranings, FICA, withholding tax and other deductions, and net wages paid for the week

more certifications that no rebates have been or will be solicited or made
more certifications about apprentices employed
more certifications about fringe benefits paid.

10. *Monthly Manpower Utilization Report* (Form 66)
This requires for each trade—and within the trade for the journeymen, helpers, apprentices, and trainees—the total man-hours of employment on federal and nonfederal projects (separately), the Negro employment, the Spanish-surnamed, etc., the percent minority man-hours of total man-hours, the total number of minority employees, and the total number of employees.

Source: Stanley Waranch, President, National Association of Home Builders, "Statement of the National Association of Home Builders . . . ," in U. S., Senate, Committee on Banking, Housing, and Urban Affairs, *Improved Technology and Removal of Prevailing Wage Requirements in Federally Assisted Housing: Hearings Before the Subcommittee on Housing and Urban Affairs . . . on S. 3373 . . . and S. 3654 . . .* , 92d Cong., 2d sess., 20 June 1972, pp. 192ff.

Although this figure is justifiable on the basis of the sample taken, it is possible that it overstates the costs somewhat. But even if it is too high by a factor of two, it is still close to $100 million per year of expense to generate paperwork which duplicates other required information and which is seldom of use to those receiving it. The reports are not even used for statistical compilations.

Another form of direct expense to contractors and their associations is that of collecting and supplying wage information for surveys to the Department of Labor. Personnel at the department charge that the trade associations, such as the Associated General Contractors, the Associated Builders and Contractors, the National Association of Home Builders, and the American

Road Builders Association, "could do a lot better job of getting us wage rate information without our having to demand it."[114]

It is undoubtedly true that the task of the Division of Wage Determinations would be considerably eased (and might show less apparent bias towards negotiated rates) if all rate data were as immediately available to the department as are the results of collective bargaining agreements. The big difference is in the cost of collecting wage information. A negotiated rate is published, stays in effect until renegotiated, covers all the organized workers in a craft over a territorial jurisdiction (which can sometimes be extensive), contemplates the same rate to the fraction of a cent for all journeymen in the trade, and in general is easily available. The contractors' associations, for their open-shop segments, are dealing with a great diversity of rates, with workmen who have the flexibility to cross lines of union craft demarcation, with skill differentials within categories, with rates subject to change at any time, and with a host of other problems. They do not have such an easy time of collecting or supplying this sort of information.

Increasingly, however, contractors' associations are driven to do this. In Texas, in North and South Carolina, in Maryland, and in other states, surveys of this sort are being performed routinely. In 1962, the cost to the Carolinas' Branch of the Associated General Contractors for wage surveys exceeded $40,000 annually, exclusive of the administrative cost to the individual firms surveyed.[115] Current costs in the Carolinas alone for this purpose are now $65,000 to $75,000 per year.[116] Although these costs are not great compared with those already discussed, they can be a significant burden to the firms and associations involved and would be immense if conducted nationwide by all the associations, as desired by the department. Making wage surveys is actually the job that the Department of Labor is supposed to do under the provisions of the Davis-Bacon Act.

Finally, the cost associated with appeals of Davis-Bacon decisions taken to the Wage Appeals Board is also modest compared with others discussed, but the conditions under which it is

---

[114] Interviews with Division of Wage Determinations personnel, U.S. Department of Labor, September 26, 1973.

[115] Statement of C.P. Street, Carolinas Branch, Associated General Contractors of America, in U.S., Congress, House, Committee on Education and Labor, *Administration*, Part 2, *op. cit.*, p. 456.

[116] Interview with contractors' association official, August 6, 1973.

incurred accentuate it. On a number of occasions previously in this study, we noted that decisions of the department stand unless protested. Protests may be made by any interested party. With rare exceptions, protests have been by or on behalf of contractors or contractors' associations in hopes of obtaining lower rates more in keeping, in their view, with those actually prevailing in the locality of the proposed construction. The burden of proof is on the protester, who must also take his own surveys if he wishes them.

Although procedures before the Wage Appeals Board are far less formal than in the courts, lawyers are almost inevitably involved. Legal rates are quite high. Costs for an appeal reported to the author in various interviews ranged from $5,000 to more than $30,000. What intensifies these amounts for the contractor is that even if he should be successful in his protest, he has no assurance (nor should he) that he will be able to win the bid on the job under the revised rates. The time spent on the protest might well have been used more advantageously to refine other aspects of his bid.

Thus, although aggregate cost of protests relative to other administrative expenses have not been large, the number of protested determinations has not been great because of the lack of either real or potential competitive advantage.[117]

INDIRECT COSTS

Indirect costs of the Davis-Bacon Act are those which arise from disruptions in local labor markets and those which institutionalize archaic training procedures and other manpower practices in the industry, impeding its progress. These items can be discussed, but they are not quantifiable. Some of the discussion which appears in the literature is highly technical and econometric. One such study, produced independently by three economists on the staff of the Council of Economic Advisors, considers the effect of Davis-Bacon on market structure and competition in the construction industry.[118] Even if the act were

---

[117] It has also been reported to the author that many contractors are unaware of their rights to protest determinations. This seems to be a joint problem of the Department of Labor and the contractors' associations.

[118] Ronald G. Ehrenberg, "The Economic Impact of Davis-Bacon Type Legislation: An Econometric Study" (unpublished; preliminary draft circulated March 1971).

perfectly administered, the equations and analyses of this study indicate that one of its effects has been to cause the demand for publicly financed and assisted construction to be relatively price-inelastic (that is, price-insensitive). The significance of this effect is that the incentives for contractors to resist high wage demands by unions is very dependent on their ability or inability to pass along high wage costs to construction users. If it is easy to pass along higher wage costs, as it is to the price-inelastic government construction user, then higher wage demands will not be as strongly resisted. The greater the proportion of Davis-Bacon work in an area, the higher the wage scale will be.

Thus, through the normal course of economic activity, and irrespective of the quality of administration of the act or the rates determined by it, the Davis-Bacon Act has the unintended consequence of increasing union power to raise wages. The cost of this consequence over the years is difficult (if not impossible) to measure. But its influence can be seen in the much higher wage rates paid construction union members than almost all other comparable skilled workmen, including those in other unions.

It is not difficult to see that there is also spillover from the union to the nonunion segment of the industry. Another very technical study by Professor John P. Gould examines certain aspects of this problem.[119] His mathematical model looks at competitive shifts in the industry resulting from inelastic government demand, and his conclusions reinforce those of the earlier study. This study will be subsequently referred to in this chapter.

High levels of econometric sophistication are not necessary to understand that in the open-shop sector, as workmen are absorbed by government-sponsored jobs, higher wage offers are necessary to secure desired employment levels. The open-shop segment of the industry must also be sensitive to wage levels on the union side. If the differential becomes too great, qualified workmen with the skills necessary for similar work will be difficult to retain. Thus, open-shop wage rates are also subjected to upward pressure by Davis-Bacon.

The differential which exists between most job rates and most Davis-Bacon rates has some further consequences which result indirectly in higher construction costs, but which have not been thoroughly analyzed. These include higher costs arising from

[119] John P. Gould, *op. cit.*

decreased morale, frictional unemployment, and disrupted work practices.

Decreased morale arises when nonunion workmen who had been working on a Davis-Bacon job complete it and go back to working on other jobs for the company at decreased pay rates. Even if the Davis-Bacon work were known to be temporary and even if the decreased pay rate did not fall all the way back to its original level, there will almost definitely be a period of lowered morale and decreased productivity. This view is supported by the General Accounting Office:

> The information [in the Comptroller General's Report to the Congress, July, 1971] . . . was based on discussions which we had with small contractors in a number of areas. They indicated to us that they were reluctant to bid on projects which were subject to the Davis-Bacon Act because if they got themselves in a position where they had to pay the higher wages and then had to go back to privately financed construction, it would disrupt their relations with their own workers.
>
> So . . . this limited to some degree the competition which would be obtained on certain of the projects for which the smaller contractors . . . might otherwise have submitted a bid.[120]

Work practices would become disrupted towards the conclusion of Davis-Bacon jobs when workmen consciously or unconsciously might be slowing down to avoid reverting to the non-Davis-Bacon rates for as long as possible. Both of these factors would be intensified in a firm whose entire work force was not used on a Davis-Bacon job. In this kind of situation, the act creates artificial inequities in wages for similar amounts and quality of work within the firm.

Frictional unemployment would arise when workmen, instead of reverting to work on non-Davis-Bacon projects, choose instead to search for work in the high wage market. As indicated, these factors have not been thoroughly researched. But to the extent that they are accurate representations, they show that an unintended side effect of the act is to drive up construction costs. The effects of Davis-Bacon on the use of apprentices and helpers, and the restrictions which the job designations place on work force utilization, flexibility, and training, have already been noted in the preceding chapter. Open-shop construction firms tend increasingly to follow industrial standards in these areas. They

---

[120] Statement of Gregory J. Ahart, Director, Manpower and Welfare Division, General Accounting Office, in U.S., Congress, Senate, Subcommittee on Housing and Urban Affairs, *op. cit.*, p. 16.

use training programs as devices to develop tradesmen rather than to restrict entry. Many of their programs, which are discussed in the Industrial Research Unit's forthcoming open-shop construction study, tend to be far shorter than union apprenticeship programs. The often excessive length of these programs reflects educational patterns and general knowledge levels of fifty years ago. To a much higher degree than the unions, and increasingly as time goes by, the larger open-shop firms pay workmen in accordance with their skill and productivity levels rather than by automatic length of service rates in an apprenticeship program or at a uniform, negotiated rate. This open-shop practice has been made possible partly by technological changes in construction which have allowed more uniform activity through the year, thus permitting firms who choose to do so to retain more permanent work forces.

Many feel that these developing patterns in open-shop construction are long overdue and give recognition to the successful development patterns of practically every other segment, organized or not, of the industrial society. They are patterns which are hindered by the Davis-Bacon Act. The cost of the disruption—a future cost of unknown size—results from the encouragement of restrictions in the supply of skilled workmen to the construction industry. Social costs are also involved, for the history of the union apprenticeship programs has often been characterized by scant opportunities for minority group members, although some progress has been noted in recent years.

It is quite possible, of course, that the patterns which have been developing in open-shop construction will continue apace even if the Davis-Bacon Act continues to discourage it. But this progress will mean that the more advanced open-shop contractors will be forced to choose between working on government contracts and maintaining their training programs. In the opinion of one contractor:

> Because of the high wages, we cannot economically employ apprentice workers on Davis-Bacon regulated projects and this has been an effect of creating a future shortage of supply of skilled craftsmen and this fact adds fuel to the fires of inflationary wages, through reduced labor supply.[121]

---

[121] Statement of W. I. Hogan, Dan Hogan Construction Company, Inc., cited in U.S., Congress, Senate, Subcommittee on Housing and Urban Affairs, *op. cit.*, p. 46.

DIRECT COSTS AND INFLATIONARY IMPACT

Many of the indirect costs of the Davis-Bacon Act are extremely difficult to quantify. Although this difficulty is also true of direct costs and the inflationary impact of the act, far better statistical estimates can be made in this area. First, some opinions:

A Contractors' Association:

> Probably no other provision of law, practice, or custom [than Davis-Bacon] has more substantially caused housing, constructed under these Federal programs, to cost more than similar, and, in many cases, identical housing built with conventional financing.[122]

An independent analysis:

> Prevailing wage laws appear to raise the relative average wages in the construction trades. . . . This . . . suggests that government construction expenditures under Davis-Bacon prevailing wage determinations may be an engine of inflation especially in periods when the amount of government construction is increasing.
>
> [T]his legislation has had undesirable consequences for almost everyone except, perhaps, unionized construction labor.[123]

A congressman:

> If the problem were solely one of mal-administration, or of excessive union influence over the "prevailing wage" determination process, new administrative regulations or Congressional clarification of the provisions and objectives of the Act might be the suitable remedy. However, in my view the problem goes much deeper.
>
> In my view, the imposition of "prevailing wage" requirements is fundamentally incompatible with the effective operation of a free market economy; it inevitably leads to inflationary pressures, mis-allocation of resources, protection from competitive forces for the favored producer group . . . and a reduction in overall economic output and public welfare.[124]

There are many similar views on the direct costs of Davis-Bacon. To what degree are they supported by statistical or

---

[122] Statement of Stanley Waranch, President, National Association of Home Builders, in U.S., Congress, Senate, Subcommittee on Housing and Urban Affairs, *op. cit.*, p. 168.

[123] Gould, *op. cit.*, pp. 28, 29.

[124] Statement of John B. Anderson, Representative in Congress from the State of Illinois, in U.S., Congress, Senate, Subcommittee on Housing and Urban Affairs, *op. cit.*, p. 390.

empirical evidence? First, the evidence arising from the Davis-Bacon freeze period might be considered.

Davis-Bacon During the Suspension

One section of the Davis-Bacon Act specifies that its provisions may be suspended during time of emergency by the president.[125] During 1970, prices and wages were rising at a rapid rate, but nowhere more rapidly than in construction. Wage increases for unionized workers in the industry averaged 15 to 18 percent during that year and were continuing apace into the spring of 1971. In an effort to curb this rampant inflation, President Nixon exercised his prerogatives, declared an emergency, and suspended the operations of the act on February 23, 1971. This suspension lasted for a little over a month. When organized labor agreed to a program of voluntary wage constraints holding increases in negotiated construction wages to an annual rate of about 6 percent, the suspension ended.

For purposes of statistical comparison, most jobs for which bids were either solicited or awarded during the thirty-four-day suspension are of no help. For them, it is impossible to say whether construction prices decreased when Davis-Bacon became inoperative, because there is no way to determine how high the prices would have been under the opposite circumstance. As an example of the sort of gamesmanship that goes on in these situations, the following situation is illuminating.

> During the 35-day suspension of the Davis-Bacon Act . . . , the Corps of Engineers advertised for bids on the Webber Falls lock and dam, power plant completion project in Oklahoma. Open-shop construction companies are strong in that area and it was known they would submit bids because of the Davis-Bacon Act's suspension. Union contractors interested in the contract knew they could not compete without wage concessions from the local unions. Two days before bid opening the union contractors met in Tulsa with union officials and asked for reductions in existing wage rates. The union officials felt their members would not consent to such reductions, but they did offer to keep wage scales at their current level for the duration of the project—36 months. The contractors accepted and each reduced his bid by approximately $300,000. The job went for slightly over $5,000,000, and the low bidder and second low bidder were Union contractors.[126]

[125] Section 5 of the Davis-Bacon Act. See Appendix B.

[126] Final report of Study Group No. 13-C to the Commission on Government Procurement, February, 1972 (an internal, unpublished staff report to the commission; in the files of the author).

Third, the average time period between the initial bid opening date and the second one was about forty-five days—long enough for inflation to have modified the bid amounts by 1 to 2 percent upwards. Despite these problems, the bids and rebids are worth analyzing. One group of jobs, however, can yield somewhat more information. When the act was suspended, all construction projects for which bids had been received but for which contracts had not been awarded were sent back for rebid at free market labor rates. No predeterminations were issued for these by the Department of Labor.

The cost comparison which can be provided by these bid and rebid jobs is far from pure. In the first place, all of the initial bids became public knowledge before the rebids, which undoubtedly influenced the later decision making. Second, a considerable amount of gamesmanship was probably going on among both open-shop and union contractors to cut bids, withhold them, raise them, or encourage new ones, as the case suited their purpose. At the time of the suspension, there were 398 projects for which bids had been accepted but no contracts awarded. Of these, 288 were for projects whose initial low bid was $10,000 or more. The contracting agencies for these rebids are listed in Table 10.

On the rebids received for these projects, 914 initial bidders submitted rebids, of which 594 showed decreases, 218 showed increases, and 102 showed no change from the initial bid amount. Summaries of the bids are shown in Tables 11 and 12. The first of these covers all bids for those bidders who submitted them on both occasions. The dollar amounts in the table are not representative of levels of construction spending or of savings to the government by virtue of the suspension, because each project may have had several bids associated with it. However, the percent decrease in the last column is useful. It shows that, on the average, in sum, and for all categories of construction except heavy construction in metropolitan and indeterminate areas, the rebids were lower than the initial ones. If competitive factors, information about the initial bids, and gamesmanship were not influencing these figures, they would have been expected to be 1 to 2 percent higher (because of inflation) instead of almost 3 percent lower; consequently, the effect of suspending the act would have been a savings of 4 to 5 percent on the government's $38 billion share of construction, or more than $1.5 billion a year.

TABLE 10.
Davis-Bacon Suspension
Rebids of Projects with Initial Low Bid Exceeding $10,000
February 1971

Department or Agency	No. of Projects
Air Force	89
Army	77
General Services Administration	31
Navy	31
Atomic Energy Commission	14
Interior	14
Veterans Administration	8
NASA	7
Housing and Urban Development	5
Transportation	5
Defense Supply Agency	4
U.S. Postal Service	2
Justice	1
Total	288

Source: Unpublished U.S. government study in author's posssesion.

It would be naïve to assume that competitive factors other than those related to Davis-Bacon were not involved, but it is difficult to estimate their effect or, in some cases, even the direction of their effect. It does seem fair to assume that contractors with low initial bids might raise them somewhat, and that those with high initial bids might lower them for competitive purposes, unless the low initial bid were quite close to the second lowest (in which case the low bidder might strive to decrease his rebid somewhat) or unless some bidder were extremely high compared with the others (in which case he might not bother to change his rebid much).

Many of the effects of competitive pressures disappear when only the lowest initial bid and lowest rebid are considered. A summary of these is shown in Table 12. In this table, for most categories except heavy construction, the low rebids were less

TABLE 11.
Davis-Bacon Suspension
All Bids and Rebids Received From Bidders
Who Entered Both
During Suspension Period
February 1971
Summary by Type of Contract and Area
(In thousands)

Type of Contract [a]	Initial Bid [b] (1)	Rebid (2)	Difference (1—2)	Percent Decrease
By type:				
Building construction:				
Metropolitan areas	$2,073	$1,943	$130	6.27
Non-metro areas	3,461	3,289	172	4.97
Indeterminate areas	12,760	11,818	942	7.38
Total building	18,294	17,050	1,244	6.80
Heavy construction:				
Metropolitan areas	1,076	1,078	(2)	(0.19)
Non-metro areas	14,978	14,130	848	5.66
Indeterminate areas	44,267	44,315	(48)	(0.11)
Total heavy	60,321	59,523	798	1.32
Highway construction	11,748	10,489	1,259	10.72
Residential construction	36,921	35,380	1,541	4.17
Indeterminate type	170,939	167,052	3,887	2.27
By area:				
Metropolitan areas	28,784	27,391	1,393	4.84
Non-metro areas	21,192	20,006	1,186	5.60
Indeterminate areas	248,247	242,097	6,150	2.48
All bids	298,223	289,494	8,729	2.93

Source: Developed from data in the author's possession.

[a] All categories or types of area are estimated from project descriptions. Where insufficient descriptive information was available, the project was classified as indeterminate.

[b] Total number of bidders: 914.

TABLE 12.
Davis-Bacon Suspension
All Low Bids and All Low Bids Received
During Suspension Period
February 1971
Summary, by Type of Contract and Area, of All Low Bids
(In thousands)

Type of Contract [a]	Initial Bid [b] (1)	Rebid (2)	Difference (1−2)	Percent Decrease
By type:				
Building construction:				
Metropolitan areas	$485	$483	$2	0.41
Non-metro areas	751	774	(23)	(3.06)
Indeterminate areas	2,455	2,391	64	2.61
Total building	3,691	3,648	43	1.16
Heavy construction:				
Metropolitan areas	327	354	(27)	(8.26)
Non-metro areas	4,018	4,186	(168)	(4.18)
Indeterminate areas	7,593	7,915	(322)	(4.24)
Total heavy	11,938	12,455	(517)	(4.33)
Highway construction	2,750	2,670	80	2.91
Residential construction	12,911	12,392	519	4.02
Indeterminate type	49,284	48,901	383	0.78
By area:				
Metropolitan areas	8,798	8,350	448	5.09
Non-metro areas	5,551	5,761	(210)	(3.78)
Indeterminate areas	66,225	65,955	270	0.41
All low bids	80,574	80,066	508	0.63

Source: Developed from data in the author's possession.

[a] All categories or types of area are estimated from project descriptions. Where insufficient descriptive information was available, the project was classified as indeterminate.

[b] Total number of projects included 1263. On 23 other projects, the initial low bid is not known, because low bidders did not rebid.

than the low original bids. In heavy construction they averaged 4.33 percent higher, almost offsetting the decreases in building, highway, residential, and other types of construction. Nevertheless, the difference between the original low bids and the low rebids amounts to 0.63 percent, exclusive of any factor to account for the inflationary impact of the delay between bids and rebids. This percentage is probably a fair representation of actual savings to the government as a result of the suspension. Projected over the estimated current government spending total of $38 billion for construction work, it represents a savings of about $240 million a year. In other words, by this estimate, the cost to the government of the Davis-Bacon Act is $240 million a year. Corrected for expected price rises due to inflation during the bidding period, the figure would rise to between $620 million and $1 billion.

Naturally, this figure, too, must be interpreted with some care. These low bids are also subject to competitive and gamesmanship pressures, although they are less influenced by them than are the aggregated figures previously presented. Nevertheless, it is probably the most direct comparison of costs with and without Davis-Bacon rates that could be produced.

Looking at the breakdowns within Table 12, one can see that the differentials varied by both type of construction and type of area. Although such information cannot be summarized in the table, it is apparent from the raw data that the extent of unionization in a particular area is even more important than these factors. In highly unionized areas, the differentials (and therefore the impact of the suspension) were negligible. In predominantly open-shop areas, however, the impact was often substantial. This effect is in keeping with what one would expect if the Davis-Bacon rates were, as alleged, often taken as the union rate even in open-shop areas. When the act was suspended, the open-shop contractors rebid on the basis of their own lower wage rates.

GAO Cost Estimate

During its several investigations into Davis-Bacon administration, the General Accounting Office studied 28 federally financed housing projects of various types and a water storage dam, as well. The total construction involved about $88 million. In the comptroller general's view, improper wage determinations and other administrative problems were responsible for extra costs on these 29 projects of $9.1 million.[127] The government, in other words, paid 10 percent more for this construction than it should have or than a different purchaser would have.

Naturally, this 10 percent extra cost cannot be applied to all federal construction, unless it were assumed that all federal construction rates contain the same errors. But the General Accounting Office did estimate an annual excess cost of $60 million, in the housing area alone, resulting from improper administration.[128] This figure may somewhat understate the case, as the following quotation from an interview shows:

> This [$60 million] is the public number. GAO actual estimate was on the order of $300,000,000, but higher-ups got scared, and reduced the amount before submitting it to Congress.[129]

Other Cost Estimates

There is no convenient way to make accurate projections for the percentage figure or either of the previously quoted dollar figures to the entire constellation of Davis-Bacon construction projects. Virtually no set of reasonable assumptions about the cost of Davis-Bacon, however, results in costs of less than hundreds of millions, at least.

To give a crude example, it has been alleged previously that 20 percent of wage determinations fail to reflect actual local conditions accurately. If we assume that the overwhelming majority of these are high, rather than low, and that the amount of inaccuracy is 10 percent (conservative), then labor rates on Davis-Bacon work are 2 percent high. Labor as a proportion of total job costs varies with the type of job from less than 20 percent to over 60 percent. Taking the lowest figure and applying it to the $38 billion of Davis-Bacon work, we find that some $7.6 billion of this work is in labor costs. If excess costs on this labor are 2 percent, the excess amounts to $142 million yearly.

Many other similar examples can be calculated from estimates and assumptions. Perhaps the best and most sophisticated is that prepared by Republican Congressman John Anderson of Illinois, who based his work on one of the mathematical models developed

---

127 Comptroller General, *Report* (B-146842), 1971, *op. cit.*, pp. 9, 10.

128 *Ibid.*

129 Interview with General Accounting Office personnel, June 13, 1973.

by John Gould of the University of Chicago, mentioned previously.[130] The following is adapted from that source:

I. $$AWa = (U)\ (Wu) + (1-U)\,Wn$$

Where: AWa = average construction wage

U = amount of unionization of workforce (assumed to be 65%, or 0.65)

Wu = union wage rate. (In 1970, the year for which this calculation was made, Wu was $5.71. By October, 1973, this figure had risen to $7.74. The earlier figure will be used, because of its consistency with the other parameters.)

Wn = non-union wage. (It is assumed that there is a 33 percent differential between Wn and Wu. Thus, Wn + 0.33 Wn = Wu, or Wn = Wu/1.33.)

So: $$\begin{aligned} AWa &= (U)\,(Wu) + (1-U)\ (Wu)/1.33 \\ &= (0.65)\ (5.71) + (0.45)\ (5.71)/1.33 \\ &= \$5.21 \end{aligned}$$

Because of the prevailing wage law, there is excessive demand for union-rate construction workers. If the law were repealed, this excessive demand would be shifted in part to the open-shop wage sector, and the equilibrium average wage would decrease. The amount of the decrease is a measure of the cost of the prevailing wage law:

II. $$AWb = (U-g)\ \ (Wu) + [(1-U) + g]\ \ (Wn)$$

Where: AWb = average wage if Davis-Bacon repealed.

g = degree of demand shift resulting from repeal of Davis-Bacon. (Estimated by Anderson to be 22.5%, or .225.)

Other symbols: see equation (I).

So: $$\begin{aligned} AWb &= (0.425)\ (5.71) + (0.575)\ (4.30) \\ &= \$4.90 \end{aligned}$$

The difference between AWa and AWb is 6.5 percent. In 1970, the construction industry accounted for over 6.6 billion

---

130 Statement of John B. Anderson, Representative in Congress from the State of Illinois, in U.S., Congress, Senate, Subcommittee on Housing and Urban Affairs, *op. cit.*, p. 391.

man-hours. So during that year, the approximate cost of the act to the economy was over $2.1 billion. The cost to the government, which purchased or financed about 27 percent of all construction that year, was thus $567 million.

One could argue that this last figure should be a bit less, because the type of construction purchased by the government would not be as greatly affected by demand shifts. The conclusion, however, must remain the same: on any reasonable set of assumptions about the Davis-Bacon Act, the costs to the government in higher-priced construction is hundreds of millions of dollars annually. To put this conclusion in context, it might be noted that the annual cost of the entire federal judiciary is $171 million and of the entire legislative branch is $477 million. The cost of the Davis-Bacon Act is probably somewhere between these two.

SUMMARY

If increased construction costs to the federal government were the only effect of the Davis-Bacon Act, its effect would be largely confined to the government, which is receiving less for its expenditures than other customers are—or, in other words, wasting several hundred million dollars a year on the construction that it purchases or finances. But the inflationary impact of Davis-Bacon is much broader than supply price changes to the government. Here are some other impacts, most of which have already been discussed:

1. *Shifts in demand*—Price-inelastic demand by the government causes transfer of resources in the nongovernment market, thus increasing competition for labor and driving up its cost. There are no offsetting productivity advantages, so the result is inflationary. Anderson's estimate was $2.1 billion annually in 1970.
2. *Mortgage increase*—In situations where government-guaranteed or government-financed private construction is subject to the act, any increased costs resulting from it are magnified by mortgage interest rates, which will typically more than double them over the life of the mortgage. If the unit is for housing, these magnified costs may make rent requirements noncompetitive.
3. *Average as minimum*—Examination of wage surveys reveals that in most cases the rates set are higher than the

weighted average of rates in the survey. But even if they are taken as the average, the operation of the act turns the average into the minimum on the proposed work. In the open-shop sector, where skill levels are recognized within crafts, this effect disrupts the system and puts pressure on the non-Davis-Bacon wages that are less than the designated minimum. In the union sector, it ensures less resistance to higher wage demands at the next round of negotiations, because the government will pay any rate negotiated.

4. *Spreading high wages*—Through improper or imprecise administration, union rates are spread into the nonunion sector and urban rates into the suburban and rural areas. These higher than normal or higher than necessary rates change workers' expectations and put pressure on increasing wage rates.

5. *Restricting supply*—A long-term inflationary effect of Davis-Bacon is on the supply of skilled craftsmen in the industry. By not recognizing helper, learner, or trainee categories (except in a very few instances), the act discourages their use and the use of on-the-job training. This circumstance restrains the supply of skilled craftsmen (often restricting the training opportunities of minority group members) in the industry and, through normal competitive pressures, results in higher construction wages and costs.

6. *Changing work patterns*—High labor costs, occasioned in part by Davis-Bacon, generate higher construction costs in other areas. To cut down on high on-site labor costs, contracttors go to off-site work, a situation which often increases costs in other areas. For example, to save on high cost on-site carpentry, contractors use large sheets of siding which require less installation. But the large sheets are more expensive to buy and haul. So the high labor cost is hidden in higher materials and transportation costs, but over-all costs increase anyway.

7. *High rates perpetuated*—The inflationary impact of incorrect determinations would lessen if they were applied only to the incorrectly determined job. But the rates perpetuate themselves because previous Davis-Bacon jobs are included in surveys for proposed new work. This inequity prompted one trade association official to comment that "high rates are like the parade of elephants," with the snout of one elephant—the new determination—hooked to the tail of the one before him.[131]

8. *Operation of the act*—The direct operation of the act

[131] Interview with a trade association official, September 10, 1973.

has produced annual costs by government and contractors of $100 million or more for its administration, indirect costs of an indeterminate but significant amount, and direct costs, for higher priced construction, that total several hundreds of millions of dollars.

These and other factors which cause and perpetuate inflation in wages and costs in the construction industry are what caused Congressman Anderson to style the Davis-Bacon Act an "engine of inflation," [132] and newsmen Haynes Johnson and Nick Kotz, of the *Washington Post*, to note:

> The construction industry has stirred resentment in the rest of society among consumers who cannot afford housing or a repairman, workers envious of the far higher wages paid construction tradesmen, and other union and business executives who feel that construction provides most of the gasoline for an inflationary engine which hurts everyone.[133]

The unions have argued, along with the Department of Labor, that the Davis-Bacon Act does not influence the level of construction wage rates but merely reflects existing conditions of wages and fringe benefits.[134] This argument would be inaccurate even if none of the administrative problems or incorrect determinations shown by the historical evidence existed. As we explained previously, even at its best, the act takes the average rate found in an area and makes it the minimum. Except in the special case of a single existing rate, where the average and minimum are the same, it is axiomatic that the average will be higher than the minimum. (Although, under the 30 percent and majority determinations, it sometimes happens that the lowest, or minimum, rate is the rate taken as the Davis-Bacon minimum, this is an infrequent occurrence, affecting fewer than one-tenth of one percent of cases. In most other circumstances, the 30 percent or majority determination has an even greater upward influence on wage rates than the determination based on survey averages.)

The other major cost-related argument of the unions is that wage rates are not responsible for inflation in construction

---

[132] Statement of John B. Anderson, Representative in Congress from the State of Illinois, in U.S., Congress, Senate, Subcommittee on Housing and Urban Affairs, *op. cit.*, p. 387.

[133] Haynes Johnson and Nick Kotz, "Construction Industry Has Destruct Mechanism," *Washington Post*, April 15, 1972.

[134] "Davis-Bacon Act Under Attack Once Again," *The Laborer*, July 1972, p. 2.

costs, or at least not as much as increased costs of materials, land, financing, or other construction inputs.[135] It is quite true that other inputs are skyrocketing in price and are now a larger proportion of total construction costs compared to labor costs. This effect is particularly the result of the changing work patterns previously discussed, which result in hiding higher labor costs in higher materials and delivery costs. But it is also true that these other inputs are becoming more expensive themselves. In fact, everything is more expensive. That is precisely the nature, and the evil, of inflation.

Economic opinion has long been divided on whether inflation is caused by prices pulling up wages or wages pushing up prices, or both. Whether all inflation is demand-pull or cost-push is, in regard to Davis-Bacon, an academic question. Evidence piled on evidence demonstrates that changes in wage levels alone created by the Davis-Bacon Act or its administration result in hundreds of millions of dollars annually of unnecessary expenditures; and the act and its administration modify competition and supply-demand relationships in the industry, in turn encouraging inflationary wage rates throughout the industry. Davis-Bacon is certainly not the only culprit in high construction costs, but there is certainly evidence that it is a culprit.

The minimum increased cost estimate for the federal government alone is $60 million annually, as determined by the General Accounting Office. But this estimate, as indicated, may have been understated for political reasons. If one uses rough calculations of labor and administrative cost increases (again for the federal government alone), the estimate increases to more than $150 million. This estimate is taken from the most conservative of the figures for labor rate increases and administrative expenses incurred by the government and by contractors. Annual increases estimated from the activities during the Davis-Bacon suspension are at least $240 million. Congressman Anderson estimated $567 million. All of these estimates are on the low end of the range, and none of them includes any indirect costs. The higher figures range to as much as $1.5 billion a year. Davis-Bacon may not be solely responsible for escalating construction costs and accelerating inflation. But it certainly must be counted among the major causes of both.

---

[135] Statement of Frank Bonadio, President, Building and Construction Trades Department, AFL-CIO, in U.S., Congress, Senate, Subcommittee on Housing and Urban Affairs, p. 216.

CHAPTER VII

Case Studies and Examples

Davis-Bacon cases do not evolve in the kind of atmosphere that encourages public attention. Little of the kind of drama that attracts newsmen is associated with them. They cannot even get into the court system, except peripherally, and prior to the formation of the Wage Appeals Board in 1964, there was no reason to write up any protests because there was no appeals procedure at all. Collecting the specific information required to verify individual rate findings of the Department of Labor is no easier for an outside observer than it was for the department to set the rates in the first place. In fact, it may be considerably more difficult, because the department's presumption is often in favor of published rates, whereas the outside observer would actually have to make a survey.

These are a few of the reasons why the number of actual case write-ups of Davis-Bacon examples is somewhat limited. A few cases were presented by individual persons or associations in the various public hearings about the act and its administration, a number were written up by the General Accounting Office, and a few others have appeared in the studies of Davis-Bacon referred to in earlier chapters or cited in the notes of this book. To a large extent, the Wage Appeals Board, individual contractors, and contractors' associations provide the only sources for new materials.

The purpose of this chapter is to provide some examples of cases from each of the preceding sources. The General Accounting Office cases, however, have already been given wide coverage in hearings and other studies.

GENERAL ACCOUNTING OFFICE CASES

The General Accounting Office maintains that the legislative history of the Davis-Bacon Act indicated the intent of Congress that the determined rates should be based on the wage rates established by *private* industry.[136] Over a number of years, the GAO reviewed wage rate determinations in specific cases of military housing, federally financed housing, building, and heavy construction in order to form an opinion on whether this intention was actually being carried out. In the cases which it studied, it usually found that this was not the case and that the Davis-Bacon Act was being improperly administered.

Capehart Housing at the Marine Corps Schools at Quantico, Virginia, in 1962, is perhaps the best known of these case write-ups, but there were also others covering federally financed housing in the southeastern areas of the United States (1964), in Dallas-Fort Worth, Texas (1965), and in the Washington metropolitan area (1968). Building construction in New England (1965) and construction of a dam in Georgia (1966) were also covered. Citations for all of these cases can be found in subsequent footnotes.

In 1970, another critical review of Davis-Bacon determinations was made of certain federally financed low-rent housing and military family housing built between 1966 and 1969 in New Jersey, Pennsylvania, Oklahoma, and Virginia at an estimated total cost of approximately $37.4 million.[137] Because these are more current and have been less frequently written about than the others, they are included here, along with the General Accounting Office findings relating to them.

Project Descriptions

LOW INCOME PUBLIC HOUSING, MILLVILLE, NEW JERSEY. Five fixed-price contracts totaling approximately $1.5 million were awarded by the Millville Housing Authority in 1966 for the construction of one hundred units of low-rent public housing, divided equally into units for low-income families and units for low-income senior citizens. The fifty units for senior citizens were located on a separate site from those for the low-income families, and consisted of seven one-story buildings with brick veneer and cedar siding exteriors. The low-income family units

---

[136] U.S., Comptroller General, *Report* (B-146842), 1971, *op. cit.*, p. 6.

[137] U.S., Comptroller General, *Report to the Congress: Construction Costs for Certain Federally Financed Housing Projects Increased Due to Inappropriate Minimum Wage Rate Determinations*, B-146842 (Washington, D.C.: General Accounting Office, 1970), p. 4.

were of the same materials, but were two stories high. The project architect stated that the projects were similar to private housing construction in the Millville area.

LOW INCOME PUBLIC HOUSING, LANCASTER, PENNSYLVANIA. The Lancaster Housing Authority awarded four fixed-price contracts in 1966 for a project called Franklin Terrace, the total value of which was about $1.8 million. This project contained 124 apartments in 41 two-story buildings of frame construction with brick veneer exteriors. The similarity of the Franklin Terrace project to local private housing was substantiated by the project architect.

The General Accounting Office also examined two low-income housing projects in Oklahoma City, Oklahoma, and one in Hampton, Virginia. These projects were similar to the previous examples and were each determined to be similar to private housing in their areas.

MILITARY FAMILY HOUSING, LANGLEY AIR FORCE BASE, VIRGINIA. In 1968, the Department of the Air Force awarded a $1.5 million fixed-price contract for the construction of one hundred military family housing units at Langley Air Force Base, Virginia. This project consisted of two-story town houses in 23 separate buildings. Each building had a brick exterior on the first floor and wood siding on the second floor. Both the chief engineer at Langley Air Force Base and a private residential contractor familiar with the Langley area agreed that the project was similar to private residential construction in the Langley area.

MILITARY FAMILY HOUSING, TINKER AIR FORCE BASE, OKLAHOMA. Also in 1968, the Department of the Air Force awarded a $3.2 million fixed-price contract for the construction of 162 units of military family housing at Tinker Air Force Base, Oklahoma. The Tinker housing project consisted of 162 units in one- and two-story duplex and row buildings. The similarity of the Tinker project to local residential housing projects was confirmed by the project architect.

GAO Case Findings

In each case, the General Accounting Office found that the minimum wage rates, as determined by the Department of Labor, were well in excess of those paid for similar private residential housing projects. The Department of Labor's inflated wage determinations increased the costs of the seven projects by an estimated $2.4 million, or more than 15 percent of the total estimated costs.[138] Table 13 shows the cost increase for each project. It should be added that the GAO's estimated increase in costs pertains to direct labor costs only, and it does not include any other costs or profit factors which could have been based on direct labor costs and included in the contract bid prices.

The wage rates of various worker classifications on each project as determined by the Department of Labor are compared in Table 14 with the wage rates paid on private housing projects. In almost every case, the department's determination is higher than the private housing rate, and in many instances the difference exceeds 50 percent.

As part of its study, the General Accounting Office interviewed several private contractors. These contractors stated that they would not bid on federally financed construction projects because of the high wages they would have to pay, even though they would be reimbursed for the higher wage rates. They felt that paying the higher wage rates, as dictated by the Department of Labor, would cause a disruption in their labor forces because the workers on federally financed construction would receive higher wages than the workers on the company's private construction projects; this difference would lead to morale problems which would be intensified later, when the federally financed project was completed and the workers who had been working on it would go back to working on private construction at relatively reduced wages. The general contractor for the low-rent public housing project in Lancaster, Pennsylvania, offered the local housing authority a $114,000 price reduction if the wage clause on his bid requiring the payment of the higher wage rates were removed from the contract.[139]

Improper Determinations

In these cases, the General Accounting Office found several basic shortcomings in the Department of Labor's procedures to determine wage rates for federally financed housing projects, a process which led to the adoption of inflated wage rates. It found that the wage rate information on file at the Department

---

[138] *Ibid.*, p. 17.

[139] *Ibid.*, p. 19.

TABLE 13.
The Davis-Bacon Act
Increase in Construction Costs
Attributed to Davis-Bacon
By General Accounting Office

Housing Project and Location	Number of Units	Contract Cost	Estimated Increase in Contract Cost
Government financially assisted:			
NJ 61-1, Millville, New Jersey	100	$1,460,439	$200,000
Hamilton Court, Oklahoma City, Oklahoma	400	5,312,000	1,026,000
Okla. 2-14, Oklahoma City, Oklahoma	50	1,166,462	208,000
Franklin Terrace, Lancaster, Pennsylvania	124	1,804,390	273,000
VA 17-1, Hampton, Virginia	100	1,149,998	100,000
Government constructed:			
Langley Air Force Base, Virginia	100	1,524,100	188,000
Tinker Air Force Base, Oklahoma	162	3,157,710	431,000
Total	1,036	$15,575,099	$2,426,000

Source: U.S., Comptroller General, Report to the Congress: *Construction Costs for Certain Federally Financed Housing Projects Increased Due to Inappropriate Minimum Wage Rate Determinations,* B-146842 (Washington, D.C.: General Accounting Office, 1970), p. 17.

of Labor was grossly inadequate to determine the prevailing wage rates properly. On-site surveys required for the residential-type construction had not been made for several years. Most of the wage rate data in the Department of Labor's files consisted of data from negotiated union agreements that were submitted by local labor organizations. The department's data did not specify the types of construction work for which the union rates were and were not being paid. Neither the number nor the proportion of workers who were receiving the union-negotiated and other wage rates was known.

Although regulations stipulate that whenever the data on hand are considered inadequate, a field survey in the area of the proposed project may be undertaken, the department seldom

TABLE 14.
The Davis-Bacon Act
Federally Financed Construction Projects
Wage Rates Determined by the Department of Labor
Compared with Similar Private Housing Construction Rates
Fiscal Years 1966, 1967, and 1968

Classification	Millville, New Jersey			Oklahoma City, Oklahoma			Lancaster, Pennsylvania		
	Minimum Rate Deter-mined Apr. 12, 1966	Private Housing Rate	Dif-fer-ence	Minimum Rate Deter-mined Apr. 8, 1968	Private Housing Rate	Dif-fer-ence	Minimum Rate Deter-mined Mar. 9, 1966	Private Housing Rate	Dif-fer-ence
Bricklayers	$4.55	$4.31	$0.24	$4.975	$3.25	$1.725	$3.95	$3.00	$0.95
Carpenters	4.95	3.03	1.92	4.25	2.50	1.75	3.75	2.57	1.18
Electricians	5.54	3.25	2.29	5.095	2.50	2.595	4.65	2.88	1.77
Laborers	3.25	1.79	1.46	2.975	2.00	0.975	2.35	2.18	0.17
Painters	4.00	2.45	1.55	4.15	2.75	1.40	3.275	2.41	0.865
Plumbers	5.20	3.39	1.81	4.90	3.15	1.75	4.30	3.13	1.17
Sheet Metal Workers	5.00	—	—	4.82	2.58	2.24	4.35	2.68	1.67

TABLE 14 (Continued)

Classification	Hampton, Virginia			Langley Air Force Base, Virginia		
	Minimum Rate Determined Dec. 13, 1965	Private Housing Rate	Difference	Minimum Rate Determined Oct. 17, 1967	Private Housing Rate	Difference
Bricklayers	$4.15	$3.00	$1.15	$4.30	$4.00	$0.30
Carpenters	3.35	2.50	0.85	3.60	2.82	0.78
Electricians	4.19	2.70	1.49	4.49	3.50	0.99
Laborers	1.90	1.50	0.40	2.20	2.25	−0.05
Painters	3.00	2.50	0.50	3.00	3.00	—
Plumbers	4.12	2.60	1.52	4.52	3.19	1.33
Sheet Metal Workers	3.80	—	—	4.05	3.00	1.05

Source: U.S., Comptroller General, Report to the Congress: *Construction Costs for Certain Federally Financed Housing Projects Increased Due to Inappropriate Minimum Wage Rate Determinations,* B-146842 (Washington, D.C.: General Accounting Office, 1970), p. 17.

Note: The private housing rates shown above were compiled using the Department of Labor's own regulations and formula for determining prevailing wage rates. The minimum rates determined and the private housing rates, as shown above, consist of the basic hourly rate and applicable hourly fringe-benefit payments.

conducts any actual surveys. Wage data used in the determination for the Oklahoma City projects consisted partially of survey information. For the eleven worker classifications covered, however, the General Accounting Office found that: (1) several of the survey wage rates for workers on private housing projects were considered to be inapplicable by the Department of Labor because they were lower than what the department considered equitable; (2) the wage data collected in the survey were not considered sufficient to alter prescribed union wage rates; and (3) some of the wage rates for other worker classifications were ignored because they were lower than the rates the department recognized as prevailing.[140]

The department's attitude resulted in the continued use of union-negotiated wage rates for construction of the federally financed housing projects in the Oklahoma City area, despite evidence in the hands of the department showing the lower commercial rates were prevailing in Oklahoma City. The same situation was generally found in determinations for other projects studied. Union-negotiated rates were used even when other residential rates were available, and no surveys were conducted to determine which rate was actually prevailing. In addition, it should be noted that commercial building construction rates, regardless of how they are determined, should not be used on a residential housing project because of the different nature of the construction required for each.

Once a determination has been made using commercial rates on a residential construction project, or using union-negotiated rates where they do not, in fact, prevail, future determinations in the same area use those rates as a base, thus perpetuating them. Increased project costs either reduce the amount of construction or inflate its costs to the taxpayer. These results, in the view of the General Accounting Office, are contrary to the spirit and purpose of the Davis-Bacon Act.

WAGE APPEALS BOARD CASES

The Wage Appeals Board was set up within the Department of Labor in 1964. It is not a court, and its decisions are not appealable to the court system. Nevertheless, it allows review of prevailing rate decisions by a different section of the Labor

---

[140] *Ibid.*, p. 22.

Department than the one that set the rates in the first place; this review system allows an opportunity for some diversity of opinion and some checks and balances to rate setting procedures. The Wage Appeals Board has not processed an overwhelming number of cases. During its first five years, it handled fewer than ten cases per year, and only eighteen cases during the entire five years manifested any aspect significant enough in any particular of Davis-Bacon coverage, rates, or enforcement—or even procedures before the board—to warrant inclusion in the digest of the board's decisions during that period.[141] Currently, utilization of the board is said to be about twice as great as during its first five years, but even that is very modest usage.

The board is quasi-judicial rather than investigative, so many of its decisions cover items which would not be relevant here. Two are included, however.

The first, Metro C-7, deals primarily with application of building rates to heavy construction and is covered in detail. The second, Mountain Park Dam, deals with the definition of locality for rate surveys and with Davis-Bacon administrative procedures. It is also covered in detail but is not so lengthy.

Metro Segment C-7, Arlington County, Virginia, 1971-1972

The Washington Metropolitan Area Transit Authority has been building a subway system for the District of Columbia for a number of years and will still have work in progress into the 1980s. The method of building much of this subway is "cut and cover." That is, a ditch is first dug; then, in the ditch, a conduit to carry the subway trains is built; then the conduit is covered with dirt, or sometimes a roadway is built on top of it for surface traffic. Work of this sort is very unusual for the District of Columbia, which has few railroads, tunnels, elevated highways, hydroelectric projects, breakwaters, or other projects which would be classified as "heavy" construction rather than "building" or "highway" construction. By tradition in the district, heavy construction is performed at building rates. In other parts of the country, and in particular in Virginia, heavy construction is performed at its own rate schedule or at highway rates, either of which are usually considerably lower than building rates for the same job categories.

---

[141] *Decisions of the Wage Appeals Board, op. cit.*

In October, 1971, a new section of the subway contract was opened for bids. This was a feeder section entirely in Arlington County, Virginia, consisting of a station 814 feet long at Pentagon City, 2,339 feet of cut and cover reinforced concrete box section, and 1,268 feet of two-way earth tunnel. A few small structures such as air tower shaft and pump housings were contemplated, but not the laying of rails or electrification of the tunnel. The amount of the contract was estimated to be about $27,000,000.

The secretary of labor, through the Division of Wage Determinations, issued a wage determination for this project, known as Virginia Segment C-7, Metropolitan Rapid Rail Transit System, on October 8, 1971. This determination set basic hourly rates for some 91 job titles or job categories (most of which would have no applicability to a project of this sort), ranging from a low of $2.75 plus $0.12 per hour for health and welfare (plus some other modest fringe benefits) to be paid dump truck and fuel and oil truck drivers, up to a high of $8.35 plus $0.55 hourly for fringe benefits to be the minimum for bricklayers. The average for all 91 rates was $5.597, plus hourly contributions to health and welfare of approximately $0.22 and to pensions of about $0.18. Some additional fringe benefit rates for vacation and apprenticeship training existed for certain trades. (The entire rate decision is included as an example in Appendix F of this study.)

The Virginia Road Builders Association, at the request of one of its members, examined the rate decision and the character of the work to be performed under the contract. It was the association's feeling that much of the work, including all cut and cover and concrete work, was highway-type construction, similar in character and requirements to work then being done in Arlington County on a very complex interchange of Interstate Route 95, known as the Shirley Highway "Mixing Bowl," involving some thirty lanes of traffic, tunnels, etc. The association also felt that the predetermined Davis-Bacon wage rates were District of Columbia building construction rates, which were not only much higher but were from an entirely different polity than that in which the C-7 segment was to be built. Accordingly, the association took steps to protest the rates.

The burden of proof in contesting wage rate determinations lies with the protester. Otherwise, the rate schedule fixed upon by the Department of Labor stands. Before a protest can be taken to the Wage Appeals Board, the petitioner must first request a reconsideration of the issued determination from the Branch of Construction Wage Determinations (which issued it) and raise sufficient question to gain a review. This procedure often requires considerable time, effort, and expense to the petitioner in conducting his own investigations into the way the survey rates were calculated, determining what projects were included, and securing wage rate surveys of his own.

The petitioner here included wage rates then being paid workmen on the Route 95 project—rates which had not been taken into account by the Department of Labor survey—and further supported his request for reconsideration by letters from a number of influential people such as a senator from Virginia and the federal highway administrator. Some of the language in a letter from the highway administrator follows:

> The Federal Highway Administration believes that wage decision AM-5,434 will have an unwarranted inflationary effect upon the cost of future construction in Arlington County, including highway construction. We further believe that the wage decision is incorrectly, if not arbitrarily and capriciously, formulated.
>
> The wage schedules in AM-5,434 are obviously, from their captions, District of Columbia schedules. We have no knowledge of the prevalence of such rates for building construction, building demolition, cut and cover tunnel work, or utility alteration in Arlington County (Virginia). Presently under way are several large contracts for reconstruction of Shirley Highway in the immediate vicinity of the proposed segment of the subway project. Much of the work actually now being accomplished under the highway contract is similar construction to the subway work proposed. The rates being paid for such work should, we believe, form the basis under the law for determining the minimum rates applicable to the initial subway construction rather than rates imported across a State line from another political jurisdiction.
>
> * * * *
>
> To illustrate our concern with the inflationary aspects of this matter, the hourly wage rate now predetermined for common laborers on the Shirley Highway work totals $2.87. In AM-5,434, the common laborer's rate is $5.72, or over 100 percent greater. It is obvious that this action, if permitted to stand, would have a monumental adverse effect on the cost of future highway work in the area. In addition, it could even be impossible to retain an adequate workforce on our highway work since the contractors on highway work could not raise the wages of their workforces to compete for the available labor market in view of the present and contemplated future wage controls.[142]

---

[142] Letter from F.C. Turner, Federal Highway Administrator, U.S. Department of Transportation, to W.D. Landis, Assistant Administrator, Wage and

This letter raised a number of serious questions about the wage determination issued, particularly in regard to the similarity of the proposed work to an existing project a few yards away in the same county and to the importation of building rate wages across a state line. It was sent on November 5, 1971.

On the same day, the Department of Labor responded:

> We have given careful consideration to the information and arguments contained in your letter and have reviewed the wage rates listed in AM-5,434 in the light of the description of the project provided us by Metro. On the basis of this review wage determination AM-5,434 is hereby affirmed as issued.[143]

In the face of this abrupt refusal of reconsideration, the petitioners exercised their option of filing for a hearing before the Wage Appeals Board. To support their case, the petitioners collected opinions about the character of the proposed work and made their own survey of wages being paid on heavy and highway work in Arlington County. This effort resulted in a stack of fifty exhibits (about one inch thick), which had to be secured with great rapidity and without the benefit of any coercive authority. Bid opening on the C-7 contract was scheduled for November 24, and any action changing the wage determination would have to take place at least ten days before the opening date to ensure that any changed rates would be reflected in the contract specifications.

In view of the time constraints and because the Wage Appeals Board may refuse to hear a case if it feels it would be inappropriate to do so because of lack of timeliness, the petition was filed on November 9. The case was docketed and set for hearing on November 18.[144] (On November 16, the Washington Metropolitan Area Transit Authority agreed to delay the bid opening date until December 8, 1971.)

The issue, principally, was whether the Department of Labor erred in predetermining rates from District of Columbia Metro rates (which were "building and heavy" rates) and whether it should have predetermined the Arlington County "heavy and highway" rates. It might be helpful to point out here the

---

Hour Division, U.S. Department of Labor, November 5, 1971 (in the files of the author).

[143] Letter from W.D. Landis, U.S. Department of Labor, to F.C. Turner, U.S. Department of Transportation, November 5, 1971 (in the files of the author).

[144] Wage Appeals Board, Case No. 71-4, November 18, 1971.

requirement under which the rates were originally set and review the operating procedures for ascertaining them.

Section C-7 of the Washington Metro was being contracted for by the Washington Metropolitan Area Transit Authority Compact, in whose enabling legislation the Davis-Bacon Act was included by reference:

> The Board shall take such action as may be necessary to insure that all laborers and mechanics . . . shall be paid wages at rates not less than those prevailing on similar construction *in the locality* as determined by the Secretary of Labor in accordance with the Davis-Bacon Act, as amended.[145]

The wage determination provisions of the Davis-Bacon Act require:

> minimum wages to be paid various classes of laborers and mechanics which shall be based upon the wages that will be determined by the Secretary of Labor to be prevailing for the corresponding classes of laborers and mechanics employed on projects of a character similar to the contract work in the city, town, village or other civil subdivision of the State in which the work is to be performed.[146]

The pertinent provisions of the Department of Labor's regulations are as follows:

> In making a wage rate determination projects completed more than 1 year prior to the date of request for the determination may, but need not be considered.
>
> If there has been no similar construction within the area in the past year, wage rates paid on the nearest similar construction may be considered.[147]

In its brief for the Wage Appeals Board, the Wage and Hour Division argued that it was justified in applying the District of Columbia negotiated "building and heavy" rate to the project because the only "heavy" construction it could find in Arlington County was covered by this rate. It also argued that it could find no existing agreements in Arlington County applicable to tunnel projects (apparently differentiating between heavy construction and tunnel building) and so was justified in looking to the rates paid on the nearest similar construction,

---

[145] Metro Compact, P.L. No. 89-774, 80 Stat. 1324, Article XIV.

[146] 40 USC 276a-276a-5.

[147] 29 CFR, 1, Sec. 1.6. (These procedures were modified October 5, 1972. The same language is found in the current procedures as Sec. 1.8.)

which was, of course, in the District of Columbia. The division further supported its position by contending that the Wage Appeals Board had, in the past, often reaffirmed the differentiation of rates based on different character of work between "heavy" and "highway," citing the Carter Dam case and the Tombigbee Lock and Canal case.[148]

The petitioner of record (who was the Federal Highway Administration) and various intervenors (including the American Road Builders Association, the Virginia Road Builders Association, the Virginia Department of Highways, the County Manager of Arlington County, and four construction companies), in appearing before the board on November 18 argued, in essence, that the predetermined wage rates were considerably higher than rates paid for similar work in Arlington County, and that the character of the proposed work was generally similar to a large amount of highway construction in progress in the area. They argued that the effect of implementing the predetermined rates would be two-fold: first, it would set the pattern for other segments of the Metro system to be built in Virginia, even though work on future segments was anticipated to resemble highway work even more; second, it would have a serious inflationary effect on other projects in progress and might, because of the wage differential, have a disruptive impact on them, as well, through loss of personnel, increased hiring and training costs, and possible project delays.

A total of 36 persons, 8 of whom made presentations, appeared before the board to support one side or the other, but because the bid opening date had been postponed until December 8, the Wage Appeals Board decided to defer an immediate decision in the case and give all interested parties ten days to file posthearing briefs. During this period, the petitioners prepared documentation on the similarity of the work proposed to work then in progress on the $52,000,000 Shirley Highway "Mixing Bowl," which, it contended, also considerably involved cut and cover reinforced concrete box sections and some 576 feet of earth tunnels of about the same size and sunk to the same depth as the subway. They also presented the wage rate data collected for the 50 ongoing projects or projects completed within the past twelve months in Arlington County or the nearby Louisa and Surry Counties. The supplemental brief from Wage

---

[148] Carter Dam, Wage Appeals Board, Case No. 65-1, March 1, 1965. Tombigbee Lock and Canal, Wage Appeals Board, Case No. 71-2, July 26, 1971.

and Hours Division dwelt on the alleged lack of similar "heavy" construction in Arlington and on precedents for the solicitor to cross state lines to find rates for similar construction when necessary. As requested by the board, both sides gave their impressions of the congressional intent concerning the word "locality" as it is used in the Washington Metropolitan Area Transit Authority Compact previously quoted; they argued whether "locality" was meant to define the entire Washington metropolitan area for inclusion in wage surveys and therefore controlled the survey extent, or whether it was a descriptive term as used in the Davis-Bacon Act, defining area for inclusion in wage surveys as a political subdivision of a state.

The Wage Appeals Board exercises no investigative functions of its own. It acts on information brought before it. It accumulated this information through November 29, and issued its decision (WAB Case No. 71-4) on December 7, 1971, eight days before the bid opening (which had been again postponed from December 8 to December 15 by the Transit Authority.)[149] The board generally accepted the petitioners' views on the definition of "locality" and on the character of the work being done in the "Mixing Bowl," and ordered that a new wage predetermination for the project be prepared.

The new rate predetermination was prepared and released on December 13, 1971. It contains rates very similar to those issued previously but specifies that these are "building rates." It includes another set of rates specifically for "heavy construction." Table 15 gives a few of the key rates for comparison. They show that average rates are approximately one-third lower for heavy construction than for building rates.

It is characteristic of the confusion surrounding Davis-Bacon rates that a newspaper story released on the day the revised rates were issued talks of the rates almost as though they were taking pay away from workers. Under the headline, "Metro Pay Rates Cut," the lead paragraph reads:

> Pay scales for workers who will build the subway in the Pentagon area today were ordered cut to keep them in line with wages of employees on the Shirley Highway "Mixing Bowl" project.[150]

---

[149] It is an established practice of the Wage Appeals Board not to request agencies to change bid opening dates. If an agency chooses not to do so, a WAB case could be mooted for lack of timeliness.

[150] "Metro Pay Rates Cut," *Washington Star*, December 14, 1971.

TABLE 15.
The Davis-Bacon Act
Comparative Rates for Key Heavy Construction Job Titles Under Different Rate Determinations of the U.S. Department of Labor And Some Arlington County Highway Contracts

Selected Job Titles	Metro Rate #1	I-95	Arlington Highway	Metro Rate #2 (Building)	Metro Rate #2 (Heavy)	% Difference, Metro Rate #2 (Heavy) to Metro Rate #1
	(1)	(2)	(3)	(4)	(5)	(6)
Air Compressor Operator	6.07	3.12	3.87	7.16	3.00	50.6
Backhoe Operator	6.65	3.37	5.33	7.74	4.50	32.3
Bricklayer	8.90	5.65	5.00	8.90	4.00	55.1
Bulldozer Operator	5.85	3.22	4.55	7.14	4.33	26.0
Carpenter	7.37	4.90	5.17	7.37	5.06	31.3
Common Laborer	5.72	2.87	3.17	5.72	3.00	47.6
Cement Mason	7.24	5.70	4.83	7.24	6.80	6.1
Iron Worker-Reinforcing	7.12	4.45	4.50	7.48	4.45	37.5
Loader Operator (over 2 yards)	5.95	3.22	5.20	7.59	4.75	20.2
Motor Grader Operator (fine)	5.95	3.37	4.87	6.94	4.90	17.6
Pipelayer	5.92	3.25	3.97	5.87	4.35	26.5

TABLE 15 (Continued)

Powderman	6.37	3.25	—	6.90	—	—
Truck Driver (dump)	4.07	2.87	3.88	4.47	3.25	20.1
Truck Driver (multi-axle)	4.17	2.97	3.25	4.57	4.00	4.1
Average, 14 rates (mean)	6.24	3.73	4.43	6.79	4.34	30.4

Sources:

(1) Decision AM-5,434, October 8, 1971.

(2) "Mixing Bowl" determination, reported by Arlington County Manager.

(3) Arlington County highway contracts (average of five) actually being paid, November 26, 1971, as reported by Arlington County Manager.

(4) Decision AM-9208, December 13, 1971, building rates.

(5) Decision AM-9208, December 13, 1971, heavy rates.

(6) Percentage decrease computed by Industrial Research Unit.

Although the article is generally accurate in its factual presentation, talking of "wages cut to keep them in line" rather than "wage rates redrafted to reflect conditions actually prevailing" creates unwarranted inferences.

The next phase of the case opened December 15, two days after the revised rates were issued. (Bid opening had again been postponed, this time until December 22.) The Building and Construction Trades Department of the AFL-CIO sent a telegram to the Department of Labor requesting revision and review of the revised wage determination. This request was turned down, and on December 17, the AFL-CIO filed a petition for review with the Wage Appeals Board, alleging a number of imperfections in the Wage Appeals Board decision, particularly concerning the definition of "locality" (as used in the passages previously quoted here from the Davis-Bacon Act and the Metropolitan Area Transit Authority Compact) and also concerning the equivalence of the proposed job to the "Mixing Bowl" project. A hearing on the petition was scheduled for January 20, 1972, but in the meantime the often postponed bids were opened on December 22, and contractors were selected on the basis of those bids which reflected the December 13 rates.

In something of a break with tradition, although the complex timing of the bids and the appeals and reappeals may have provided adequate reason, the board decided not to moot the new appeal, but to go ahead with the January 20, 1972, hearing. Subsequent to it, the board issued its decision. This decision, Case 71-5, dated February 18, 1972, affirmed the earlier definitions of "locality" and "similarity," but remanded the case to the Division of Wage Determination to make yet another wage survey in Arlington County; the survey was to take into account the personnel employed on another segment of the subway system, part of which was in the county, even though the rates predetermined for that segment had not been contested when issued and were extensions of the Washington building rates, and even though only a few feet of that segment were in Arlington County (and that by accident, arising from the designer's confusion over the exact location of the Virginia state line).

The wage determinations, revised for the second time, did not change significantly, however, and no further protests were lodged. Under the actual job rate schedule, the government could anticipate considerable cost savings on the construction of this segment of Metro and, of course, on subsequent segments to be built in the Virginia and Maryland suburbs. Department of Transportation statistics indicate that labor costs are about 25 percent of primary construction costs for highway work (and presumably other heavy earth-moving work such as that involved here).[151] With a contract estimated to cost some $27 million, of which 25 percent was in labor costs for which an average savings of 30.4 percent could be effected under the revised rates, savings to the government could be anticipated as over $2,000,000 on this segment alone.

Unfortunately, the savings were not realized. Although the taxpayers should have saved some money on segment C-7 itself—the low bid accepted was about $4 million less than the anticipated cost—this savings did not occur, and there were no continuing benefits for later work. The job went to a joint venture of two open-shop firms whose experience was principally in sewer construction in other parts of the country. Shortly after starting work, these firms began to experience trouble getting subcontractors to work for them and found that most of their employees in certain trades were hired away for days at a time, disrupting work progress. Somewhat higher rates had to be offered than the scheduled minimums in certain trades, and job costs went up while job progress fell behind schedule. Metro found it convenient to terminate the original contractors in the spring of 1974.

In addition, before work was even begun on Segment C-7, another segment of the Metro in Arlington County was advertised for bids. This segment was even more similar to standard highway construction than C-7 was. But the prevailing rates attached to it were again the Washington building rates. No one noticed who might have protested, and as a result this segment was bid and let on the basis of union building rates for the District of Columbia.

The combination of these two problems has probably now ensured that any heavy construction and probably, though not necessarily, any complex highway work with federal involvement taking place in Arlington County or other areas of northern Virginia will be constructed at Washington union construction rates.

---

[151] Wages were reported to be 25.5 percent, 25.7 percent, and 25.5 percent of Federal-Aid primary construction costs for the years 1968, 1969, and 1970, respectively. U.S., Department of Transportation, "Highway Statistics," various years.

CONCLUSIONS. This case illustrates several points which prompted its inclusion. First, the procedure for Davis-Bacon rate determinations allows the rate to stand unless challenged. Second, the burden of proof is on the challenger; he must provide the wage surveys and other documentation necessary to show that the Department of Labor rate is incorrect. Third, the expense of a challenge and petition to the Wage Appeals Board requires considerable expenditure of both time and money. Fourth, the challenger of a rate, if a private firm, is in no improved competitive position for receiving the work, even if his challenge is successful and results in lower rates; in fact, he may be in a worse position because of the time and effort he expends in challenging the rate rather than preparing his bid. Fifth, if the challenger is an association, it can expect to derive no benefits at all from the challenge. Sixth, a challenger may receive adverse publicity when he is successful in getting a lower rate because of the confusion which can easily arise between establishing a correct rate reflecting prevailing wages in the area and "cutting" the previous, erroneous rate. Seventh, appeals are on a case-by-case basis, and great vigilance is required to ensure that practices found to be erroneous are not continued; the practice must be challenged (again at considerable cost) each time it arises until the pattern is rectified.

In addition to these items, the most important factor which this case illustrates involves the great interpretive problems in the Davis-Bacon wording and procedures. Definitions of "locality" and "similar work" were contested here, and in the second rate revision the timeliness of the appeal and the time span over which other similar work in the past should be considered were also contested. Interpretations of the statute are done by the Department of Labor. The setting of prevailing rates, including the selection of area, time span, and projects to be included in the survey, is done by the Department of Labor. The Wage Appeals Board is part of the Department of Labor. Except in very unusual circumstances, no appeals can be made on its decisions anywhere other than to the Department of Labor itself. Finally, it appears from the case that stopping the spread of urban wage rates to the suburbs and building rates to heavy and highway work is extremely difficult when a major government job is involved.

Mountain Park Dam, 1972

The Mountain Park Dam, located in Kiowa County, Oklahoma, is a $2.8 million project.[152] It uses thin arch concrete construction techniques. Invitations for bidding were issued on September 2, 1972. The invitations contained wage decision AM-3,606, dated August 25, 1971. This wage decision was for highway construction and was an "area" determination from the *Federal Register.* The International Union of Operating Engineers protested the inclusion of wage decision AM-3,606 on the grounds that highway rates were inapplicable for projects such as the Mountain Park Dam. The Bureau of Reclamation requested that the Employment Standards Administration of the Department of Labor issue a project wage determination for "heavy" construction. This request was granted. A new decision (72-OK-569) was issued November 27, which the Bureau of Reclamation received on November 30, 1972. The bid opening date had been postponed from November 16 to December 12 to allow time for the new survey.

Three days after it issued its revised decision, and on the same day that the Bureau of Reclamation received it, the Department of Labor issued a modification on the new project wage determination. This modification was made after the International Union of Operating Engineers submitted data concerning the wages being paid on another Bureau of Reclamation project, about 225 miles distant from the Mountain Park Dam site, called Hugo Dam. In the modification, the wage rates for power equipment operators were increased significantly—an average of more than 30 percent for the eight rates for job titles identical on both schedules. These wages were formulated on the basis of the latest rates on the Hugo Dam project. The Bureau of Reclamation's Denver office did not receive the modification in the mail until December 4. Department of Labor regulations relevant to timing state:

> All actions modifying an original project wage determination prior to the award of the contract or contracts for which the determination was sought shall be applicable thereto, but modifications received by the Federal agency . . . later than 10 days

[152] The source for much of the information in this case is Construction Labor Reports, Nos. 906, 921, and 923, in addition to the briefs and rate determinations filed with the case and letters to the Wage Appeals Board from the files of the U.S. Department of the Interior.

> before the opening of bids shall not be effective except when the Federal agency . . . finds that there is a reasonable time in which to notify bidders of the modification.[153]

Because the modification was received only eight days before the opening of bids, the contracting officer of the Bureau of Reclamation decided that there was not a reasonable period of time in which to notify all the bidders of the wage modification. He therefore concluded that the modification was not to be effective under federal procurement regulations. One day before the scheduled bid opening, Local 627 of the International Union filed a suit in U.S. District Court for the Western District of Oklahoma to secure a restraining order preventing the opening of the bids because the modification had been excluded from the project specifications. A hearing was held the next day at 8:30 A.M., the day of the bid opening. The bids were scheduled to be opened at 10:00 A.M. Because it was readily apparent that the hearing might not be concluded until a short time before that hour, the contracting officer arranged to have someone standing by to receive word by telephone about whether or not the injunction had been issued.

During the course of the hearing, the court determined that although the Bureau of Reclamation did not receive the modification in the mail until December 4, it had become aware of the existence of the modification during a phone conversation with the Department of Labor on December 1. This meant that the bureau did have ample time to notify the bidders of the modification. The court decided that irreparable damage could result if the bids were opened under these circumstances and then issued a preliminary injunction. A deputy U.S. Marshal was instructed to call the contracting officer's phone number to inform him of the injunction. This was done at 9:53 A.M., just seven minutes before the bids were scheduled to be opened. However, the contracting officer did not receive the message until four minutes after the hour. By that time, four bids had already been opened. He decided to open the remaining seven because he felt that there would have been a great deal of criticism from all of the contractors had not all of the bids been revealed at that time.

At a later hearing, the court voided all of the bids opened on December 12. The court also permanently enjoined the awarding of the Mountain Park Dam contract on the basis of those

---

153 29 CFR, 1, Sec. 1.7(b)(1) (1972).

bids and ordered the Bureau of Reclamation to include in the project specifications the wage determination "with all modifications thereto, as properly determined pursuant to the Davis-Bacon Act." The court went on to criticize the contracting officer for not trying to determine the disposition of the hearing before opening the bids. For this reason, the officer was held to be in contempt of court when he opened the first bid. Because the bureau knew of the modification more than ten days before the bid opening, the court criticized it for its capricious action and "callous attitude" in not accepting the wage modification.

In the meantime, the Department of Labor was petitioned by the Bureau of Reclamation to cancel the project wage rate modification covering operating engineers. In response to the bureau's request, a statewide area wage survey was undertaken. This statewide survey included such projects as Hugo Dam (225 miles from Mountain Park), Kaw Dam (200 miles away), Optima Dam (200 miles away), and Waurika Dam (only 75 miles away). The relative location of Mountain Park Dam and the others is shown in Figure 5.

Upon completing this survey, the Department of Labor issued a new wage determination to replace the previous one. At this point, the Bureau of Reclamation filed an appeal with the Wage Appeals Board. The bureau hoped to secure reinstatement of the original project determination, but without the operating engineers' modification. Concurrently, the International Union of Operating Engineers filed a second petition with the Wage Appeals Board. The union felt that the final determination issued by the Department of Labor did not fully take into account the peak period of employment at the Hugo Dam project. The union also contended that the determination failed to use the top rates paid at the end of the Hugo Dam project.

It was quite evident, and all parties agree, that the Waurika project should be included in any wage survey. However, both sides differed beyond this point. The operating engineers believed that any survey should include every dam in Oklahoma and use the peak pay period at Hugo Dam. The Bureau of Reclamation, on the other hand, contended that there were several other projects in the vicinity of Mountain Park which could be used should a survey beyond Waurika Dam be required. These projects included highway and railway con-

FIGURE 5
Mountain Park Dam, Oklahoma

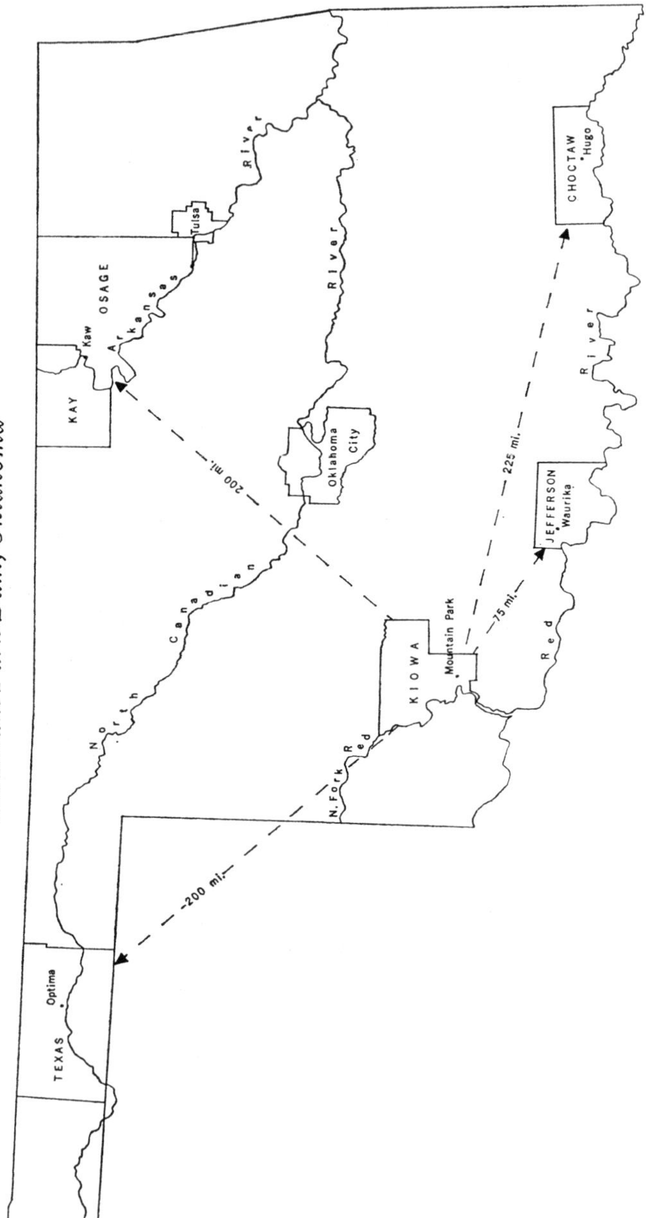

Redrawn from original material supplied by U.S. Department of Labor, Wage Appeals Board

struction related to the Mountain Park Dam and several local mining operations.

In its decision, the Wage Appeals Board decided that the relevant area for the wage survey was the Waurika Dam. It felt there was no valid reason to extend the survey beyond that point. "Waurika has a set of rates that are being paid and the Board sees no need here to move the inquiry a step further back to determine the justification for the rates at Waurika Dam," the panel said.[154] The higher wages in the modification were terminal rates paid only during the last days of construction at Hugo under a previously agreed upon arrangement. At the time of the survey, Hugo Dam was 98 percent complete, and only six mechanics and six bulldozer operators were shown on the payrolls at that time. In contrast, the payrolls for the Waurika project showed two mechanics, three oilers, eighteen laborers, one tractor operator, two roller operators, five bulldozer operators, four scraper operators, two motor patrol operators, and one semi-trailer operator. The higher, terminal rates at the Hugo Dam site were not being paid at Waurika Dam. For purposes of wage determination, the department had no justification to "leapfrog" the then current project at Waurika and disregard it for terminal wage rates on a nearly completed project some 225 miles distant. Thus, the original project determination, minus the modification, was reinstated.

Although the Wage Appeals Board and the court may appear to be in conflict, this is not the case. The court ruled that the Bureau of Reclamation was obligated to include any modifications issued in a timely fashion according to the rules. In contrast, the Wage Appeals Board concluded that the modification was not called for in the first place. The end result is that bidding should take place under the original project determination, but the Bureau of Reclamation is not excused from its actions.

CONCLUSIONS. Several observations can be made from this case. First, many contracting agencies (such as the Bureau of Reclamation) would rather not became embroiled in prevailing rate decisions and administration. Second, the Department of Labor, in making surveys for Davis-Bacon purposes, uses very flexible definitions of "locality" and "similar work." There was no apparent need to leapfrog a nearby project in search for

[154] Wage Appeals Board, Case No. 73-5, 1973.

rates 225 miles away. Third, artificially high rates (such as those set as terminal, bonus rates at Hugo Dam) can be perpetuated in later decisions—thus escalating rates rapidly—unless great care is exercised by interested observers who are sufficiently familiar with local rates to know that such determinations are artificial.

Two undetermined questions of Davis-Bacon surveys are also clearly illustrated. First, how many rates are sufficient to establish a survey base before extending the survey search beyond the immediate locality of the proposed work? Second, if it is decided to look at rates over the past year's time, what rates or numbers of workmen should be included—the maximum numbers employed at some rate, the number employed at the maximum rate, or some other variation? This decision can be very important, particularly on open-shop jobs where rate levels are not fixed by contract but can vary during the life of the project.

NEW CASES

The case examples in the preceding section were "new" cases; they have not been previously written up in other studies. But because they were based on cases taken to the Wage Appeals Board, they were included separately. In this section, three additional new cases are presented which do not have that association. The first, Delta Electric, deals with apprentices and Davis-Bacon procedures. The second, Portage Realty, illustrates problems which can arise when a contractor is caught between a federal contracting agency and the Department of Labor. The third is a short example concerning a state's prevailing wage act.

Delta Electric, 1970

The Delta Electric Construction Company, Inc., is a Texas-based corporation which has its home office and principal place of business in San Antonio (Bexar County), Texas. On February 13, 1970, Delta entered into a standard "Form 23" construction contract with the Department of the Navy, Naval Facilities Engineering Command. Under the terms of this contract, Delta was to make modifications and additions to the airfield lighting systems at both the Corpus Christi and Kingsville Naval Air Stations.

Each wage determination, AJ-7,426 and AJ-7,425, for construction at Corpus Christi and Kingsville, respectively, contained wage rates for both building construction and heavy-highway construction. Although the two determinations contained wage rates for both types of construction, the work to be performed by Delta consisted of only heavy-highway construction. The determinations specified $4.60 per hour wage rate for electricians involved in heavy-highway construction. No wage rates for electrician helpers were involved in either determination.

Shortly after entering into the two contracts with the Naval Facilities Engineering Command, Delta submitted a request for authorization of additional classifications and wage rates for electrician helpers, junior and senior. This request was sent to the authorized representative of the commander, Naval Facilities Engineering Command. Included in this request were data from the Texas Highway Department, the Texas Highway-Heavy Branch of the Associated General Contractors of America, and other sources to verify the use of electrical helpers in the area in which the work was to be performed. Delta requested a wage rate of $3.25 per hour for senior electrician helpers and a wage rate of $2.25 per hour for junior electrician helpers.

On April 13, 1970, the officer in charge of construction denied Delta's request for additional classifications and wage rates on the grounds that electrician helpers could not be used on the work at Corpus Christi and Kingsville instead of "properly indentured apprentices." Delta operates an open shop. Instead of an apprenticeship program approved by the Bureau of Apprenticeship and Training, it operates its own extensive training programs which include a correspondence course, classroom training conducted by its supervisory personnel, and on-the-job training. Delta had previously used its electrician helpers on projects done for the Texas Highway Department and the U.S. Army Corps of Engineers.

After the officer in charge of construction denied Delta's request for additional classifications and wage rates, Delta requested a final written decision from the commander of the Naval Facilities Engineering Command. This request was made under the disputes clause of the contract so that an administrative appeal might be made. The disputes clause of Delta's contract provides that:

> Except as otherwise provided in this contract, any dispute concerning a question of fact arising under this contract which is not disposed of by agreement shall be decided by the Contracting Officer, who shall reduce his decision to writing and mail or otherwise furnish a copy thereof to the Contractor.[155]

Clause 6 further provides for administrative appeal and the opportunity for the contractor to be heard and to offer evidence in support of his appeal. The first request for a written decision was made by letter dated April 21, 1970. Additional requests were made on June 3, July 8, and July 31, 1970. Delta received no response to any of these requests; however, by letter dated September 4, 1970, the officer in charge of construction forwarded to Delta a copy of a letter from the associate administrator, Division of Wage Determinations, U.S. Department of Labor. In this letter, the associate administrator agreed with the decision of the officer in charge of construction to deny Delta's request for the approval of the classification of electrician helper, junior and senior. The officer in charge of construction advised Delta that "the matter of additional classifications does not fall within the items which may be appealed under the Disputes Clause." This decision was in apparent contradiction with the section of the disputes clause that was stated earlier.

Because the contracting officer never made a final written decision on Delta's request for additional classifications and wage rates, Delta was not entitled to any sort of administrative appeal. The company therefore went to court to petition it to require the contracting officer to furnish a final written decision that would be subject to administrative appeal. If the court ruled that the decision of the Department of Labor to deny Delta's request for additional classifications constituted a final administrative decision, Delta was prepared to ask that it be set aside on several grounds. First, the decision of the Department of Labor was arbitrary and capricious. It totally disregarded the evidence presented by Delta showing that the use of electrician helpers was an established practice in the area and had been used on projects involving the Texas Highway Department and the Army Corps of Engineers. Second, the decision by the Department of Labor discriminated against Delta's employees by depriving them of an opportunity to learn the electrical trades without first joining a union and entering a union-sponsored apprenticeship program.

---

155 Delta Electric Construction Company, Inc., contract, General Provisions, clause 6.

Finally, Delta argued that the decision was contrary to the intent of Title VII of the Civil Rights Act of 1964, because the vast majority of the people to be used as electrician helpers would be members of a minority group, a status which mitigated against their being accepted as participants in a union-sponsored apprenticeship program.

The United States District Court dismissed Delta's case. It ruled that the matter of the decision rested within the jurisdiction of the secretary of labor and was not subject to any form of judicial review. Thus, the decision of the Department of Labor was affirmed and Delta was not afforded the opportunity to secure an administrative appeal.

Portage Realty, 1971-1973

On November 29, 1971, the Portage Realty Corporation of South Bend, Indiana, received a firm commitment from the Department of Housing and Urban Development (Case No. 073–35095–PM) to build an apartment house complex known as Creekside Terre Apartments, in Mishawaka, Indiana. These apartments were to be two-story walk-up buildings of wood frame construction with brick and aluminum exteriors. The complex was also to contain a community building with a pool. Construction costs were estimated to be about $2,000,000.

Because the commitment was issued under the federal program known as Section 221(d)(4), it was subject to the Davis-Bacon Act. The wage rate predetermination under which the project was to be built, AM–8,171, was issued December 20, 1971; it was received by Portage Realty on January 8, 1972. With the firm commitment and the necessary wage rate schedule in hand, Portage proceeded with final negotiations with various subcontractors and requested a rapid preconstruction conference so that work could be started earlier, if possible, than the anticipated starting date of March 1, 1972.

On February 11, more than a month after it had received the rate schedule and less than three weeks before work was to commence, Portage received word from the Indianapolis office of HUD that rate decision AM–8,171 was being withdrawn and the start of construction postponed. Despite protests, a new project determination, 72–IN–45 was not issued until March 29. This new decision contained wage rates about 50 percent higher than in the earlier one and reflected the union scale for commercial construction in St. Joseph County.

Portage immediately protested both the revised rates and the fact of their being issued so soon before work was to start and after the company had already made financial commitments based on the earlier rate. This was not a bid job in the same sense as a direct government contract would be. Section 221(d)(4) is an interest guarantee clause rather than a procurement clause, so it is the start of work rather than bid opening which controls the latest date for changing prevailing rate determinations. It did not, however, appeal to the Wage Appeals Board—perhaps because it was not aware of the board's existence. Because of its commitments, Portage decided to go ahead with the job. Work at the new rates commenced July 19, 1972, four and one-half months later than initially anticipated.

Portage continued to seek an explanation of the revised rate schedule. Early in 1973, the answer began to become apparent. The original survey which had been conducted for the first rate decision (AM–8,171) had been conducted in October 1971 by personnel of the U.S. Department of Housing and Urban Development. This followed the procedure which had been recently established, in which HUD and the Department of Labor were to cooperate in determining residential building rates, with HUD field personnel actually conducting surveys to supplement the (usually) union-rate-only information otherwise relied upon by the Department of Labor.

When the resulting rate schedule was published, many protests —said to be accompanied by wage data—were received by the Department of Labor. Because of them, the department felt it had to do something, so it cancelled the previous rate and made a survey of its own. This survey found the union rate to be prevailing for "projects of a similar character," although it is not known whether this was a 30 percent rule or actual majority determination; neither is it known how "projects of a similar character" was construed. There is a very good possibility, however, that these two-story brick and frame buildings were distinguished in character from single-family residences, some 822 of which had been built in St. Joseph County during the preceding twelve months. Although single-family residential construction far exceeded multi-family low-rise residential construction in the county, Department of Labor guidelines will not accept single-family wage data if *any* multi-family data are available. Because HUD personnel had recently started making wage surveys, they may have misinterpreted this guideline, thus producing the lower rates. The conflict, in other words, may have been primarily between two government agencies over interpretation of a Davis-Bacon definition, with the contractor caught in the middle.

By April 1973, Portage Realty estimated the increased costs to that date on the project (then 65 percent complete) to have been at least $71,081.06, thus indicating excess costs of more than $100,000 for the over-all project, or about 5 percent of the total. It continued its protests vigorously throughout 1973, pointing out the inflationary effects of the revised wage schedule, but without any noticeable results.

Mercersburg School System

Sometimes the problems created by importation of wage rates can pervert the purpose of the Davis-Bacon Act to the point that its effect is to deny local contractors and workmen the opportunity for work at all. This can also be the case under the states' prevailing wage laws. One recent situation under a state law involved the proposed construction of a new school in the small town of Mercersburg, Pennsylvania. Because no federal funds were involved, the Davis-Bacon Act did not apply, but the Pennsylvania prevailing wage statute applies to school construction where state funds are involved, which was the case here.

Mercersburg is in Franklin County. The largest metropolitan area in it, Chambersburg, has a population of less than 20,000. The local carpenter rate there was estimated by an area contractor to be "probably about $2.00 per hour." In the far corner of the county, however, 12 carpenters were working on a turnpike tunnel at a wage rate of $8.25 per hour. Actually, when an aerial survey of the tunnel project was made by a contractors' association, it was found that the tunnel project was really in the neighboring Allegheny County. Nevertheless, the $8.25 rate was determined for the school, which so increased the costs that the local school system had to abandon the effort to build it.

The Vermont Situation

Construction in the state of Vermont has always been heavily open shop—since 1969 almost completely open shop.[156] Nevertheless, the U.S. Department of Labor has continued to impose union rates on Vermont construction, sometimes imported from

[156] Information based on field survey of Vermont by Industrial Research Unit for open-shop construction study, spring, 1974.

New York or New Hampshire. By September 1974 the department had apparently made only one recent wage survey in Vermont—Franklin County, building, 1973. Since, in all revenue sharing projects, where 25 percent of the funds are provided by the federal government, Davis-Bacon rates apply, Davis-Bacon wage determinations of rates higher than those truly prevailing have become a significant problem for Vermont municipalities and contractors. As a result, the Associated General Contractors of Vermont (AGC/VT) employed a wage analyst and undertook a series of surveys of wages actually paid. Following are excerpts from a report issued by William J. Keogh, Executive Director, AGC/VT, September 20, 1974.

HIGHWAY CONSTRUCTION

The first wage survey was in highway construction in Rutland County. The results were accepted by the Dept of Labor and published in the Federal Register in February, 1974:

Trade	D-B Rate	Survey Rate	Trade	D-B Rate	Survey Rate
Carpenters	$6.60	$5.30	Truck Drivers	$5.00	$3.25
Masons	7.30	6.00	Spec Equip	5.25	4.75
Electricians	7.35	5.48	Backhoe	8.55	4.00
Laborers	4.00	4.00	Bulldozer	8.10	5.24
			Gradall	8.55	5.25

Thus, it was established, at least in one county, that the D-B wage determinations for highway construction, state-wide, did not reflect truly prevailing wages. It proved that D-B determinations were higher, thus inflating the cost of construction.

The Dept of Labor Wage Administration continues to issue state-wide highway construction rates, except for Rutland County. Yet, highway construction is negligible in rural counties like Grand Isle and Essex. The rationale used by the Dept of Labor to inject union rates in these counties is that the labor force is available in a contiguous county, even though the contiguous county may be completely different in character (urban or rural) and economics.

A highway survey was done in Addison County, another rural county in Vermont. Of the seven construction projects surveyed, one was D-B and the contractor had to pay the higher D-B rate. Because the contractor had to pay the higher single rate (per trade), the D-B rate was prevailing. (Under D-B rules, if 50% of the tradesmen get a single rate, then that rate is determined prevailing. If the 50% rule is not applicable, then the 30% rule applies, similarly. Should the first two not apply, all other rates are averaged.) Other than the single Federally-supported project, the otherwise truly prevailing rate was much lower than the D-B determination.

An interstate project was out for bid when it was discovered that the D-B wage determination of $5.42 was considerably higher than the previous determination of $4.00. The $5.42 figure was the amount negotiated between some non-Vermont contractors and the laborers' union. The wage was never paid to anyone, yet published by the Dept of Labor in the Federal Register as "prevailing". A protest was registered by AGC/Vt and carried directly to Washington. No payment evidence to establish the $5.42 was submitted to the Dept of Labor. To establish its position, AGC/Vt had to conduct a wage survey in a couple of days. The survey showed the $4.00 to be actually prevailing. The contractor estimates the incorrect figure would have cost the Vermont Highway Department an additional $60,000.

HEAVY CONSTRUCTION

Because of the time involved in conducting wage surveys in highway and building construction, AGC/Vt is unable to address itself to this type of survey, even though surveys are needed. Therefore, a surveyed and non-surveyed situation like this can and does exist. The prevailing rate for the laborer in Rutland County in highway construction has been determined at the surveyed rate of $4.00. The laborer in heavy construction in the same county without a survey, has a determined rate of $6.25.

BUILDING CONSTRUCTION

An owner of a proposed roofing job was shocked at the $9.25 D-B determination for roofers in Chittenden County. On a query to the Dept of Labor as to the source of the $9.25, it was ascertained that the roofers' union in Albany, NY was contacted for its rate and this was the figure. So the Dept of Labor cranked this dollar amount into its "prevailing" determination. It should be noted that there is no union roofer operating in Vermont. A rate of $8.69 was conceded for the roofer. The engineer's estimate for that job was $36,000. The lone bidder was given the job for the price of $82,000. Others would not bid the project due to the high roofer rate. An actual survey of roofers in Chittenden County shows the prevailing rate approximately of $4.00. Payment evidence supporting this rate has been pending in the Dept of Labor for over three months.

There is no painters local in Vermont. Because the union agreement had an increment increase, the wage determination for Bennington County was raised from $6.07 to $8.58 for brush painters and from $8.09 to $11.04 for spray painters. The rate was increased without a survey and even though the rate was never paid, no payment evidence was sought to substantiate the higher rate. Yet the determination was made.

There are few union ironworkers in Vermont. The Dept of Labor gets its "prevailing" wage determinations from the union in Manchester, NH. A total wage package of $9.37 has been determined for Vermont for structural ironworkers and reenforcing ironworkers. Much of this kind of work involves tying reenforcing bars in advance of pouring concrete. This reenforcing work is being done either by carpenters or laborers and does not require the greater skill of a structural ironworker. The D-B determination of $9.37 is higher than is actually prevailing for both the structural worker and the reenforcing worker. It has to be a long, slow, documentary process to convince the Dept of Labor to separate the reenforcing ironworker rate from the more skillful structural ironworker's rate. Meantime, the inflated rate is built into the cost of the project, paid by the owner.

The union rate for electricians has consistently been determined as prevailing in the State, currently $8.52. A survey in Chittenden County indicates the truly prevailing rate is $5.96. Payment evidence to support the $5.96 has been submitted to the Dept of Labor. Only one Vermont electrical contractor has signed with the Union and that is for a single industrial site in Chittenden County. On an actual survey, the Dept of Labor would have little basis to support its contention that the union rate prevails across the State. This statement would apply to many other trades as well.

The first evidence that the electricians' rate termed prevailing by the Dept of Labor was in fact not prevailing, surfaced during a building survey in Rutland County done by AGC/Vt and found acceptable by the Dept of Labor. The results of the entire survey:

Trade	D-B	Survey	Trade	D-B	Survey
Bricklayers	$7.95	$7.80	Sheetmetal	$7.64	$7.64
Carpenters	7.10	5.65	Truck driver	4.65	3.61
Cement masons	7.95	6.55	Backhoe	8.45	3.81
Electricians	7.73	4.85	Gradall	8.85	4.10
Laborers	6.20	3.61	Loader	8.85	4.10
Jackhammer	6.45	4.00	Paver	8.45	8.45
Painters	4.25	3.61	Bulldozer	8.45	8.45
Plumbers	7.65	8.20	Roofers	8.69	4.60

A LOOK AT VERMONT CONSTRUCTION

For reasons of their own, the vast majority of construction workers in Vermont choose not to belong to construction unions. Traditionally, contractors employ their main work force most of the year, thus offering a more stable and constant income. . . .

Union contracts have been signed by Vermont-based contractors in Chittenden County. Two contractors have bricklayer agreements; at least two have plumber agreements, one has signed with the carpenters and agreements have been signed with the glaziers and sprinkler-fitters. There is no evidence of any other building construction contracts with any of the other trades.

When the D-B wage determination is the union rate and the negotiated contract calls for an increase, the increase automatically goes into the determination as prevailing, even though the new wage has not been paid and despite the fact no local union exists in the area.

The imposition of union rates as prevailing, when in most cases they are not, results in the higher construction costs for the owner and a disruption of the local economy. Actual surveys and pending surveys already show a material difference in the supposed prevailing rate by the Dept of Labor and the actual survey data.

In its own surveys, AGC/Vt makes every effort to be objective. It is not unusual, for example, to come up with the union rate in an AGC/Vt survey. Union bricklayers, plumbers, sheetmetal, sprinkler fitters, operators, glaziers can frequently establish the D-B rate. Of course, these union rates, though frequently "prevailing" under Dept of Labor regulations, are generally much higher than the average wage rate.

The need for wage surveys throughout Vermont to determine truly prevailing wages is obvious. AGC/Vt has conducted wage surveys using the procedures and forms prescribed by the Dept of Labor to substantiate the payment evidence required. But the Dept insists on double-checking each employer's submission. This imposes on the Department a workload it is not prepared to assume, apparent from the delays already experienced in roofers and electrician payment evidence. Additional surveys have been presented to the Dept of Labor and there is no telling when a determination will be made on the basis of the payment evidence.

The delay is due, in part, to the regulation which requires all interested parties be notified when a wage survey is being made. In the case of AGC/Vt surveys, unions having jurisdiction in Vermont (even though they may not have a signed agreement), are asked to submit payment evidence. There appears to be an inconsistency in that, when a change in the determination is about to be made, AGC/Vt is not notified.

A request for additional personnel to be added to the Dept of Labor Boston office to conduct wage surveys in Vermont resulted in the creation of the position of Clerk-Typist. Hardly a solution to the problem.

Appended to this report is a summary of surveys. . . . Some have been approved; some are pending [Table 16].[157]

---

157 William J. Keogh, "Davis-Bacon Fuels Inflation in Vermont," duplicated study (Montpelier, Vt.: Associated General Contractors of Vermont, 1974).

TABLE 16.
The Davis-Bacon Act
Davis-Bacon Wage Determinations
Compared with Wage Surveys in Vermont
1973-1974

1. Building Construction

Trade	Washington County			Rutland County			Chittenden County			Orange County			Addison County		
	D-B	Survey	+ or —	D-B	Survey	+ or —	D-B	Survey	+ or —	D-B	Survey	+ or —	D-B	Survey	+ or —
Bricklayer	8.86	7.00	+1.86	7.95	7.80	+ .15	8.41	7.76	+ .65	8.86	8.42	+ .44	8.41	7.30	+1.11
Carpenter	7.00	5.47	+1.53	7.10	5.65	+1.45	7.40	6.41	+ .99	7.02	6.35	+ .67	7.85	5.66	+2.19
Cement Mason	8.86	7.00	+1.86	7.95	6.55	+1.40	8.41	7.76	+ .65	8.41	8.42	— .01	8.41	7.30	+1.11
Electrician	8.52	5.04	+3.48	7.73	4.85	+2.88	8.12	5.96	+2.16	8.52	8.05	+ .47	8.52	5.00	+3.52
Laborer	6.25	3.36	+2.89	6.20	3.61	+2.59	6.25	4.37	+1.88	6.25	3.27	+2.98	6.25	3.50	+2.75
Painter	5.40	4.99	+ .41	4.25	3.61	+ .64	5.40	3.50	+1.90	5.40	5.30	+ .10	5.40	3.50	+1.90
Plumber	8.47	5.20	+3.27	7.65	8.20	— .55	8.02	6.60	+1.42	8.47	8.02	+ .45	8.47	7.33	+1.14
Roofer	8.70	4.04	+4.66	8.70	4.60	+4.09	8.70	3.82	+4.88	9.25	4.26	+4.99	8.70	3.61	+5.09
Sheet Metal Workers	7.64	5.88	+1.76	7.64	7.64	same	7.64	7.64	same	7.64	4.35	+3.29	7.64	7.36	+ .28

TABLE 16 (Continued)

	2. Highway Construction						3. Building Construction			
							U.S. Dept. of Labor Survey			
	Rutland County			Addison County			Franklin County			
Trade	D-B	Survey	+ or —	D-B	Survey	+ or —	Trade	Survey	Trade	Survey
Carpenter	6.60	5.30	+1.30	7.30	4.50	+2.80	Bricklayer	5.00	Truck Driver	3.70
Cement Mason	7.30	6.00	+1.30		no date		Carpenter	5.72	Power Operator:	
Electrician	7.35	5.48	+1.87		no date		Electrician	5.30	Backhoe	3.00
Laborer	4.00	4.00	same	4.00	3.75	+ .25	Iron Worker	5.15	Crane	5.00
Truck Driver	5.00	3.25	+1.75	5.15	3.00	+2.15	Laborer	3.38	Dozer	5.88
Backhoe	8.55	4.00	+4.55	9.10	4.75	+4.35	Painter	5.05	Loader	3.25
Gradall	8.55	5.25	+3.30	8.85	4.00	+4.85	Roofer	4.29	Paver	4.25
Dozer	8.10	5.24	+2.86	8.65	3.58	+5.07	Sheet Metal	6.50	Roller	4.25

Source: William J. Keogh, "Davis-Bacon Fuels Inflation in Vermont," duplicated study (Monpelier, Vt.: Associated General Contractors of Vermont, 1974).

CASES AND SITUATIONS REPORTED IN CONGRESSIONAL HEARINGS

Case examples, personal experiences, and sample situations have always played a role in congressional and public hearings. In the most recent hearings, in 1972, a number of specific instances were mentioned at least briefly.[158] These were hearings into wage requirements in federally assisted housing, so the cases are all in that area. Also, several of the examples reflect the suspension of the Davis-Bacon Act, which had taken place during the preceding year.

Scottsboro, Alabama, low-rent public housing.

Rates imported for an unusual, large-scale construction project were imposed on a local housing project.

Rockdale, Maryland, electrical installation.

A 22 percent saving was realized on a project during the Davis-Bacon suspension.

Swampscott, Massachusetts, rehabilitation center for the aged.

A 23 percent saving was realized on a project during the Davis-Bacon suspension.

Alabama, housing project.

Firm usually paid skill differentials for carpenters, with rates ranging from $3.50 to $6.50 per hour. Rate determined for a Davis-Bacon job was $6.50. Firm could not afford to employ its own trainees.

Tampa, Florida, housing project.

A 6 percent saving was realized on a project during the Davis-Bacon suspension.

Newton, Iowa, center for the aged.

A 10 percent lower cost bid was made possible for a particular contractor because of the Davis-Bacon suspension.

---

[158] U.S., Congress, Senate, Subcommittee on Housing and Urban Affairs, *op. cit.*

Prince Georges County, Maryland, high-rise apartment complex.

To receive an interest cost subsidy to build an apartment complex for moderate-income families, Davis-Bacon rates were required. But the high Davis-Bacon rates more than offset savings, eliminating the project.

Philadelphia, Pennsylvania, "236" housing.

Additional cost estimated by builder because of Davis-Bacon rates was $222,750, or 15 percent of the contract cost.

Camden, New Jersey, "236" housing project.

Wages on a Davis-Bacon job were 63 percent higher than those paid on an adjacent, conventionally financed project. The wage difference amounted to 12.36 percent of total project cost.

Dallas-Ft. Worth, Texas, "236" housing project.

Wage rates for the same trades up to 62 percent higher on the "236" project than conventional housing less than two miles away.

Arkansas, 50-unit FHA project.

Contractor appealed wage determination. After a one-year delay, appeal was successful. Average hourly rate was reduced by 44 percent.

Keene, New Hampshire, Bean Construction Company.

Comparative jobs, side-by-side, one subject to Davis-Bacon rates, and the other bid during the suspension, were in progress simultaneously. Savings on the noncovered job was 12 percent of the total contract price of $220,000.

Madison County, South Dakota, county hospital.

Davis-Bacon rates were considerably higher than the job contractor had been paying.

Fremont, Michigan, housing for the elderly.

All local contractors refused to bid on a job when Davis-Bacon rates were assigned to it. Nonlocal contractor bid price was 45 percent higher than a local (withdrawn) bid. The project was abandoned.

Walnut, Iowa, home of the aged.

Davis-Bacon rates determined for the job were imported 60 miles from a metropolitan area in another state. Project was abandoned.

Atlanta, Georgia, low-rent housing.

Davis-Bacon rates determined were much higher than local available rates.

Cullman, Alabama.

Davis-Bacon rates imported from a city 55 miles distant were 62 percent higher than the local rates.

CONCLUSIONS

After the first few cases in this chapter, individual conclusions were not attached to the examples presented. To have done so would have created needless duplication. Although the cases were selected to provide as broad a range of examples as possible, two factors are common to almost all of them: various aspects of the administrative problems discussed in Chapter V and many illustrations of the way Davis-Bacon rates drive construction wage costs above what open market competition for the available labor supply would allow, as discussed in Chapter VI. Insofar as these cases are representative, they substantiate the conclusion that the act is both badly administered and inflationary.

But the cases also illustrate other aspects of the operations of the act which have not yet been fully discussed. In several of them it is seen that wage determinations will remain in effect unless protested; in others, local contractors are unable to protect local wage rates or work practices; in yet others, local contractors are unable or unwilling even to bid on work covered by Davis-Bacon determinations. These problems go to the very heart of the act. Does it fulfill the functions it was designed to serve in 1931—to protect local wage rates from predatory itinerant contractors? Does that function remain socially necessary today? These questions are discussed in the next chapter.

CHAPTER VIII

Rationale and Other Issues

From case studies and analyses of the preceding three chapters, the conclusion is inescapable that Davis-Bacon administration leaves something to be desired. It is also difficult not to conclude that the act exerts considerable upward pressure on construction wage rates, is expensive to administer, and promotes inflation. Most of the questions raised there had to do with administration, and the point has been made by supporters of Davis-Bacon that administrative and procedural reform would prevent necessary repeal or modification of the act.

In addition, they argue that financial, administrative, or other problems are inconsequential compared with the benefits the act offers and are a small price to pay for them. The costs involved in Davis-Bacon, even under conditions of perfect administration, have been discussed in Chapter VII. Here is it necessary to examine the act's consequences on the construction labor market, and then to consider the question of whether the act fulfills its original purpose and whether the rationale which sponsored it has remained valid.

THE LABOR MARKET

As mentioned often enough previously, the specific language of the Davis-Bacon Act is in terms of geographic locality. Nevertheless, from time to time, the Department of Labor has extended this concept and has chosen to justify doing so on the basis of labor supply. For some considerable period of time, the department contended that when the labor supply in the immediate vicinity of a job was too small to staff the complement of workers necessary to complete a particular project and the rate for such workers was less than that in adjacent labor supply areas, the contractor would probably not be able to import sufficient workmen at the lower rate. Therefore, in making surveys for such jobs, the department felt justified in extending into adjacent areas until a sufficient labor supply was found and in using those rates for the predetermination. According to one study:

> In order to have rates high enough to attract the necessary labor for a very large project, it is sometimes necessary for the Department of Labor to predetermine rates based on rates paid in another state.[159]

A former solicitor of labor is quoted in another study:

> The legislative history of the Davis-Bacon Act indicates that Congress intended the Secretary to have sufficient administrative discretion to take the source of labor supply into account in predetermining wage rates.[160]

Actually, it is very difficult to derive this interpretation from the legislative history of the act. The former solicitor seems to have been placing his reliance on the phrase "other political subdivision," which appears in the statute which discusses "projects of a character similar to the contract work in the city, town, village,—comma—*or other political subdivision of the State in which the work is to be performed.*"

The interpretation of the Department of Labor in extending "other political subdivision" to include other states or major sources of labor supply (usually the nearest metropolitan area) was brought under scrutiny in congressional hearings on amendments to Davis-Bacon in 1962; it seemed to many observers that this was an unwarranted interpretation. At that time, spokesmen for the Department of Labor indicated that the department was no longer following that interpretation, and in fact had dropped any reference to the source of labor supply from its labor regulation. Nevertheless, it continued to discuss labor supply concepts as justification for setting the normal geographic unit for predetermination surveys at the county level, rather than "city, town, [or] village." [161]

Current departmental regulations continue to use the county as the principal basis for rate predeterminations. In rural or sub-

---

[159] David B. Johnson, "Prevailing Wage Law," *op. cit.*, p. 250.

[160] W. S. Tyson, "Prevailing Wage Determination in the Construction Industry: Some Legal Aspects," *Labor Law Journal* 3, Journal 776 (1952), in J. R. Serumgard and F. A. Steward, "The Davis-Bacon Act, Analysis and Recommendations," duplicated study (Washington, D.C.: Chamber of Commerce of the United States, n.d.).

[161] Testimony of Charles Donahue and John H. Dent (U.S. Department of Labor) in hearings on H.R. 9656 and 9657, March 8, 1962, pp. 195, 196.

urban areas of counties which are dominated by a metropolitan city, this decision has the effect of ensuring that the metropolitan rate is determined in most cases. Metropolitan rates are usually union rates. In rural or suburban areas of counties which are separated from or not dominated by a metropolitan area, the department may still exercise its option to decide that the available labor supply is not great enough to provide a good survey for predetermination; thus, it may survey in adjacent counties until enough of such work is found. The amount of flexibility the department exercises is demonstrated by its determinations in the Mountain Park Dam case in the preceding chapter. But also to be considered is the effect on the local (that is, the rural or suburban) labor market. If a major government job is done in a rural or suburban area, any succeeding government jobs done during the following year in that county will carry the same labor rates. Furthermore, the wage expectation levels of workmen, regardless of whether they were actually working on the project, will escalate to match the project rates. This situation creates potentially disrupting and certainly inflationary pressures within the local labor market.

Davis-Bacon as an Organizational Tool

Davis-Bacon can be used by the unions in jurisdictional disputes and as an organizational tool. Some observers have gone so far as to suggest that its use as such is the principal reason why the construction unions want to keep the act on the books:

> they [the construction unions] obviously don't need it to keep wages up. They have a very potent reason to want to keep it on the books—the Davis-Bacon Act, in the hands of a helpful and understanding Labor Department, is a wonderful weapon for winning jurisdictional disputes.[162]

The jurisdictional disputes to which this comment refers are those which arose a few years ago between the construction unions and the industrial unions representing production and maintenance employees in publicly owned plants (for example, plants owned by the Atomic Energy Commission but operated by a private contractor). At that time, the basic criterion for determining applicability of the Davis-Bacon Act to particular work was whether it fell within the traditional work of a con-

[162] Thomas F. Hilbert, "Federal Wage and Hour Laws," *Proceedings of New York University Twelfth Annual Conference on Labor*, ed. Emanuel Stein (New York: Matthew Bender and Co., 1959), p. 133.

struction union. In a publicly owned plant, electrical work, painting of plant surfaces, rigging, plumbing, carpentry, and other functions which would normally be carried out by maintenance men perhaps organized by some industrial (as opposed to building trades) union might well have been determined to be Davis-Bacon work. As such, it would have had to be performed at construction wage rates. Because the employer could not have paid the high Davis-Bacon rates to some of his maintenance personnel without causing serious disruption to his entire wage structure, he would have had to subcontract the work in question to outside construction contractors whose employees were represented by the various construction trades unions. Thus, the Davis-Bacon Act would have resulted in assignment of work to building trades members rather than to the maintenance employees represented by industrial unions.

Although jurisdictional problems of this sort were much more common fifteen years ago (particularly on the missile sites which were then being set up) than they are today, and even though current Department of Labor regulations exclude "force account" labor, applicability problems continue to be a hazard of Davis-Bacon. In such situations, Davis-Bacon might well be used as a lever of jurisdictional disputes among unions.

Davis-Bacon has also found use as an organizational tool. In his remarkably candid history of the International Union of Operating Engineers (IUOE), Garth Mangum outlines this function in some detail:

> The Davis-Bacon Act provides that a wage rate common to the majority of the employees in a particular classification in an area (or 30 percent if there is not a majority paid at the same rate) shall be determined as the prevailing rate which all in that classification must be paid. This being the case, once the Joint Heavy and Highway Construction committee was successful in signing the employers of a majority of the members of their crafts in an area, they could appeal to the Department of Labor and have those wage agreements become binding upon all other employers upon construction projects in which the federal government was involved. The unions then suggested that the contractors form a statewide association, if they had not already done so, and bargain as a group. Whatever wages were negotiated became the prevailing rate, and, since the contractors were more interested in relative than absolute costs as long as they were established in advance of the bidding, rates could be increased to a level more acceptable to the union member.

He continues:

> Once the union scale became prevailing, there were advantages to using the union as a labor supply source which usually brought in the nonunion contractor. If not, interrelations between union and nonunion contractors could be used as a lever for organization. The familiar pattern of persuading a union contractor to break off relations with a nonunion subcontractor is well known. An example of a more direct technique was one case where union engineers refused to hoist some quick-drying concrete which a nonunion subcontractor was attempting to pour.[163]

The principal time period when federal prevailing wage laws were the major organizing tool of the Operating Engineers was in 1954, when a four-way pact was made among the engineers, teamsters, carpenters, and laborers under the direction of Hunter Wharton, then assistant to the general president of the IUOE, and John Brunozzi, formerly with the Davis-Bacon division of the Labor Department. This pact was formed to stave off inroads being made in many construction areas by the catchall organization, District 50, then affiliated with the United Mine Workers and since merged with the United Steelworkers. So, to some extent, this organizational drive was also a jurisdictional dispute. The pact dissolved in 1958 and is no longer a factor. But the tactics which it employed, with the Davis-Bacon Act the focal point, are significant.

The recent order of the secretary of labor, noted in Chapter III, which attempts to bring owner-operators of trucks under the act's purview, may also have been prompted by an attempt of the Department of Labor to aid Teamster organizing. One AGC chapter wrote the secretary:

> you are aware that compliance will require payroll status for all owner operators. We would point out that by your administrative action you have accomplished for the Teamsters what that union has been unable to accomplish through collective bargaining for many years—forcing employment status on owner operators.[164]

Another chapter noted that the secretary's order could endanger minority contractors to which it had subcontracted the truck work.[165] It should be noted in this regard that the Teamsters'

---

[163] Garth L. Mangum, *The Operating Engineers: The Economic History of a Trade Union* (Cambridge, Mass.: Harvard University Press, 1964), pp. 257, 258.

[164] "Davis-Bacon Policy on Owner Operators Rescinded," *Constructor* 56, No. 10 (October 1974): 11.

[165] *Ibid.*

Union has been found in an earlier Industrial Research Unit study to have had a less than favorable record insofar as utilization of black truck drivers is concerned.[166]

The Extension Principle

In Western Europe, wage scales negotiated by unions in an industry may be made automatically binding on nonunion employers by law or government action. Thus the union scale is protected. The Davis-Bacon Act performs a similar service for unions in the construction industry. The act extends wage setting without forcing the unions to organize additional employees.

Craft Union Classifications

Another consequence of Davis-Bacon felt by construction labor markets does not seem very dramatic but has considerable long-range impact—classification of craft union workers. Construction was one of the first industries to be unionized; then, the labor philosophies of the time plus the somewhat special working conditions of the industry combined to produce the still-existing job classification pattern and single rate structure of the industry. All journeymen in a craft were to be paid at the same rate and for the knowledge they all needed to become journeymen, not for what each of them could do on the job.

As developing technology created new crafts, and as workmen split others into smaller units for better leverage, craft classifications began to multiply. What used to be done by approximately a dozen basic trades at the same number of wage rates now requires different rates running into the hundreds. Davis-Bacon has exacerbated this profusion. In the sample Davis-Bacon determination included here as Appendix E, ninety-one separate rates are listed. There are three different categories of line construction groundmen, eight categories of truck drivers, and five different categories of laborers. (Incidentally, can anyone say with certainty that a well-point installer laborer is really worth five cents more per hour than a non-metallic clay and concrete pipe caulker laborer? Or that a trestle scaffold builder over one tier high should be paid the same as a scaffold erector, steel or wood?

---

166 Richard D. Leone, "The Negro in the Trucking Industry," in Herbert R. Northrup *et al.*, *Negro Employment in Land and Air Transport*, Studies of Negro Employment, vol. 5, part 3 (Philadelphia: Industrial Research Unit, The Wharton School, University of Pennsylvania, 1971).

For work on a trestle scaffold only one tier high, should the laborer get a different rate? None is specified.)

In addition, different rates are set for different types of construction—building, heavy and highway, etc. In some cases, the equipment (for example, a dumptruck) operated for one work classification is the same equipment, operated in the same way, as that for another work classification. Only the classification changes; the different rates make no sense at all. In other cases, different skill levels are required, so the wage differences are more understandable; however, they are contrary to the established scheme of one rate for journeymen.

The job classification scheme was designed to support the flexibility required of the construction industry. But the conditions of the industry have been undergoing evolutionary change. Improved technology and larger scale operations have helped stabilize work forces. They work longer during a year, are less sensitive to seasonal variations, and work longer on the same projects. Open-shop firms, which are not as constrained by the closed apprenticeship systems of the unions, have been better able to move towards breaking down the artificially restrictive craft designations. On-the-job training, certification, and pay for various levels of skill development—the common practice in most of the industrial working world—are evolving among modern nonunion firms. These are very healthy developments; they allow greater opportunity for workmen than the closed systems do—especially for minority workmen. But most importantly, they overcome the needlessly restrictive practices of overspecialized trades and work against the trend towards "professionalization" of, and job rights in, unskilled, manual work.

By establishing up to a hundred or more rates for some contemplated government job, and specifying job content to be covered, in some cases, down to the brand name of the equipment to be utilized, Davis-Bacon denies contractors the flexibility necessary to improve or to make more efficient work practices on the job. Open-shop contractors can still avoid some of the restrictive work practices of particular trades, but they are nevertheless compelled by Davis-Bacon to categorize their employees according to rate determination listings. If an open-shop contractor is to contemplate any Davis-Bacon work at all, he cannot very well employ a work force consisting of "building constructors A, B, and C," unless he is also willing to keep the records necessary to apportion their time each day into the various rate categories of his Davis-Bacon determination. Therefore, to an even greater degree than wage rates, work categories specified in Davis-Bacon determinations spread through and influence the market organization of construction labor.

The point of these examples of the influence of Davis-Bacon on local labor markets is not to show poor or improper administration of the act. The effects (although perhaps not their magnitude) are the same, whether the act is well or poorly administered. Neither does it matter if a particular practice involving Davis-Bacon is or is not currently sanctioned by Department of Labor regulations. The point is that the act can have these effects, has had them in the past, and is not prevented from having them again in the future.

RATIONALE

The events which led up to the Davis-Bacon Act were outlined in Chapter II and will not be repeated here, but it is well to recall that Davis-Bacon was protectionist legislation, as much triggered by the public relations appeal of its issues and by union pressures as by fears of itinerant contractors. Thus, the real purposes of the act were somewhat different from its rationale.

In 1931, when the act was passed, Keynesian economics and deficit spending had not yet been introduced. The economics of J. B. Say still controlled thought on such matters. In this view, when the supply of a commodity, even labor, outstripped demand for it, either the price had to fall until the market cleared or supply had to be curtailed. Government, when forced to take action, usually tried to limit supply. (Later in the depression, government would seriously adopt a deficit spending for demand stimulation, but that was the new, Keynesian approach.)

The real purpose of the Davis-Bacon Act was to try to uncouple wage levels from the market for labor in the construction industry and to minimize the effect of the oversupply of labor by restricting wage competition. The tenor of the times would not yet contemplate general legislation for this purpose, but federal construction was certainly within the purview of Congress. The Davis-Bacon Act did not affect supply directly; but, by requiring prevailing local wage rates to be paid workmen on federal construction, it ensured that workmen would not be competing with one another by offering their services at reduced wages, nor that contractors would be competing with one another on the basis of low wage rates. It was not part of the purpose of the act, but economically inescapable, that although wage levels would be partially maintained, less work would be available as a result. Oversupply would be reduced because the growing numbers of persons displaced from other jobs would be discouraged by the few job opportunities from seeking work in the construction industry.

The rationale of the act, on the other hand, was that the federal government should not contribute to falling wage rates by insisting on the lowest-priced bids for the construction work it desired. If all contractors bidding on such work were required to pay the same wage scale (that which prevailed in the local community), then wages would be taken out of competition and contractors could not compete with each other on the basis of being able to get workmen at low rates. Itinerant contractors importing low wage rates from the South or other areas would not have any advantage over those operating in the local community, and the industry would be stabilized on both fronts, with only the government bearing the cost of the stabilization. It is this rationale, rather than the act's purposes, around which questions were asked and defenses raised.

Through the years, and increasingly as the economy has overcome the conditions of the depression, observers within and outside the construction industry have questioned whether the rationale of the act remains a useful pursuit. For example, the president of the National Association of Home Builders expressed this view in 1972:

> While there may have been at one time a need for requiring the payment of prevailing wages in connection with federally assisted projects, this is no longer the early 1930's and the conditions that then prevailed are no longer with us. We are not in the depths of a depression and the union and the working man in general are now in a much better position to bargain for and obtain wages in a community which are commensurate with the cost of living. We do not have vast unemployment with the concomitant problem of men willing to work for almost nothing, thereby driving down the wage level for all. In fact, in most places, such as here in the Washington metropolitan area, we have the exact opposite, without enough trained construction workers to fill the jobs available.[167]

---

[167] Statement of Stanley Waranch, President, National Association of Home Builders, in U.S., Congress, Senate, Subcommittee on Housing and Urban Affairs, *op. cit.*, pp. 168, 169.

Others have gone even further by maintaining that the rationale of the act has been so completely abrogated that it now serves the reverse of its original purpose:

> When enacted during the depression days of 1931, the Davis-Bacon Act could boast merit in expressing the public policy that local wages should not be depressed by the expenditure of Federal funds on Federal projects. At the same time, however, it can be argued today quite convincingly that public policy demands that local wages should not be *inflated* by the expenditure of Federal funds on federally assisted projects [Emphasis added].[168]

Many other similar views were expressed in the most recent hearings on the Davis-Bacon Act.[169] On the other hand, some observers feel that Davis-Bacon is as much needed as ever to prevent the chaotic cheap labor conditions of an earlier day. According to a union spokesman,

> [If a bill is passed to abolish Davis-Bacon] the country may revert to the chaotic conditions of the early 1930's with itinerant contractors traveling from locality to locality, underbidding local contractors and causing local unemployment.[170]

The Department of Labor seems to take a related but slightly different view—Davis-Bacon repeal would disrupt the construction industry. Excerpted from the hearings already mentioned is the following statement from the under secretary of labor:

> Moving in the direction of Davis-Bacon repeal will only sow the seeds of discord that will hinder the modernization of the industry.[171]

From the preceding opinions, it is easy to see that positions on Davis-Bacon adhere to what might be considered a classical labor-management dichotomy, each side seeing the issue through different eyes and arriving at opposite conclusions. Often, when

---

[168] Statement of Senator John Tower, in U.S., Congress, Senate, Subcommittee on Housing and Urban Affairs, *op. cit.*, p. 3.

[169] In U.S., Congress, Senate, Subcommittee on Housing and Urban Affairs, *op. cit.*; see statements of: Yale Brozen (University of Chicago), pp. 397 ff.; Robert T. Thompson (Chamber of Commerce), pp. 59 ff.; Senator Peter H. Dominick (Colorado), pp. 40 ff.; Congressman John B. Anderson (Illinois), pp. 386 ff.

[170] Statement of Frank Bonadio, President, Building and Construction Trades Department, AFL-CIO, in U.S., Congress, Senate, Subcommittee on Housing and Urban Affairs, *op. cit.*, p. 221.

[171] Statement of Laurence H. Silberman, Under Secretary of Labor, in U.S., Congress, Senate, Subcommittee on Housing and Urban Affairs, *op. cit.*, p. 25.

conclusions on both sides are derived from feelings, opinions, and views, their divergence in essential points is so great that empirical observations become meaningless. Management argues economics (costs) and labor argues need (benefits). All possible statistics collected by one side will fail to convince the other because the bases of the arguments arise from different premises. Usually in such cases, actual experimentation or trial solution is impossible. This is not true, however, of Davis-Bacon.

The relevant question is: would the chaotic conditions of 1931 return if Davis-Bacon were repealed? Readily available evidence indicates that it would be highly unlikely. If Davis-Bacon applied to all construction, this would be a very difficult matter to test. But it does not. Counting all federal construction, federally assisted projects, and projects done under the similar state prevailing wage laws, Davis-Bacon directly or indirectly affects about 40 percent of the country's construction activity. This is significant, but it does leave the other 60 percent uncovered. Many large factories, commercial structures, housing developments, and the like are built purely on competitive bidding, the contract being awarded to the lowest bidder. Sometimes the lowest bidder is a union contractor, sometimes open shop. The two types compete effectively, neither one nor the other the preordained winner. There are few complaints (none has ever been brought to the author's attention) about itinerant cheap labor contractors snapping up all of this work and forcing local wage rates down; nor is there any evidence of union contractors being forced to do exclusively government work because of their high wage structure, at least outside of homebuilding.

Therefore, there would be little reason to suppose that, were the Davis-Bacon Act to be repealed, cutthroat competition would arise in the industry. Nor is there any reason to suppose that conditions in the entire construction industry would be any different than they are now in the nongovernmental sector of it—unless the assumption were made that Davis-Bacon rates on government jobs provide some sort of stabilizing influence on rates in the private sector. On this point, the opponents and supporters of Davis-Bacon find themselves involved in a role reversal. The construction unions and the Department of Labor have argued that Davis-Bacon does not influence private rates, but simply determines what the rates are in a county and applies them to government work to be done in that county. Thus, Davis-Bacon could exert no stabilizing influence over private rates, because it follows rather than leads them. On the other hand, opponents have demonstrated in many specific cases that Davis-Bacon rates do not simply reflect area practice, but are often higher than those actually prevailing and are frequently at the union scale. To the degree to which these higher rates influence the private sector, they may be considered either a stabilizing or an inflationary influence, depending on whether the economy is in an expansionary or a depressed state.

Under either contention, the best that could be said of Davis-Bacon is that it exerts a stabilizing influence during depressions. Only in such circumstances would the rationale of the act be sustained. And during times of depression, the minimum wage laws, unemployment compensation, and the whole structure of the welfare system—all of which are new since 1931—would ensure that the intolerable conditions of falling wages and deteriorating working conditions which existed then would not happen again. Even during a depression, Davis-Bacon is unnecessary.

Nonlocal contractors perform large amounts of the Davis-Bacon construction in the country (just as they perform private construction). It is a matter of conjecture whether these nonlocal contractors might be considered itinerants shielding themselves from labor cost competition by Davis-Bacon and snapping up government jobs, thereby denying work to local contractors and local workmen. Were it so, the Davis-Bacon rationale would indeed be operating backwards. Actually, the point is a bit far-fetched. But it is no more so than the contention that low-wage itinerant contractors would reappear were Davis-Bacon repealed. The entire controversy is contrived to accord with the published rationale of the act rather than with the act's purpose. Senator Peter Dominick, in the 1972 hearings, noted:

> [The Davis-Bacon Act] was an emergency measure aimed at stabilizing wages when the cards were stacked in favor of management. Today, the building trades unions hold the high cards and no longer need this type of government help.[172]

This statement goes to the actual heart of the matter.

---

172 Statement of Senator Peter H. Dominick, in U.S., Congress, Senate, Subcommittee on Housing and Urban Affairs, *op. cit.*, p. 42.

CHAPTER IX

Survey Results

During the late spring and summer of 1974, a detailed questionnaire was mailed to every other member (alphabetically by location) of the Associated General Contractors, the Associated Builders and Contractors, the American Road Builders Association, the National Electrical Contractors Association, the Associated Independent Electrical Contractors, and the Mechanical Contractors Association.[173] A total of approximately 10,000 questionnaires were mailed. These associations were chosen to provide a good cross section of the construction industry. Some are oriented towards union firms, some towards open shop, some towards larger firms, some towards smaller. The National Association of Home Builders (mostly open shop) was not included because its vast number of members (about 28,000) would have overbalanced the results towards that sector of the industry. A copy of the questionnaire is found in Appendix D.

PROFILE OF RESPONDENTS

There were 1,402 usable responses which were received in time to tabulate. They show some interesting aspects of Davis-Bacon effects and make very clear that a majority of firms of all types is opposed to the act. The survey results also shed some light on some characteristics of the industry which are not well known. For example, the survey shows that on the average, 40.4 percent of the respondents are unionized, 50.4 percent are open shop, and 7.1 percent are doublebreasted. Although these proportions may not give a precise reflection of the over-all structure of the industry, they do show that in most

[173] The other 50 percent of the members of these associations were mailed a similar questionnaire relating to the Industrial Research Unit's open-shop study.

parts of the country the number of open-shop firms is greater than it is often assumed to be.[174]

Table 17 shows that the areas of greatest union strength are in the Pacific and East North Central regions, and the areas of greatest open-shop strength are in the South Atlantic and East South Central regions. This distribution was expected, but open-shop firms (responding to the survey) outnumbered union firms in the New England and Mid-Atlantic regions also, which was not expected. Doublebreasted firms have become a significant factor in the industry, particularly in the East South Central area.

The firms which responded to the survey are not exclusively small firms. On the average, they did $5,856,740 of business during 1973 and employed 132 employees. Although this result is skewed by the thirty firms which reported more than 1,000 employees, the plurality of firms responding indicated annual volumes of business of between $1 million and $5 million, and between 20 and 49 employees. This set of figures was for all of the firms, but the finer breakdowns show that on the average the open-shop contractors are slightly smaller.

All types of construction are represented in the survey, as shown in Table 18, and among the more than 180,000 employees represented are workmen in every major trade. Laborers, employed by 73.6 percent of the firms on their own payrolls, are the most widespread, but more than half of the respondents also had carpenters, power equipment operators, and truck drivers, and almost half also had cement masons on their own payrolls. As expected, more union shops (82.9 percent) than open shops (59.8 percent) employ apprentices. These are mostly in carpentry, but also in plumbing, electrical work, and cement work. The proportion reverses for helpers, where 71.1 percent of open shops and 16.1 percent of unionized firms employ them for carpenters, electricians, power equipment operators, or cement masons. One aspect of work force composition which is somewhat surprising is that 22.3 percent of union firms as well as 77.5 percent of open shops report paying some form of differential rates within the same craft, excluding helpers and apprentices. This result is difficult to understand unless the respondents were thinking about the different components of the power equipment operators or were including geographical differences or some other factor unrelated to skill.

[174] This is brought out clearly in the open-shop questionnaire.

TABLE 17.
Survey Responses, Davis-Bacon Questionnaire
Degree of Unionization, by Region
1,402 Contractors, Summer 1974

		Percent of Responses by Union Status of Respondent				
Region	Number of Responses	Union Shop %	Open Shop %	Double-breasted %	n.r.[a] %	Total Percents[b]
New England	96	37.5	51.0	6.3	5.2	100.0
Mid-Atlantic	215	33.5	58.6	5.6	2.3	100.0
East North Central	210	61.0	31.4	5.7	1.9	100.0
West North Central	119	48.7	41.2	10.1	—	100.0
South Atlantic	259	13.9	79.9	4.2	1.9	99.9
East South Central	99	21.2	63.6	14.1	1.0	99.9
West South Central	146	29.5	59.6	8.9	2.1	100.1
Mountain	75	46.7	42.7	6.7	4.0	100.1
Pacific	136	82.4	7.4	8.1	2.2	100.1
Region not reported	47	53.2	38.3	8.5	—	100.0
Average		40.4	50.4	7.1	2.1	100.0

[a] Unionization not reported.

[b] Percentages may not add to 100.0 because of rounding.

TABLE 18.
Survey Responses, Davis-Bacon Questionnaire
Principal Type of Construction Work Done
1,402 Contractors, Summer 1974

Heavy	12.7
Highway	12.2
Industrial/institutional	34.9
Commercial/residential highrise	25.4
Residential/homebuilding	7.4
Other	6.8
No response	0.6

Most of the union firms are working exclusively in urban areas, and most open-shop and doublebreasted firms are working in suburban or rural areas. All three types feel that the amount of open-shop work activity has been increasing in their areas. Perhaps because the labor characteristics of an area have a big influence on the way a new firm will organize to do business, most union firms believe that the other contractors and subcontractors in their area are also mostly union, whereas most open-shop firms believe that they are open shop. These views are tabulated in Table 19.

EFFECTS OF DAVIS-BACON: RESPONDENTS' VIEWS

The preceding tables and information are mostly for background and to show that our survey sample is a representative one. But what is of greatest interest is how these contractors relate to the Davis-Bacon Act and what their views and opinions concerning it are. Eighty to 90 percent of the contractors surveyed had bid on Davis-Bacon jobs during the preceding two years. They had, in fact, submitted an average of 25.2 bids each, and won an average of 10.1 bids. (Here, again, these figures are skewed upwards by the presence of a few very large, or very active, firms. The median figures would be somewhat lower—about 13 bids and 9 jobs won.)

Davis-Bacon work generally amounted to 40.6 percent of all the work done by the respondents, which is somewhat higher than the established nationwide proportion of Davis-Bacon work to all construction. A higher proportion of open-shop firms (49.0 percent) than union shops (35.1 percent) do less than 25 percent of their work under Davis-Bacon, and a lower proportion of open-shop firms (17.8 percent) than union shops (29.9 percent) do more than 75 percent of their work under Davis-Bacon. There are few contractors among the respondents who do no Davis-Bacon work (8.2 percent) or all Davis-Bacon work (7.6 percent). Davis-Bacon is thus seen as somewhat more important to the unionized firm.

Are Davis-Bacon rates different from contractors' own rates? Open-shop firms state that they are, whereas unionized firms state that they are usually not. Those who replied that they were different were asked to give examples. The results, which are tabulated in Table 20, show that the differences usually involve higher rates for Davis-Bacon. This was sometimes the

TABLE 19.
Survey Responses, Davis-Bacon Questionnaire Respondent Location and Views on Extent of Unionization 1,402 Contractors, Summer 1974

Survey Question	Percent of Responses		
	Union Shop	Open Shop	Doublebreasted
Area in which majority of work is performed:			
Urban	51.8	28.0	31.0
Suburban-rural	28.4	48.4	42.0
Combination	17.8	20.9	25.0
Total work [a]	98.0	97.3	98.0
Proportion which feels open-shop activity has increased in home-base area	69.8	77.4	84.0
Views on extent of union organization of other contractors in home-base area: [b]			
Mostly union	76.9	19.9	44.0
About even	13.1	18.4	29.0
Mostly open shop	7.1	54.5	23.0
Total views [a]	97.1	92.8	96.0

[a] Totals do not add to 100.0 because some firms did not respond to this question.

[b] Subcontractors follow almost identical patterns.

case even for unionized firms. More than any other aspect of the survey, this response demonstrates the powerful inflationary impact of Davis-Bacon. With average Davis-Bacon labor reported to be 31.1 percent of the total job costs and average rate increases calculated to be 36 percent for approximately one-half of all the firms responding, total job cost increases can be calculated to be 5.60 percent. On total federal construction of $38 billion, this is a direct inflationary impact of more than $2.1 billion of annual excess cost, with no offsetting productivity benefits.

TABLE 20.
Survey Responses, Davis-Bacon Questionnaire
Davis-Bacon Rate Comparison to Usual Rate
1,402 Contractors, Summer 1974

I. Were the wage rate determinations (for Davis-Bacon) greatly different in either rate or benefits from your own on private work?

	Respondent answers (percent)	
	Yes	No
Union firms	10.8	89.2
Open shops	78.0	22.0
Doublebreasted	54.1	45.9

II. Rate comparisons:

	Average of rate examples submitted by all categories of contractors		
Trades	Own rate	Davis-Bacon rate	Percent increase
Carpenters	$5.514	$7.299	32.4
Cement Masons	5.305	6.954	31.1
Laborers	3.719	5.229	40.6
Plumber/pipefitters	5.871	7.784	32.6
Other	5.480	7.849	43.2
Average increase			36.0

III. Davis-Bacon labor as percent of total job costs: 31.1 percent.

In addition to the general inflationary impact, in the view of both union and open-shop firms, Davis-Bacon harms profits, decreases work force productivity, harms morale, and leads towards decreased minority employment possibilities. Feelings are mixed on whether it improves or harms general recruiting. Somewhat more open-shop firms believe that it helps in recruiting (probably because of the ability to offer higher wage rates) than believe the opposite. These views are in Table 21.

The survey questionnaire also presented a list of seventeen statements and asked respondents to check whether they strongly agreed, agreed, had no feelings or did not know, disagreed, or strongly disagreed with them. The responses show that few

TABLE 21.
Survey Responses, Davis-Bacon Questionnaire
Davis-Bacon Effects on Contractors
1,402 Contractors, Summer 1974

Factors	Proportions of Contractors Seeing Effects Noted		
	Union Shop %	Open Shop %	Doublebreasted %
More profits	3.2	4.1	5.0
Less profits	17.7	28.0	42.0
More productivity	1.6	1.3	5.0
Less productivity	18.9	24.2	36.0
Better morale	2.8	6.9	8.0
Worse morale	12.5	22.6	23.0
Improved minority employment	8.8	4.1	7.0
Decreased minority employment	10.2	11.9	24.0
Improved general recruiting	4.2	7.5	14.0
Decreased general recruiting	9.7	6.1	16.0

Note: Firms not reporting or reporting "no change" in these factors can be determined by subtracting the "more" and "less" figures from 100.0.

contractors see many benefits arising from Davis-Bacon. On a weighted strength scale of ten,[175] they disagreed at a level of nine with the statement, often used as justification for continuance of Davis-Bacon, that "Davis-Bacon adds stability to the industry and is desirable in the event of an economic downturn." They disagreed at a level of five that "Open shop firms make more profits when they are working on Davis-Bacon jobs." They also disagreed at a strength level of eight that "Minority employment possibilities are improved by the Davis-Bacon Act,"

[175] The strength scale is calculated simply by assigning a factor value of two, positive or negative, to "strongly agree" and "strongly disagree," of one to "agree" and "disagree," and of zero to "?" The percentage distribution of response is weighted by these factors, summed, and regulated to a 10-point scale.

and agreed at a level of six that "Davis-Bacon hinders on-the-job development of craftsmen."

Concerning administration, they agreed with strength three that "Time required to administer Davis-Bacon provisions is a major deterrent to bidding on covered work," and expressed their strongest disagreement (a level of ten) with the statement, "When Davis-Bacon rates are in error, it is easy to have them corrected."

The survey questionnaire presented three statements which could serve as recommendations. To these, the respondents disagreed at a level of seven that "Davis-Bacon should set a rate for 'construction workers,'" agreed at a level of five that "The *average* rate in a given area for any given type of construction should be used as the Davis-Bacon rate," and were undecided about the advisability of "All contractors should be required to report their wages periodically to a trade association or the government so rate determinations can be more accurate."

Conclusions

The firms surveyed concluded at a strength level of eight in each case that the Davis-Bacon Act does spread union wage rates to the nonunion sector and urban wage rates to the nonurban areas. They disagreed at a (modest) level of three with the statement, "Any Davis-Bacon rate lower than the union rate automatically excludes the union contractor," and also disagreed (but at an even more tentative level of one) that "Without the Davis-Bacon Act, the construction industry would probably go heavily nonunion." At a level of six, they felt that local contractors do not need protection from itinerant low-range contractors.

Finally, they strongly agreed (level of eight) with the statement, "My firm would be better off if the Davis-Bacon Act were repealed," and, at a higher strength level than for any other statement—a level of ten—they agreed that "The Davis-Bacon Act should be repealed." A summary of all the responses to the statements in the order in which they were presented on the questionnaire is contained in Table 22.

Since they hold opinions of this sort, one might suppose that most contractors would not be interested in doing much Davis-Bacon work. Actually, the statistical results of their opinions

TABLE 22.
Survey Responses, Davis-Bacon Questionnaire
Views and Attitudes About Davis-Bacon
1,402 Contractors, Summer 1974

Attitudes	Percent Distribution [a]				
	SA	A	?	D	SD [b]
Davis-Bacon adds stability to the industry and is desirable in the event of an economic downturn.	5.0	9.4	10.8	32.5	39.6
Without the Davis-Bacon Act, the construction industry would probably go heavily nonunion.	11.4	24.0	14.1	34.9	12.7
Open-shop firms make more profits when they are working on Davis-Bacon jobs.	6.1	10.7	24.3	35.7	20.5
The Davis-Bacon Act spreads union wage rates to the nonunion sector.	28.0	47.0	8.0	11.3	3.4
The Davis-Bacon Act spreads urban wage rates to the nonurban areas.	26.5	43.7	12.6	11.1	2.4
Davis-Bacon rates are usually the same as union rates.	35.9	41.7	6.6	10.0	2.9
All contractors should be required to report their wages periodically to a trade association or the government so rate determinations can be more accurate.	17.5	26.2	10.8	17.3	24.6
The *average* rate in any given area for any given type of construction should be used as the Davis-Bacon rate.	27.1	32.7	10.4	14.6	12.2
The Davis-Bacon Act should be repealed.	50.9	18.9	13.6	9.2	4.2
Any Davis-Bacon rate lower than the union rate automatically excludes the union contractor.	11.3	17.0	15.4	38.5	15.0
Minority employment possibilities are improved by the Davis-Bacon Act.	1.8	12.0	19.5	37.6	26.5
Local contractors need protection from itinerent low-wage contractors.	5.7	16.3	10.7	40.4	23.8
When Davis-Bacon rates are in error, it is easy to have them corrected.	1.7	4.6	26.1	26.0	38.6
Davis-Bacon should set a rate for "construction workers."	4.9	11.8	21.6	27.8	29.5
Davis-Bacon hinders on-the-job development of craftsmen.	26.5	30.7	20.5	15.6	4.0

TABLE 22 (Continued)

Attitudes	Percent Distribution [a]				
	SA	A	?	D	SD [b]
Time required to administer Davis-Bacon provisions is a major deterrent to bidding on covered work.	17.5	31.3	15.1	29.0	3.3
My firm would be better off if the Davis-Bacon Act were repealed.	37.9	23.0	18.8	11.8	4.6

[a] Distribution does not total 100.0 for each question because some respondents did not answer all questions.

[b] SA = Strongly agree with statement.
A = Agree with statement.
? = Do not know, or have no opinion.
D = Disagree with statement.
SD = Strongly disagree with statement.

show them to be more indifferent to it than hostile. Union firms, as might be expected, are a bit more interested than open-shop firms. But a majority of all firms responding stated that they are either indifferent to Davis-Bacon work or are willing to try for it if there is no other work around. The statistical results are in Table 23.

Special Comments

Space was left on the questionnaire to supply comments beyond those required for answering the questions of the survey. About two hundred such responses were received. These covered the entire range of questions about Davis-Bacon, from administration to inflation, and some of them were quite heated. The ones presented below were selected as representative comments about specific aspects of the act. None of the really heated comments is included. Only six of the replies could be considered favorable to continuation of the Davis-Bacon Act, and the majority of those were qualified. Here are the six:

> Davis-Bacon should not be repealed, but there is room for revisions to the DB act.
>
> Repeal of Davis-Bacon could be good if it were replaced by legislation based on all of our experience. We would be in bad shape if Davis-Bacon were repealed and not replaced with anything.
>
> The principal [sic] is OK but it is still union-oriented.

TABLE 23.
Survey Responses, Davis-Bacon Questionnaire
Contractor Views About Future Work Covered by Davis-Bacon
1,402 Contractors, Summer 1974

Concerning future work covered by Davis-Bacon type wage requirements, would you say your firm was:	Distribution of Response		
	Union shop	Open shop	Double-breasted
Anxious to obtain it to the exclusion of other work?	4.6	0.8	1.0
Interested in obtaining it?	33.4	16.8	22.0
Indifferent to it?	28.8	19.8	27.0
Willing to try for it if nothing else around?	20.1	34.2	36.0
Not interested in bidding on it?	5.5	20.2	10.0
No response	7.6	8.2	4.0
Total	100.0	100.0	100.0

> The requirements of the DB Act are not oppressive when one has been thru the procedure several times. However, many contractors could be discouraged from bidding work covered by DB.

> As long as we have strong union laws where contractors must work with restrictive work practices of unions we need the DB Act for union contractors to operate. The DB Act would make no difference if we had a "right to work" act.

> The Davis-Bacon Act has some good points, but on most of our construction projects it is cumbersome.

Although all of the remaining comments did not call specifcally for repeal of the act, a great many of them did; others complained of the administration of the act or raised other problems. A number questioned the continuing need for the act.

> The Davis-Bacon Act was enacted in a time of depressed national economy. If I understand it correctly it was for the purpose of putting a floor under wages paid on government funded work for the purpose of getting the wages up to a level that then was considered desirable. Now with inflation being what it is and in my opinion with the construction industry being the culprit that is leading the pack there cannot be any logical reason for continuing the Davis-Bacon Act except that we are blind to the fact and refuse to eliminate the crutch that is holding up the high construction wages.

> Although we are a union contractor we feel strongly that Davis-Bacon's value has long passed and that the prevalence of unionism has swung too far in their favor.
>
> I cannot help but feel that the Davis-Bacon Act is completely out of keeping with the times and is certainly not necessary to keep outside contractors from paying established local wages. We are far more concerned about outside contractors coming into our area and paying well over the established wages, excessive overtime, or other fringes that make it hard for us to keep our local crews. Construction wages are obviously far higher than they should be compared to other segments of our economy, and it is due to the enormous power the construction unions have at the bargaining table, and once wages are established by this unbalance, then the wages are projected to the non-union contractors for all the public type work. There is no question in my mind but that removal of Davis-Bacon would encourage a more realistic attitude of the construction unions at the bargaining table.

The feeling that unions are the principal beneficiaries of the Davis-Bacon Act and that there is a close relationship between the unions and the "prevailing rates" set by the act is a common one. More comments were received on this point than on any other.

> Davis-Bacon is strictly a union tool. It makes little difference to us as union contractors, except for the additional time and money to file all the payroll reports and police our subs on furnishing same. The average cost of forms, time, postage, etc. is $3,000 per project (without the aggravation factor).
>
> The Davis-Bacon Act does little more than encourage union participation.
>
> Speaking selfishly, we like the Davis-Bacon Act because it eliminates the local contractor from bidding on government funded jobs in the outlying areas. This is because the so-called wage determination is just a verbatim copy of the local union scales.
>
> The law exists and will continue to exist because of union political power.
>
> Davis-Bacon is a tool of unions to force their wishes on the rest of the industry. We have "little" Davis-Bacon in Minnesota and it is being used by government officials to reward unions.
>
> Davis-Bacon rates are almost always union rates, and the total union membership in the USA is approximately 22 percent of the total work force, yet the legislation protecting their inflated wages is supported by all members of the public in every tax dollar spent for unproductive work.

The influence of the unions on administration of the act and on the Department of Labor was also frequently alleged:

> There are four primary deterants [sic] to realistic Davis-Bacon rates:
>
> 1. Urban areas are assumed union and no surveys made without a considerable amount of reports submitted by open-shop contractors.
> 2. The survey notification mailing lists which are furnished to the Regional Offices by the Department of Labor in Washington consist of the local union business agents. Therefore, surveys are made without open-shop firms even having knowledge that they are being conducted.
> 3. The 30% criteria in determining prevailing wages means a survey must show 71% open-shop to recommend other than union wage rates.
> 4. Survey results must be forwarded to Washington for review where they are closely monitored by International Unions.
>
> The above should indicate how this unfair law is stacked in favor of the unions.
>
> When the administrators of the Davis-Bacon Act need to know the wage rate to be paid in a given area, their investigation lacks any in-depth investigation as to the correct wage. They call the local union hall, and ask what the wage is in the area for a given trade, and that is how it is established. That in itself is the most incredible fraud perpetrated on a community by a government body.
>
> The rates that have been applied have not been the "prevailing rates in the area of construction." They have been, for the most part, the organized union rate for the metropolitan area. This is because the government has let organized labor do the paper work for them and has accepted the union figure as being the "prevailing wage."

A number of others objected to the administration of the act without specifying any relationship between it and the unions.

> From our observation, the Davis-Bacon accomplishes nothing except adding unnecessary administrative work. If rates are in error or a classification is omitted, it is a major project to get it corrected.
>
> Reporting hours by job is burdensome when a work crew of 60 work on 15 different jobs each pay period. We have furnished as much as 20 pages of payroll detail covering 50 employees.

Work force morale and training also come in for comment:

> Our experience has been that it [Davis-Bacon] creates bad feelings among the men, especially when one group is working on a private

> job and the other on a public job; there is much jealousy. The men on DB have a tendency to slow down in order to extend the job and in an effort to get the even higher overtime. (I can't really blame them.)

> Since our first job covered by the D-B act, we have not hired a single summer or part-time employee. Our best recruits have consistently come from those two sources.

> The restrictions on the number of apprentices is archaic, ridiculous when there is a crying need to attract more young men into the trades, and more importantly, more minority youngsters.

> It (D-B) has also helped the unions to keep minorities out of construction, and helped to bring about the abusive power of the unions today.

Other comments were received on a variety of topics. Of these, the ones dealing with the inflationary impact of Davis-Bacon are perhaps the most significant and make a suitable close for this chapter.

> The unions, supported by Davis-Bacon are the reason a $10 million highway project costs the government $14 million.

> Sometimes our cost of labor is more than doubled on D-B jobs. We must quote the government on the average, twice the amount for labor. To install the same amount of fence, private industry would pay one-half the labor cost and receive the identical job, workmanship wise.

> The whole thing is very inflationary.

It goes without saying that these separate opinions are those of only a few contractors from among the hundreds of thousands who operate in the United States. Nevertheless, they do provide the only cross-section of views ever solicited from contractors on this subject. The results of the survey are clear enough: if the Davis-Bacon Act is being maintained to serve the needs of contractors, it is a failure. The overwhelming majority of contractors do not want it.

CHAPTER X

Conclusions and Recommendations

Most legislation has both advantages and disadvantages, the relative proportions of which vary with time. Economic conditions, international relations, or any number of other factors may change, and when they do, the usefulness, desirability, or efficacy of the legislation may also be altered with them. This has been the case with the Davis-Bacon Act. The depressed economic conditions which spawned it have long since been replaced by general prosperity and, most recently, by economic stagnation combined with rampant inflation. The workers who needed the act's protection in 1931 to keep their wages from falling below twenty-five or thirty cents per hour are now among the best paid American blue collar craftsmen, whether their wages are measured on an hourly basis or an annual basis. Minimum rates now prescribed for them have at times exceeded ten dollars per hour, thirty times as much as the 1931 rate, and five times as much as the minimum wage protection enjoyed by other American industrial craftsmen of similar skill development.

With most legislation, the evaluation problem is one of measuring the costs of the legislation against its benefits or of weighing its advantages against its disadvantages at any given time. But with Davis-Bacon, it is difficult even to discern benefits for today's society. This may seem a harsh judgment, but it is in accord with the evidence about the act available from congressional hearings, academic studies, interviews, opinion surveys, case examples, and analyses of various sorts. This is not to say that Davis-Bacon benefits no one or that it is completely valueless—simply that its discernible advantages accrue to a limited group of beneficiaries rather than to the over-all economy, and that many of its aspects which were advantageous forty years ago can no longer be claimed to be so.

ASSESSMENTS

Advantages

There seems little doubt that when Davis-Bacon was first enacted, it slowed the downward trend in construction wages, discouraged nonlocal contractors and labor, and prevented destructive competition among contractors for government work. In those depression days before welfare, unemployment compensation, or minimum wage laws, the act had certain obvious advantages which do not apply today and would not apply again, even during a severe depression. (Whether it was then appropriate to reduce contractor and laborer mobility in support of local businesses and workers need not now be debated. It certainly seems inappropriate to continue to do so.) The notion that the United States is today on the brink of a reversion to the chaotic cheap labor conditions of that era, and that therefore the Davis-Bacon Act is essential to help prevent such a catastrophe, seems to underlie much of the argument in defense of the act. This argument is scarcely plausible. Whatever the potential harm of a severe recession, it is difficult to believe that it could be substantially mollified by the existence of the act or exacerbated by its repeal.

Although the principal advantages of the act at the time that it became law may no longer be germane, other advantages can be adduced. Some of these accrue to contractors. Open-shop contractors use their lower wage rates to obtain work in private construction. When Davis-Bacon eliminates their advantage in this area for bidding on government work—which the act often does—greater competition is promoted because the union contractors and the open-shop contractors are put on a more even wage rate footing. This aspect benefits a number of union contractors and allows them to win more work. It is, however, a disadvantage to the same number of open-shop contractors. Furthermore, although a greater level of competition might result, it does not afford the usual advantages of more competition. Usually, competition is beneficial because it results in the most efficient or lowest-priced producer's getting the job. But here the government often insists on denying itself this benefit. Construction does not necessarily go to the lowest-cost bidder, but to the bidder who has lowest costs in nonlabor areas. Because labor costs are 20 to 60 percent of most construction jobs, this difference is significant.

In specific cases, Davis-Bacon provides other advantages for some contractors. During the wage-price freezes, the act gave open-shop contractors a way to raise wages for their employees without running afoul of the regulations. In doing work outside of their home areas, open-shop contractors could raise their workmen's wages to the level of Davis-Bacon rates prescribed for that area without having to justify the raises to the Construction Industry Stabilization Commission, the Cost of Living Council, or other agency. Some open-shop contractors have also said that Davis-Bacon rates were helpful to them in bidding on jobs away from their home territory by eliminating their need to determine independently what wage rates must be offered to obtain enough workmen there. Finally, there are circumstances when work is done on a "cost-plus" basis—for instance, during wars or other emergency situations, when time means more than money; the higher the justifiable costs, the higher the profits. Davis-Bacon labor rates are certainly justifiable costs and would, therefore, result in higher profits.

These benefits of the act for contractors are rather specialized, and not all contractors can take advantage of them. Far more certain are the benefits applied to unions. Removing wages as a competitive measure among firms competing for government work makes it much easier for unions to sign up contractors. Also, by institutionalizing the building trades craft demarcations and training procedures, the act permits continued union control over job assignments. It is difficult to estimate exactly the impact Davis-Bacon has had on the degree of unionization in the construction industry, but it is generally agreed that it has been significant. However, by extending union wage rates, the government in effect protects the unions against the competition of workers whom they have failed to organize.

Finally, there can be no argument that the various effects of Davis-Bacon have encouraged, produced, and maintained high wage rates in construction—certainly an advantage of the act to the workmen receiving them. But why construction workers should be singled out as a special class for these benefits is at least open to question.

Thus, over-all, the main beneficiaries of the act appear to be construction workers, the building trades unions, and some contractors. Other advantages of the act either apply no longer or arise only in special situations. Its disadvantages are considerably more widespread.

Disadvantages

Without question, the greatest disadvantage of Davis-Bacon is its cost. Exclusive of residual, multiplying, or escalating effects, Davis-Bacon costs more to operate than the whole federal judiciary establishment, and perhaps more to run than the entire legislative branch of government. A very conservative estimate would be one-quarter to one-half of a billion dollars per year in administration and excess construction costs over what a free market would provide. To this estimate must be added the inflationary impact which Davis-Bacon creates by favoring union rates, which then spread from government construction to private construction and hence establish an escalating superminimum wage rate for the industry. Including these effects might well bring the total annual cost of the Davis-Bacon Act to $1.5 billion.

Davis-Bacon rates trend towards the union scales and favor them regardless of what rates actually prevail in a locality because:

1. The Department of Labor has insufficient personnel to make on-site inspections and surveys, even with its recent regional administration.
2. The unions have been very efficient in providing contract rate information.
3. Alternative rate information, as from contractors' associations, is very difficult and costly to obtain.
4. Davis-Bacon rate making activities are under close surveillance by the unions.
5. There are seldom adverse consequences from improper rates which accrue to administrators.

Davis-Bacon rates are correct and reflect the wages prevailing in an area—as "prevailing" is defined by Department of Labor regulations—far more often than they are incorrect. But errors can and do occur, if for no other reason than because more than 20,000 determinations are still made every year, containing perhaps as many as 1,000,000 or more separate rates. These are handled without the aid of computers or automatic systems, are subjected to the pressures towards union rates as previously listed, and are subject to flexible and varying definitional interpretations about job categories and work types. Furthermore, the spreading coverage of the country by area determinations (which go against the character and purpose of the act to reflect local wage conditions) undoubtedly forces metropolitan rates on rural areas to a greater degree than the previous project rate determinations. Other possibilities for error exist because of administrative difficulties, which are discussed in the following material.

When errors in rates do occur, they are most often errors on the high side, because pressures and conditions encourage this. If sufficient information is not available, the operating procedure of the department seems to be to put in an available rate—usually the union rate—and leave it for any protester to disprove its applicability. The dangers to the department of challenges are few and the frequency low because the expense and difficulty to a protester of making the necessary independent wage surveys, of hiring lawyers to prepare appeals, etc., are time consuming, often have no compensating benefits, and are beyond the capabilities and interests of most interested parties. In addition, there is sometimes the possibility of greater profits to contractors who do not protest the higher wage rates which the government is willing to pay.

Even if no errors are made and the act is operating perfectly within its administrative definitions, the administrative definition of "prevailing" influences rates upward. The prevailing rate is either the rate to the penny paid to 30 percent or more of the work force (which almost always means the union rate, if at least that proportion of the surveyed work force is organized) or the average of all the rates in the survey. In the overwhelming majority of decisions—those for which the union rate is higher than nonunion—this 30 percent rule means that at least 50 percent and perhaps as many as 70 percent of the rates paid local workmen would have to be modified upward, if these men worked on the government job. Contrary to the implied intention of the act, rates paid on previous Davis-Bacon jobs are included in the surveys for new Davis-Bacon work; thus, they again become part of the 30 percent or average used in setting the next rate. Therefore, the use of the modal or average rate as the minimum pushes the minimum upward. When errors are made, the escalation accelerates.

In either case, normal labor market competitive pressures—to preserve a rate hierarchy within a firm or to establish the rate level which would have to be offered to secure additional workmen from the community—ensure that the influence of Davis-

Bacon rates spreads through private as well as government construction. These effects are difficult, if not impossible, to isolate with the degree of precision necessary for a quantitative estimate. Qualitatively, their mechanism and direction can be observed, and they are cumulative over time. Since the Davis-Bacon Act was passed in 1931, it has very likely been responsible for construction wages (and therefore construction costs) of perhaps twenty billion dollars or more than the wages would have been without it. Indeed, not many advantages offset these costs.

Many problems associated with Davis-Bacon arise from the wording of the law itself and from the fact that all aspects of it are handled by the Department of Labor. The wording of the act is vague and imprecise, and it is flexibly administered by the Department of Labor, which cannot be challenged in any court for the procedures or definitions it devises. The department determines the scope of the market area, the classification of the project, and the designation of the job classification and job structure.

Procedures have changed from time to time in response to pressures brought to bear by congressional hearings, unions, or contractors' associations. At various times, the greatest attention has been paid to the following: procedures for calculating rates based on the 30 percent rule, establishment of geographic boundaries, use of county instead of village or town, use of labor market instead of geography, classification of types of construction for similarity, demarcation of job titles, coverage of force-account personnel, determination of job site location, use of apprentices and helpers, use of rates on work completed in the previous twelve months, and other considerations. All of these remain actually or potentially troublesome as long as legal challenge and judicial review remain impossible.

The courts ruled thirty years ago that, because Davis-Bacon applied only to government contracts and because no contractor was compelled to accept or seek such work, administrative regulations of the Department of Labor could not be brought before the courts. Thus, the Department of Labor is responsible solely to itself for all aspects of Davis-Bacon—rules, rates, and reviews. The solicitor establishes the rules and procedures; the Branch of Construction Wage Determinations interprets them, carries them out, and sets the rates; the Wage Appeals Board adjudicates and, when called upon to do so, reviews. For an act as economically important as Davis-Bacon, this situation seems excessively inbred and utterly lacking in checks and balances.

STATE PREVAILING WAGE LAWS. One unusual aspect of Davis-Bacon as legislation is that it does not prevent states from establishing prevailing rate laws of their own. For state construction or joint state-local construction, this is reasonable enough, because Davis-Bacon would not extend to that sort of work. But for joint federal-state construction, both prevailing wage laws are in effect, and the contractor doing the work must be responsive to both. In fact, there are a number of instances where local jurisdictions impose a third level of rates. This is true in the city of Baltimore, for example. Usually, the contractor resolves this by paying the higher of the two minimum rates. Having to be responsive both to the states' widely varying procedures for determining rates for each category of workmen on a construction job and to Davis-Bacon's own procedures, the contractor might find himself paying federal minimum rates to some workmen and state minimum wages to others; this would be administratively troublesome. To date, no such problem has been brought to the author's attention, but joint federal-state construction is becoming increasingly important and the potential for future problems exists. Even without such problems, much needless effort is expended to supply both bureaucracies with their necessary input and control information.

Conclusion

Little can be added to the conclusion about the Davis-Bacon Act drawn in 1972 by William Dunn, the Executive Vice President of the Associated General Contractors of America:

> While more and more attention has been directed toward the Davis-Bacon Act problem from the standpoint of how to improve it, the basic fact seems to escape notice, and that is that these laws are obsolete, serve no useful purpose, and only contribute to the serious problems in the construction industry without making any contributions towards their solution.
>
> While we should recognize that the Davis-Bacon laws are basically unsound, we need also recognize that they are administered in an unsound manner.[176]

[176] Statement of William E. Dunn, Associated General Contractors of America, Inc., in U.S., Congress, Senate, Subcommittee on Housing and Urban Affairs, *op. cit.*, pp. 311, 312.

RECOMMENDATIONS

Recommendations about Davis-Bacon follow two general types: those made to contractors or their associations about the best procedures to be followed under the existing Davis-Bacon Act, and those made to Congress to modify administrative procedures or to amend the act.

Recommendations to Contractors

If, because of political pressures or other problems, Davis-Bacon could not be modified or amended, it is recommended that open-shop contractors devise some better means of collecting wage information so that these rates can either be supplied and thus included by the Department of Labor in the predetermination process or used to verify the department's accuracy. The obstacles to this procedure are, however, great.

First, there are many open-shop contractors, including some who are not interested in doing government work and consequently would not be interested in supplying rate information. Second, administrative cost is associated with collecting wage rates regardless of how it is done; this cost could be extensive. (Each mailing to the members of the National Association of Home Builders, for example, costs about $2,500 in postage alone.) Third, open-shop contractors observe no uniform wage rates, as the union contracts do. Fourth, open-shop contractors classify job titles differently and often use workmen interchangeably in several different categories of jobs. Fifth, the trade associations must be careful to avoid antitrust problems which might arise if they suggested common wage rates to their members.

As a start, perhaps the contractors' associations might consider surveying their memberships regularly, using their trade association magazines as a vehicle. To save administrative costs as much as possible, this survey might best be used as a control device—instead of surveying for each craft designation for each type of construction work and sorting out all of the fringe benefits so the Department of Labor can be supplied with input data. The survey might ask only for laborer rates (and the associated fringe benefits in dollar terms) for county and type of work (residential, building, highway, heavy). Compiled by the trade associations, this laborer rate could be checked against the rate predetermined by the Department of Labor, either on a random selection or for areas where neither union nor open-shop rates clearly dominate. The Department of Labor is required to make survey and predetermination raw data available to interested parties. If the laborer rate seemed out of line, the association could appeal the entire decision or, at the very least, catalogue it for future reference during hearings or investigations into the administration of the act.

In a different vein, open-shop contractors might consider renaming their workmen, not on the basis of the tools they use, but on the basis of their skill development. There is no reason other than tradition and the organization of the building trades unions for construction labor to be so fragmented. If open-shop firms were to designate their employees as "journeymen construction workers," "learners," and "laborers" (or some other such scheme), in any area where at least 30 percent of the construction was done under these titles, under existing Labor Department operating procedures, the titles themselves would "prevail" and rates would have to be predetermined for them according to the procedures established for selecting the prevailing rate. This scheme would require no operating changes within the firms (a man can be both a bricklayer and a journeyman construction worker simultaneously) and is not as far-fetched as it might appear at first. A roughly similar procedure has been followed to obtain Department of Labor recognition of helper rates in some areas for trades in which they are not used by the unions.

Recommendations for Administration

Any number of recommendations might be made for the administration of Davis-Bacon. Many of these could be carried out by amendment to the act, but a number of others could be done only by the Department of Labor itself (its procedures and regulations not being subject to court review). Broadly, these suggestions concern means of reducing the administrative burden of the act and modifying its definitions.

1. *Contractors' reports*—The time required to complete the weekly payroll report form for Davis-Bacon is not well spent. These reports join the mouldering heaps of other unnecessary paperwork in some federal basement. They provide neither information for future jobs nor control of past ones. For whatever control purposes are necessary, the same form modified

slightly could be filed once, at the termination of the job. Millions of dollars would be saved every year, with absolutely no detrimental effects.

2. *Threshold amount*—Davis-Bacon now covers jobs as small as $2,000. About one-third of the total administrative burden could be saved by raising this limit to $10,000. This is actually less than the 1974 inflated value of $2,000 (1935), and so this limit would have no impact on the intent of the act. If the threshold were set at $500,000 or $1,000,000, the protection afforded by the act would be only modestly affected in quantity; however, its quality would improve because the Department of Labor might be able to make an actual wage survey for each job.

3. *Computers*—It is unbelievable that an agency processing the bulk of materials that the Branch of Construction Wage Determinations processes should be doing it by hand. Computers were designed for this sort of work and should definitely be used.

4. *Review*—Each rate decision should be reviewed, preferably outside the Department of Labor. Members of the Branch of Construction Wage Determinations are like students who grade their own examination papers. Undoubtedly they mean well. In addition, the rules, regulations, definitions, and procedures of Davis-Bacon should be subject to appeal outside the Department of Labor, preferably to the federal court system.

5. *Definition of work character*—The act draws wage information from "projects of a character similar to the contract work." This phrase has been taken to mean projects characterized as residential, building, heavy, highway, and a few more specialized others. One would suppose that the character of the work being done—driving a truck, for example—rather than the character of the job on which the work is being done would be more reasonable. It is, however, the practice of the industry to pay differently depending on the job, so this change could probably not be made. Nevertheless, in far too many cases, the Department seems to follow an arbitrary classification difference rather than a real work difference, particularly between heavy and highway construction. Paving an airport runway, for example, is much closer to paving a superhighway than it is to building a dam.

6. *Definition of prevailing wage*—No other aspect of Davis-Bacon is more annoying to contractors or generally questionable

than the 30 percent rule for determination of the prevailing wage. It is extremely difficult to justify taking a rate which may be higher than those paid to 70 percent of the workers and making it the minimum rate. But it is actually almost as bad to take the average of all rates and make *it* the minimum. Both are justified only by the assumption that the minimum, maximum, and average rates for journeymen are the same. Therefore, it is argued, using the average (or the 30 percent modal rate) as the minimum has no harmful effect. But in a growing segment of the industry, the minimum, maximum, and average rates are not the same, and using the averages as the minimum has deleterious effects. Either the prevailing rate should be used in some way as a required average, or the prevailing rate should be calculated in some way based on minimum wages. Neither of these is very easy to envision in operational terms; but, as the act now operates, it is unfair. The entire concept of prevailing rates as minimum rates should be reexamined to see whether the purposes of Davis-Bacon can be carried out in some other manner.

One recommendation would be to set a Davis-Bacon rate for construction laborers only. Laborers are the common denominator of the industry. If a rate were set for laborers only, competition and the hierarchy of job categories would mandate the other rates for a job, just as in private construction. This recommendation, if followed, would reduce Davis-Bacon administrative problems to reasonable levels even if the 30 percent rule were followed; however, it might be better to use averages and to set the determination up in matrix form as follows:

Average Construction Laborer Rate
Including Dollar-per-Hour Equivalents
for All Fringe Benefits

	Type of Work			
Job Location	Homebuilding	Building	Heavy	Highway
Urban (SMSA)	\$x	\$y	\$z	etc.
Suburban (or town)	etc.			
Rural				

This determination should be made separately for areas of the country corresponding to the standard census areas—New England, East North Central, etc.

Although the problem of using an average rate as the minimum would remain, the advantage afforded by determining the rate only for laborers is that it would allow the contractor some flexibility without denying workers the protection the act seeks to provide.

Recommendations for Repeal or Major Amendments

The recommendations made so far were in case the Davis-Bacon Act, because of political pressures, could not be repealed. Repeal has been recommended by most industry and academic observers. They agree that the act is anachronistic, obsolete, inflationary, and unnecessary for normal or expansionary economic conditions. But against the possibility that the country might again find itself in the grips of a massive, crippling depression, something like the Davis-Bacon Act held in readiness to serve its original purpose might be a comfort.

Probably the best way to achieve this status would be to repeal Davis-Bacon and, if a depression occurs, evaluate its conditions and pass some similar prevailing wage measure to meet the conditions found. History does repeat itself, but very seldom in detail. What was effective for 1931 might not be so again. Repeal of Davis-Bacon is the general recommendation.

As an alternative to outright repeal, Davis-Bacon could be amended in order to retain whatever comforts or benefits it might offer during depression and yet relieve the construction industry and the country from the burdens of maintaining it during periods of expansion, general prosperity, or inflation, when it is not needed. This measure could be taken by reversing the emphasis of sections 276a-4 and 276a-5. These sections now read:

> a-4 *Effective date of sections 276a to 276a-5*
>
> Sections 276a to 276a-5 of this title shall take effect thirty days after August 30, 1935, but shall not affect any contract then existing or any contract that may thereafter be entered into pursuant to invitations for bids that are outstanding on August 30, 1935.

a-5 *Suspension of sections 276a to 276a-5 during emergency*

> In the event of a national emergency the President is authorized to suspend the provisions of sections 276a to 276a-5 of this title.

This language could be amended so that these sections, combined, would read as follows:

a-4 *Invocation of sections 276a to 276a-4 during Emergency*

> When, in the opinion of the President, a serious depressed economic condition exists, creating an emergency, he is authorized to invoke the provisions of 276a to 276a-4 of this title. Sections 276a to 276a-4 of this title shall take effect thirty days thereafter, but shall not affect any contract then existing or any contract that may thereafter be entered into pursuant to invitations for bids then outstanding. Sections 276a to 276a-4 of this title shall not remain in effect longer than 180 days consecutively.

It is unfortunate that during the congressional debates in 1931, legislators did not accept the advice of A.P. Greensfelder, then President of the Associated General Contractors of America, and consider Davis-Bacon as an emergency measure for the duration of the depression only; that is really what it should have been. It should have died when the depressed conditions which spawned it changed, or at the latest when its functions were taken over by the Fair Labor Standards Act, passed in 1938. The Davis-Bacon Act makes little sense under conditions of prosperity and expansion and provides far too few benefits to offset its immense costs.

Appendix A

The Construction Industry

Construction, one of the most complex and important industries in the United States, accounts for 14 percent of the total gross national product. It employs between 5 and 6 percent of the total labor force.[177] In 1973, new construction was valued at $135.4 billion, of which more than one quarter was publicly owned or sponsored.[178] By 1974, the amount of government owned or sponsored construction had risen, partially because of the inflation of the period, to between $38 and $40 billion.

Construction may be briefly defined as a group of interrelated production activities involving the erection and maintenance of physical structures such as residential, commercial, and industrial buildings, highways, and earthworks.[179] The construction production process is vastly different from that of most manufacturing concerns in that it involves the fabrication and assembly of unique, custom designed productions at a special location.

LOCAL NATURE OF CONSTRUCTION

The first significant characteristic of the construction industry that may be drawn from the preceding definition is that the vast majority of all construction work must be performed at a specific site selected by the customer.[180] In some instances, there is some off-site prefabrication of components, such as window assemblies, climate control systems, and elevators, but beyond this, very little or no construction activity is undertaken in ad-

---

[177] Daniel Q. Mills, *Industrial Relations and Manpower in Construction* (Cambridge, Mass.: MIT Press, 1972), p. 4.

[178] U.S., Department of Commerce, "Statistical Series: Construction Put in Place," *Construction Review* 20, No. 5 (June 1974): 18 (Table A-1).

[179] Mills, *loc. cit.*

[180] Milton Derber, *Building Construction,* Labor-Management Relations in Illini City, Case Study No. 5, Vol. 1 (reprint ed., Urbana, Ill.: Institute of Labor and Industrial Relations, University of Illinois, n.d.), p. 666.

vance or at a location that is different from the actual construction site. The typical construction firm, except in rare cases, has no inventory of finished products ready for immediate sale.

Most contractors perform the majority of their business within their home state. This means that wage rates are most often determined locally. In 1967, 88 percent of the total receipts received by construction firms were generated from contracts within the home state of the contractor. With the single exception of heavy (nonhighway) construction activity, in no sector of the construction industry were home state receipts less than 89 percent of the total sector receipts. Even the heavy construction sector received the majority (62 percent) of its receipts from home state projects. Somewhat surprisingly, the highway construction sector also does the preponderance of its work in the home state of its contractors—in 1967, 91 percent of the highway sector receipts came from home state projects.[181]

Besides the preponderance of on-site erection, the local nature of the construction industry is also attributable to several other significant factors. As this study has shown, most construction firms are relatively small. This means that they do not have sufficient resources to undertake projects far away from their home base of operations. In addition, the importance of close business or political relationships in obtaining contracts prevents most construction firms from working far away from home. In many areas of the United States, local and state political conditions dictate that contractors must have a certain "rapport" with influential public officials in order to obtain public construction contracts. It is difficult for a contractor in one state or other political subdivision to establish this type of relationship in another state or similar political subdivision, thus limiting his operation to his home state unless federal relationships affect contractor selection.

LACK OF PRODUCT STANDARDIZATION

Most construction projects are built according to unique specifications for several reasons. Each building site is unique, and varying topography and land use criteria dictate a lack of building standardization. An urban setting often requires the construction of a high-rise building, while a rural setting will

---

181 Mills, *op. cit.*, p. 8.

allow the construction of a low-rise one. Because buildings and other structures are designed to fulfill the precise needs of the customer, no two buildings are exactly alike. The specifications of a library are very different from those of an office building. Differences in building codes are also reflected in design differences. The design of a building in California must be more concerned with the possibility of earthquake than the design of a building in New York. Terrain considerations make it impossible for any two dams, bridges, or highways to be constructed in exactly the same manner. The absence of product standardization has important implications for the construction industry.[182]

Use of Construction Machinery

To be economically feasible, a machine must be useful on many projects, or else it must be able to replace a large number of workers. As a general rule, except in earthmoving, machinery has not yet become sophisticated enough to achieve a level of performance warranting widespread use in the industry. In the instances where useful equipment has been perfected, contractors have often found it cheaper to rent than to purchase. In other instances, contractors have found it more desirable to use labor rather than to attempt to use new equipment.

Capital requirements do, however, vary greatly with the size of the contractor and with the type of construction work performed. Firms that specialize in heavy construction activity are more likely to invest in labor-saving equipment than firms specializing in building construction. Heavy construction contractors usually perform most of the work on a project themselves instead of subcontracting it. This characteristic makes it more attractive financially for them to purchase and use their own equipment. In contrast, building contractors often rent the necessary equipment for a particular project or will subcontract out a large proportion of the work to lessen the need for capital investment.[183] As a general rule, equipment investment climbs in proportion to the firm size, but in 1973, diversified contractors whose incomes ranged from $25 to $49 million had a median in-

---

[182] Derber, *op. cit.*, p. 668.

[183] Peter J. Cassimatis, *Economics of the Construction Industry*, Studies in Business Economics, No. 111 (New York: National Industrial Conference Board, 1969), p. 23.

vestment of $85,000 for each million in contracts, whereas diversified contractors with incomes of $50 to $99 million had a median investment of $42,000 for each million in contracts. These investment figures are greatly exceeded by the highway-heavy sector, which averages $420,000 in equipment investment for each million in contracts.[184] Such a high labor utilization makes wage determinations critically important.

Labor Costs

The absence of product standardization in the construction industry requires that a high proportion of skilled labor be available to cope with ever-changing job requirements. Because each construction project is different, in many cases vastly so, the construction worker in each craft needs a broader range of skills within his particular craft than his counterpart in a typical manufacturing firm would. To achieve the necessary skills, construction workers are often required to serve several years as apprentices before being classified as journeymen. Some critics charge that apprenticeship training lasts far too long and that much of the training is ancillary to the real needs of the workers. These charges and apprenticeship training as a whole will be more fully discussed shortly.

Besides having a higher ratio of skilled to unskilled labor, the construction industry also has a higher ratio of labor to nonlabor costs than most industries. Table A-1 shows the distribution of inputs for a number of types of construction projects. With the exception of dam construction, labor usage involves at least 25 percent of the total inputs for the typical projects listed. In the construction of public housing, college housing, hospitals, and public buildings, the labor input approaches or exceeds one-third of all inputs. Thus, a contractor's wage bill constitutes a sizable part of his total costs. A small increase in wages through an improper determination can greatly increase a project's costs.

Subcontracting

Finally, the lack of construction standardization has led to the widespread use of specialty contractors and subcontractors. Many primary contractors subcontract large phases of work on

[184] "The ENR 400," *Engineering News Record* 192, No. 15 (April 11, 1974): 49.

TABLE A-1.
The Construction Industry
Per Cent Distribution of Inputs for Typical Construction Projects
1959-1962

Type of Projects	Materials	Labor	Depreciation Allowance on Equipment	Over-head & Profit	Cost of Typical Project
Single family houses	47.0%	25.7%	1.0%	26.3%	$ 14,000
Public housing	45.0	39.2	2.5	13.3	1,300,000
College housing	52.6	32.7	1.6	13.1	1,000,000
Industrial buildings	53.0	25.0	5.0	17.0	5,000,000
Commercial buildings	54.0	28.0	3.0	15.0	33,000,000
Schools	54.0	29.8	1.4	14.8	730,000
Hospitals	53.3	32.6	1.2	12.9	1,500,000
Public buildings	51.3	32.0	1.9	14.8	3,000,000
Highways	50.6	25.2	12.0	12.2	4,000,000
Sewer systems	47.0	27.0	10.0	16.0	2,000,000
Civil works	35.0	26.2	20.0	18.8	1,200,000
Dams	32.0	22.0	24.0	22.0	30,000,000

Source: U.S. Bureau of Labor Statistics:

Labor and Material Requirements for School Construction, Bulletin No. 1299, 1961.

Labor Requirements for Federal Office Building Construction, Bulletin No. 1331, 1962.

Labor Requirements for Hospital Construction, Bulletin No. 1340, 1962.

Labor and Material Requirements for Highway Construction, Bulletin No. 1362, 1963.

Labor and Material Requirements for Civil Works Construction by the Corps of Engineers, Bulletin No. 1390, 1964.

Labor and Material Requirements for Public Housing Construction, Bulletin No. 1402, 1964.

Labor and Material Requirements for Private One-Family House Construction, Bulletin No. 1404, 1964.

Labor and Material Requirements for College Housing Construction, Bulletin No. 1441, 1965.

Labor and Material Requirements for Sewer Works Construction, Bulletin No. 1490, 1966.

most of their large projects. Electrical and plumbing work are most often subcontracted out because the specialty contractor is able to do the work more efficiently than the general contractor and has access to the necessary skilled labor.

Contractual and subcontractual relationships are often very complex in the construction industry. The general contractor subcontracts the parts of the job that he does not desire to undertake or is technically unable to perform himself. Subcontracting, therefore, acts to lower the general contractor's capital requirements and allows him more flexibility. Without subcontracting, small contractors would be seriously limited in the type and size of projects they could pursue and would be dominated more often by larger firms which could afford required capital outlays. In some instances, each part of a project may be independently assigned to a different contractor. In other instances, the subcontractor may also subcontract certain aspects of a project. The 1967 *Census of Construction Industries* showed that 44 percent of gross construction receipts were received by subcontractors. Census data also show that general contractors subcontracted 63 percent of their total receipts and that specialty contractors subcontracted 15 percent.[185]

Table A-2 shows the employment patterns between general, highway-heavy, and specialty contractors. During the 1967-1972 period, the proportion of construction workers employed by general building contractors fell slightly from 31 percent in 1967 to 29.2 percent in 1972. During the same period, special trades employment rose from 47.9 percent of all construction employment to 49.5 percent, while highway-heavy construction employment rose slightly from 21.1 to 21.3 percent. This trend suggests that the construction industry may be becoming more specialized. It may also suggest that some elements of the nonresidential building sector have achieved some gains in productivity during recent years.[186]

WORK BY CONTRACT

The great majority of all construction work is performed under the provisions of some type of contract. In many instances the contractor has come to regard himself as a sort

[185] Cited in Mills, *op. cit.*, pp. 9, 10.

[186] *Ibid.*, p. 9.

TABLE A-2.
The Construction Industry
Number of Construction Workers on Contract Construction Payrolls
By Type of Contractor
(In thousands)

Period	All Contract Construction	General Building Construction		All Heavy Construction		All Special Trade Construction	
		Number	Percent	Number	Percent	Number	Percent
1967	2,708	840.5	31.0	570.0	21.1	1,297.6	47.9
1968	2,768	847.5	30.6	583.0	21.1	1,337.6	48.3
1969	2,896	898.7	31.0	600.3	20.7	1,397.1	48.3
1970	2,820	847.8	30.1	607.2	21.5	1,365.2	48.4
1971	2,832	833.2	29.4	606.6	21.4	1,391.8	49.2
1972	2,908	849.9	29.2	620.1	21.3	1,437.8	49.5
1973	3,011	880.1	29.2	636.5	21.2	1,494.1	49.6

Source: *Construction Review*, February/March 1974, p. 56.

Note: Adjusted to March 1971 benchmarks.

of middleman between the customer and the workers. The nature of many construction contracts affords the contractor the opportunity to attempt to shift the burden of risks from himself to the customer.

During World War II and shortly thereafter, many construction contracts began being written on a cost-plus basis. This type of contract affords the contractor the opportunity to pass on added costs directly to the customer. Some other contract types also contain clauses allowing the contractor to pass on unexpected cost overruns to the customer.[187]

INSTABILITY FACTORS

Bidding

Bidding for construction work has often been seen as a stimulus to competition in the industry. Most firms bid on a relatively large number of projects to ensure that they will be able to secure enough work to stay in business. If the number of projects bid on can be roughly equated with the level of competition, then it is generally agreed that competition varies inversely with the business cycle.[188] When the business cycle is near its peak, the competition is usually less intense because firms tend to bid on fewer jobs than when the cycle is on the down-turn. During a boom, firms usually have adequate amounts of work to remain solvent and, in fact, may be unable to undertake any additional projects. In contrast, during an economic slowdown, the level of competition usually becomes much more intense because each firm must bid on a greater number of projects if it is to secure enough work to remain solvent. During such periods, large firms have a tendency to bid in areas usually dominated by smaller firms. On the other hand, during a boom it is usually impossible for smaller firms to reciprocate by bidding on large projects because such projects are beyond the capabilities of most small firms.[189]

In some cases, however, the existence of bidding can reduce, rather than enhance, the level of competition. One reason is the widespread use of "prequalification of bidders." This practice rates each contractor through a complete analysis of his assets, experience, credit rating, and past performance on other

[187] Derber, *loc. cit.*

[188] Cassimatis, *op. cit.*, pp. 39, 40.

[189] *Ibid.*, p. 40.

projects. Consequently, as the scope of a project increases in size and complexity, new or small construction firms find it more difficult to qualify to enter bids. New firms face an additional barrier to entry because they are often unable to underbid the more experienced, established firms.

Economic Instability

Wide fluctuations exist in the total number of job opportunities available from month to month and from year to year. This variability fosters economic instability, another characteristic of the industry.[190] Table A-3 shows how the month-to-month employment patterns changed for several areas of the construction industry during the years 1968 through 1973. As logically expected, construction employment is higher during the warmer months of the year, and usually peaks during July and August. The seasonal employment variations reflect the fact that much construction work is done outdoors, and therefore, weather is a significant factor. Seasonal variations also reflect the traditional patterns of bid letting and other institutional practices that act to inhibit winter work, such as penalty pay provisions that cover employees who fail to receive a minimum number of hours of work each week. Such provisions encourage contractors to suspend work for longer periods than would otherwise be necessary.[191]

In addition to seasonal fluctuations in the number of employees, the average weekly hours of employment also vary considerably. Table A-4 gives the average weekly hours of employment per worker for the same categories as Table A-3. Employment appears to fluctuate most in the heavy construction sector and least in the special trades sector. In the case of highway construction, monthly employment more than doubled each year between January and July or August. In 1973, highway construction employment rose 132.8 percent between January and August.[192]

---

[190] Derber, *op. cit.*, p. 669.

[191] U.S., Department of Labor, *Seasonality and Manpower in Construction*, Bureau of Labor Statistics, Bulletin No. 1642 (Washington, D.C.: U.S. Government Printing Office, 1970), p. 4.

[192] U.S., Department of Commerce, *Construction Review* 20, No. 2 (February/March, 1974) : 56.

TABLE A-3.
The Construction Industry
1968-1973 Average Monthly Employment Variations, by Type of Contractor
(In thousands)

Month	All Contract Construction	General Building Contractors	All Heavy Construction	All Special Trade Contractors
January	2,478	764.0	437.9	1,276.5
February	2,478	762.8	444.1	1,271.1
March	2,574	786.7	479.0	1,308.6
April	2,742	822.4	557.4	1,362.6
May	2,864	840.8	634.8	1,388.5
June	3,035	893.0	696.8	1,444.7
July	3,109	921.0	717.9	1,469.8
August	3,159	936.7	727.2	1,495.3
September	3,114	917.5	714.0	1,482.6
October	3,100	918.3	700.3	1,481.6
November	3,000	898.5	644.9	1,456.2
December	2,816	852.6	553.2	1,409.7

Source: *Construction Review*, February/March 1974, p. 56.

Note: Adjusted to March 1971 benchmarks.

TABLE A-4.
The Construction Industry
1968-1973 Average Variations in Weekly Hours of Employment
By Type of Contractor

Month	All Contract Construction	General Building Contractors	All Heavy Construction	All Special Trade Contractors
January	35.6	34.8	38.0	35.4
February	36.0	35.4	38.6	35.4
March	36.8	36.1	39.8	36.2
April	37.2	36.1	40.4	36.5
May	37.5	36.4	40.7	36.8
June	38.2	36.6	42.3	37.1
July	38.4	36.8	42.8	37.1
August	38.6	37.0	43.1	37.3
September	37.8	36.3	41.9	36.9
October	38.1	36.7	41.8	37.2
November	36.6	35.6	39.4	36.0
December	36.7	35.8	39.1	36.4

Source: *Construction Review*, February/March 1974, p. 60.

Note: Adjusted to March 1971 benchmarks.

The instability problem is compounded by the short duration of most construction projects.[193] The widespread use of subcontracting means that the practitioners of many crafts are employed only during certain (often brief) phases of a project. The uncertainties of bidding usually create difficulties for contractors in planning their work to ensure steady employment. As a result of these employment fluctuations, only a small number of employees are considered permanently associated with a particular contractor. Nonunionized firms apparently feel the effects of this situation more often. Nonunion firms do not have access to the hiring hall and therefore tend to retain employees over slack periods in preference to rehiring new ones.

Not only is the construction industry beset with seasonal instability, but it also suffers from cyclical instability in which general market downturns and tight credit conditions have a magnified effect on it.[194] During such periods, businesses have little incentive to construct new facilities, and individual persons are typically less able to buy new houses, thereby causing a serious decline in construction demand. During the economic slowdown of 1970, the total number of construction firms declined by 3 percent, and the following year, construction employment fell by almost 2 percent. Neither employment nor number of firms surpassed the 1969 level until 1972.[195] In 1974, under continued conditions of tight money, economic stagnation, and inflation, construction demand fell precipitately. Construction unemployment in some specific markets in the summer of 1974 was reported to exceed 30 percent of the available workforce.

HIGH WAGES. As an offset to the unsteady working conditions, construction wages are generally higher than those in other industries. Table A-5 compares the weekly wages of several industries to show that construction wage rates are considerably higher than the manufacturing industries' and even higher than mining wage rates. Over the 1950-1973 period, contract construction wages rose over 245 percent, a considerably greater increase than any of the other industries listed in Table A-5. This means that, for the most part, the gap between construction and other industry wages is widening. During the

---

[193] Derber, *loc. cit.*

[194] *Ibid.*

[195] Calculated from data in Tables A-7 and A-8.

last five years, only the transportation and public utility industry has managed to narrow the gap significantly. In 1973, contract construction wages averaged 66.8 percent more than the over-all average of all industries. Table A-6 shows average construction weekly earnings and hourly wages paid by several types of contractors. Note that the special trades workers earn the highest wages. The heavy construction workers earn lower hourly wages than general building workers, but receive a higher weekly wage because they work longer hours.

Employer-Employee Relationships

Because there is a continuous fluctuation in employment, there is usually very little employer-employee attachment in the industry, particularly in the unionized sectors. Many workers drift from job to job and employer to employer. When a contractor needs a large work force with diverse skills to build a large and complex project, workers may be drawn from a wide area surrounding the work site, especially if the site is a remote one. Such instances may be the first and last time that a particular employee will work for a particular contractor. Large contractors who secure projects throughout the country have often never previously worked in the area where they are beginning a new project. Once there, they usually try to hire as many local people as possible, finish the project, and then leave, perhaps never to return to the area to perform another job there.

Some workers do, however, become permanently attached to a particular contractor. Many contractors keep a nucleus of key employees on the payroll throughout the year. Such a crew usually consists of supervisory personnel and workers who have unusual skills or who have demonstrated a particular expertise that the contractor desires. These employees can be used to work on various projects during the "slow" season when few workers are needed. When the amount of work begins to increase rapidly during the warmer months of the year, or when a large project comes along, these same exployees can provide an excellent base from which the contractor can quickly and effectively develop a larger work force.

In the unionized sector, the workers are attached to unions, which act as referral agencies, rather than to the employer. Nonunion contractors are more likely to have a more permanent

TABLE A-5.
The Construction Industry
Comparison of Wage Differentials of Various Industries With the Construction Industry
1950-1973

Year	Contract Construction (Weekly Earnings)	Private [a]		Mining		Manufacturing	
		Total	Percent Change	Total	Percent Change	Total	Percent Change
1950	69.68	53.13	31.2	67.16	3.8	58.32	19.5
1955	90.90	67.72	34.2	89.54	1.5	75.70	20.1
1960	113.04	80.67	40.1	105.44	7.2	89.72	26.0
1965	138.38	95.06	45.6	123.52	12.0	107.53	28.7
1970	195.98	119.46	64.1	164.40	19.2	133.73	46.5
1973	240.68	144.32	66.8	199.28	20.8	165.65	45.3
Average [b]	132.36	89.13	48.5	117.98	12.2	100.04	32.3
Net Change 1950-1973 Percent	245.4	171.6		196.7		184.0	

TABLE A-5 (Continued)

Year	Transportation and Public Utilities		Wholesale and Retail Trade		Finance, Insurance, Real Estate		Services	
	Total	Percent Change	Total	Percent Change	Total	Percent Change	Total	Percent Change
1950	—	—	44.55	56.4	50.52	37.9	—	—
1955	—	—	55.16	64.8	63.92	42.2	—	—
1960	—	—	66.01	71.2	75.14	50.4	—	—
1965	125.14	10.6	76.53	80.8	88.91	55.6	73.60	88.0
1970	155.93	25.7	95.66	104.9	113.34	72.9	96.66	102.8
1973	204.62	17.6	111.04	116.8	133.93	79.7	114.58	110.1
Average [b]	150.67 [c]	18.9	71.77	84.4	83.80	57.9	89.84 [c]	99.4
Net Change 1950-1973 Percent	72.9 [d]		149.2		165.1		64.1 [d]	

Source: *Employment and Earnings*, March 1974, p. 83.

[a] Data relate to production workers in mining and manufacturing; to construction workers in contract construction; and to nonsupervisory workers in wholesale and retail trade; finance, insurance, and real estate; transportation and public utilities; and services.

[b] Average calculated from yearly data from 1950-1973.

[c] The weekly contruction wage from 1964-1973 averaged $179.12.

[d] Net change, 1964-1973: wages rose 82.25 percent from 1964-1973.

TABLE A-6.
The Construction Industry
Average Weekly and Hourly Earnings in the Contractor Construction Industry
By Type of Contractor
1967-1973

Period	All Contract Construction	General Building Contractors	All Heavy Construction	All Special Trade Contractors
	Average Weekly Earnings			
1967	154.95	145.64	154.13	161.25
1968	164.93	153.79	167.68	170.09
1969	181.54	169.82	185.64	187.59
1970	195.98	184.40	196.39	202.94
1971	212.24	197.64	209.92	221.68
1972	224.22	209.07	217.88	235.95
1973	240.68	222.84	229.54	255.83
	Average Hourly Earnings			
1967	4.11	3.99	3.75	4.37
1968	4.41	4.26	4.07	4.66
1969	4.79	4.64	4.42	5.07
1970	5.24	5.08	4.79	5.56
1971	5.69	5.49	5.12	6.09
1972	6.06	5.84	5.42	6.50
1973	6.47	6.19	5.71	6.99

Source: *Construction Review*, February/March 1974, pp. 58, 59.
Note: Adjusted to March 1971 benchmarks.

relationship with their employees. This permanent relationship fosters employment stability and is the primary feature by which the nonunion ("open-shop") contractor attracts workers. In order to be able to provide full-time employment, the open-shop contractor usually requires his employees to work in several different crafts or trades. This multiple assignment of jobs gives the open-shop contractor added flexibility and increased productivity over his union counterpart.[196]

CONSTRUCTION FIRM CHARACTERISTICS

As stated previously, the majority of construction firms tend to be small and to operate primarily in their home states. The "local" nature of the industry means that the firms are geographically distributed in a manner similar to that of the demographic dispersion.[197] Generally, as the size of the firm increases, so does its area of operation. The smallest firms usually operate locally, the medium-sized firms operate on a state or regional basis, and the largest firms operate on a national basis, many of them with multinational operations.[198] In 1973, almost 14 percent of the receipts of the fifteen largest construction firms were derived from foreign contracts.[199]

Table A-7 shows the distribution of construction firms in terms of employment from 1947 to 1972. Almost 70 percent of all construction firms employed 7 people or less in 1972. This proportion has fallen slightly over the past 25 years. The proportion of firms employing 3 or fewer persons grew during the 1950s and early 1960s, but appears to be on the decline now. The proportion of firms employing between 4 and 7 workers fell through the mid-1960s, but is now increasing. The medium-sized firms (8-99 employees) appear to be increasing in proportion, although the largest firms (250 employees or more) have fallen slightly in terms of employment.

Table A-8 shows the distribution of employment in terms of firm size. More workers are employed by the medium-sized

---

[196] In a forthcoming Industrial Research Unit study of the open-shop sector, these points will be substantially amplified.

[197] G. Alexandersson, *The Industrial Structure of American Cities* (Stockholm: Almquist and Wicksell, 1956), p. 60. Cited in Cassimatis, *op. cit.*, p. 26.

[198] Cassimatis, *loc. cit.*

[199] Calculated from data in "The ENR 400," *Engineering News Record, loc. cit.*

TABLE A-7.
The Construction Industry
Comparison of Contract Construction Firms
By Size of Employment, 1947-1971

Year	Number of Businesses Reporting (In Thousands)	Classes of Firms, by Number of Employees (In Percent)							
		1-3	4-7	8-19	20-49	50-99	100-249	250-499	500+
1947	181	51.5	23.8	15.8	6.0	1.8	1.0 (100-499)		0.09
1951	248	53.1	23.6	14.6	5.8	1.8	0.9	0.2	0.08
1953	263	55.6	22.4	13.6	5.5	1.8	0.8	0.2	0.07
1956	295	56.2	20.9	14.6	5.7	1.8	0.7	0.1	0.04
1959	302	57.0	20.3	14.6	5.6	1.7	0.7	0.1	0.04
1962	296	57.9	20.0	14.0	5.6	1.6	0.7	0.1	0.04
1964	313	56.6	20.2	14.6	5.9	1.7	0.7	0.1	0.04
1966	323	54.0	20.8	15.6	6.4	2.0	0.9	0.2	0.06
1968	310	51.7	21.4	16.6	7.0	2.2	1.0	0.2	0.06
1969	308	51.0	21.3	16.8	7.4	2.2	1.0	0.2	0.06
1970	299	51.0	21.0	16.7	7.6	2.3	1.1	0.2	0.07
1971	296	50.4	21.4	17.2	7.5	2.2	1.0	0.2	0.07
1972	312	47.8	22.5	18.1	8.1	2.2	1.0	0.2	0.06

Source: Calculated from data contained in U.S. Census Bureau, "County Business Patterns," annual issues for years listed in the table.

Note: Percents may not add to 100.0 because of rounding.

TABLE A-8.
The Construction Industry
Distribution of Contract Construction Employees
By Size of Firm, 1968-1972

Year	Total Number of Employees	Firm Size by Number of Employees							
		1-3	4-7	8-19	20-49	50-99	100-249	250-499	500+
1968	3,115,958	8.9	11.0	19.6	20.7	14.7	13.8	6.0	5.3
1969	3,189,325	8.6	10.7	19.3	21.6	14.7	13.9	6.0	5.2
1970	3,197,382	8.2	10.1	18.6	21.6	14.5	14.5	6.4	6.1
1971	3,133,884	8.2	10.5	19.3	21.6	14.3	13.6	6.5	6.0
1972	3,398,188	7.8	10.7	19.9	22.7	14.0	13.3	—[a]	—[a]

Source: Calculated from data contained in U.S. Census Bureau's "County Business Patterns," annual issues for years listed.

[a] Figures withheld to avoid disclosure of operations of individual reporting units.

firms than by the small or very large firms. Although, as stated previously, almost 70 percent of all construction firms employed seven people or fewer in 1972, these same firms employed only 18.5 percent of all construction workers.

As might be expected from the fact that the overwhelming majority of construction firms are small, the majority of firms are sole proprietorships (78.3 percent in 1970). The structure of the industry appears, however, to be moving from partnerships and sole proprietorships to corporate firms. Data contained in Table A-9 show that the proportion of corporate firms has grown steadily over the past few years, as the proportion of proprietorships and partnerships has declined.

Although corporations are greatly outnumbered by sole proprietorships and partnerships, they perform a much larger dollar volume of work. Corporations receive over three-fourths of the industry's total receipts, although they comprise only about 16 percent of all firms (see Table A-10). These data indicate that the construction industry is becoming more concentrated. Although most of the firms are small and are either sole proprietorships or partnerships, the industry is becoming increasingly dominated by a relatively small number of firms, most of which are corporations. Most of the very large firms operate on a union basis, although two of the largest, Brown & Root, Inc., and Daniel International Corporation, are predominantly open shop.

Rate of Entry

Since most of the firms in construction are fairly small and require little initial capital investment, there has been an historical tendency for a high rate of entry into the industry. The rate of entry is considerably higher than most industries. The rate of failure, however, is so large that during the past few years the overall number of firms has changed very little. Data contained in Table A-7 show that the overall number of firms has remained fairly stable over the past five years and that there were actually fewer firms in 1972 than in 1964, thus reflecting the adverse economic conditions of the early 1970s.

LABOR FORCE CHARACTERISTICS

As previously stated, the construction industry provides employment for over 5 percent of the total labor force and ap-

TABLE A-9.
The Construction Industry
Comparison of Type of Firm Ownership in the Contract Construction Industry
1963-1970

Year	Total Number of Firms	Proportion of Corporations %	Proportion of Sole Proprietorships %	Proportion of Partnerships %
1963	848,487	11.4	81.5	7.1
1964	856,765	12.1	81.2	6.7
1965	876,392	12.9	80.4	6.7
1966	858,330	13.1	80.4	6.5
1967	855,982	14.4	79.5	6.1
1968	838,988	15.0	79.1	5.9
1969	900,832	14.2	80.2	5.6
1970	874,549	15.9	78.3	5.8

Source: U.S., Internal Revenue Service, *Statistics of Income, Business Income Tax Returns*, annual issues, 1963-1970.

TABLE A-10.
The Construction Industry
Comparison of Contract Construction Industry Receipts
By Type of Firm Ownership, 1966-1970

Year	Total Receipts (In Thousands)	Proportion Going To Corporations %	Proportion Going To Sole Proprietorships %	Proportion Going To Partnerships %
1966	90,058,788	70.0	21.3	8.7
1967	93,300,082	72.9	19.7	7.4
1968	99,072,137	72.9	19.5	7.6
1969	112,795,547	74.4	19.0	6.6
1970	116,647,196	76.3	17.2	6.5

Source: U.S., Internal Revenue Service, *Statistics of Income, Business Income Tax Returns*, annual issues 1966-1970.

proximately 15 percent of all skilled blue-collar workers. The construction industry labor force comprises over two dozen crafts and many more specialties.[200] A list of the most predominant crafts includes:

Laborers	Iron workers
Bricklayers	Plumbers
Equipment operators	Boilermakers
Electricians	Lathers
Roofers	Painters
Sheet metal workers	Operating engineers
Carpenters	Truck drivers
Cement finishers	

The number of crafts employed on a given project will be dictated by the nature of the project and by whether the contractor operates union or open shop. The pattern of craft use can vary from area to area and from sector to sector. General building contractors usually hire the basic trades (laborers, cement finishers, and carpenters), the subcontractors hiring various specialty journeymen. The widest use of the trades is by nonresidential building contractors. Heavy and highway contractors generally use only carpenters, cement finishers, laborers, truck drivers, and operating engineers. Because of varying labor requirements, each trade has a different employment opportunity in each sector of the industry.[201]

Union Role

The economic instability and the lack of job security in the construction industry has led to a significant role of the union in some locales, but a lesser role than is commonly assumed. Although estimates vary widely, one recent study concluded that only 39 percent of all construction workers are covered by any type of collective bargaining agreement.[202] Brown & Root, Inc., and Daniel International Corporation, firms which, as

[200] Mills, *op. cit.*, p. 14.

[201] *Ibid.*, pp. 14, 15.

[202] "AGC and ABC Officials Challenge Rationale Behind Nonunion Wage Rules in Construction," *Construction Labor Report* 965 (April 3, 1974): A-18.

previously mentioned, have open-shop operations, received over $5.8 billion in domestic contracts in 1973.[203]

Unions are usually more prevalent in large metropolitan areas and are almost always organized along craft lines. Some sectors of the industry are more highly organized than others. The residential construction sector is the least organized sector, with perhaps 80 percent nonunion workers.[204] Some of the special trades are probably the most fully organized areas of the industry.

Although less than 40 percent of all construction workers are covered by collective bargaining agreements, union wage rates and job classifications are the most widely used basis for Davis-Bacon Act wage determinations.

The Hiring Hall

The union hiring hall plays an important role in the employment process in the industry.

> A union hiring hall is a union-administered job-referral system whose referrals enjoy advantages over all other job applicants. . . . [W]hat is essential to all hiring halls as defined here is employer agreement or acquiescence in according job preference; it is both historically inaccurate and analytically useless to call union referral services "hiring halls" where there is no job preference.[205]

Prior to the passage of the Taft-Hartley Act in 1947, there were few cases where employers were required to utilize union facilities when seeking new workers. Control over hiring was exerted, not through the use of a hiring hall, but through the use of the closed shop, which was enforced by union stewards and business agents at the job site.

After the enactment of the Taft-Hartley Act, which outlawed the closed shop, the unions began adopting formal hiring hall arrangements. In some instances, these arrangements were, in effect, closed shops. In other instances, these were an elaborate set of rules establishing preferences in union referrals, based on the employee's years of experience, previous employment, and other demonstrated qualifications. There are presently few data

---

[203] Calculated from data in "The ENR 400," *Engineering News Record, loc. cit.*

[204] Mills, *op. cit.*, p. 17.

[205] Philip Ross, "Origin of the Hiring Hall in Construction," *Industrial Relations* 11 (October 1972): 366.

to show how these arrangements work in actual practice. As Philip Ross concludes,

> It is difficult to classify these exclusive hiring halls because the imposition of formal procedures upon a wide variety of local practices has produced situations where the formal hiring procedure exists next to a shadow system of job allocation which may or may not correspond to the written rules. . . . On the surface, all hiring halls conform to the legal requirement forbidding discrimination against nonmembers, however, any conflict between hiring hall rules and the attainment of union goals is inevitably resolved in favor of the latter.[206]

The Department of Labor recently undertook a survey of the formal hiring procedures specified in 291 contracts covering 1,000 workers. Of these 291 contracts, 45 percent required "exclusive" work referrals, meaning that the employer is required to use the union hiring hall as his only source of workers; 33 percent allowed the employer to hire workers from other sources; and the remaining had no referral provision at all. Exclusive referral agreements were found to be most common among electricians, operating engineers, and plumbers, and least common among bricklayers, carpenters, iron workers, painters, and teamsters.[207]

Exclusive hiring hall arrangements frequently allow the employer a certain degree of discretion in hiring workers. He is sometimes free to rehire workers whom he has hired in the past, to specify a need for a worker with special qualifications, and to reject unsuitable applicants. The open-shop contractor, on the other hand, hires his employees in the open market, although open-shop contractors in a few localities are beginning to develop their own employment exchanges, or hiring halls.

Apprenticeship Training [208]

Most formal training in the construction industry is done through apprenticeship programs. Apprenticeship programs us-

---

[206] *Ibid.*, pp. 378, 379.

[207] U.S., Department of Labor, Labor-Management Services Administration, *Exclusive Union Work Referral Systems in the Building Trades* (Washington, D.C.: U.S. Government Printing Office, 1970), p. 25. Cited in Foster, *op. cit.*, pp. 120, 121.

[208] Some of the discussion in this section is based on Howard G. Foster, "Apprenticeship Training in the Building Trades: A Sympathetic Assessment," *Labor Law Journal* 22, No. 1 (January 1971): 3-12.

ually combine on-the-job training with classroom instruction. Most apprenticeship programs in the building trades conform to standards set by the U. S. Bureau of Apprenticeship and Training, in which the building construction unions have a strong voice. These standards include the teaching of a series of manipulative skills according to a set schedule, in-school related instruction designed to supplement training on the job with some theoretical foundations of the trade, a progressively increasing wage schedule, supervision by qualified journeymen, periodic evaluation of the apprentice's performance, and a union-management committee to ensure that each apprentice receives the proper training.

Apprenticeship training programs involving unions are funded by a small assessment from each employer for every man-hour of labor employed, whether or not the employer uses apprentices. To be admitted to a training program, an applicant must meet certain requirements. Besides minimal age and educational requirements, the applicant must pass a job aptitude test. The applicants are then ranked and placed on a list. After the program is filled, those left over remain on the list as alternates to be called in the event that someone declines to accept placement in the program. Rarely do the number of openings exceed the number of qualified applicants, a condition resulting in a long waiting list of people unable to gain entrance into any apprenticeship training program.

Apprenticeship programs have drawn a lot of criticism in recent years. Many people feel that entrance requirements are highly discriminatory. Minorities are often unable to meet certain educational admission requirements. Some trades, such as electricians, require that applicants be able to pass certain mathematics requirements which the poorly educated cannot fulfill. Many contractors complain that the standards set by the Bureau of Apprenticeship and Training (BAT) are totally unrealistic, the apprenticeship taking three to five years to complete. These contractors feel that this is much too long a period. Often, the apprentice is required to learn a number of skills which he will never use as a journeyman. The rigid standards set down by the BAT have stifled attempts by some open-shop contractors to institute innovative training programs which would remove much of the current criticism aimed at the present programs. Non-union construction organizations have experienced great difficulty in securing Bureau of Apprenticeship and Training approval for their training programs, although the number of approvals has been increasing in the past few years. Unfortunately, to gain approval, these open-shop programs must adhere to the union pattern. Experimentation is discouraged.

THE GOVERNMENT AS A CONSTRUCTION CUSTOMER

The government is by far the largest customer of the construction industry. In fiscal year 1971, the federal government awarded $30 billion in construction contracts. They accounted for over 25 percent of all new construction that year.[209]

[209] Data in the author's possession.

Appendix B

DAVIS-BACON ACT

[Public—No. 403—74th Congress]

[S. 3303]

AN ACT

To amend the Act approved March 3, 1931, relating to the rate of wages for laborers and mechanics employed by contractors and subcontractors on public buildings.

Be it enacted by the Senate and House of Representatives of the United States of America in Congress assembled, That the Act entitled "An Act relating to the rate of wages for laborers and mechanics employed on public buildings of the United States and the District of Columbia by contractors or subcontractors, and for other purposes," approved March 3, 1931, is amended to read as follows:

"That the advertised specifications for every contract in excess of $2,000, to which the United States or the District of Columbia is a party, for construction, alteration, and/or repair, including painting and decorating, of public buildings or public works of the United States or the District of Columbia within the geographical limits of the States of the Union or the District of Columbia, and which requires or involves the employment of mechanics and/or laborers shall contain a provision stating the minimum wages to be paid various classes of laborers and mechanics which shall be based upon the wages that will be determined by the Secretary of Labor to be prevailing for the corresponding classes of laborers and mechanics employed on projects of a character similar to the contract work in the city, town, village, or other civil subdivision of the State in which the work is to be performed, or in the District of Columbia if the work is to be performed there; and every contract based upon these specifications shall contain a stipulation that the contractor or his subcontractor shall pay all mechanics and laborers employed directly upon the site of the work, unconditionally and not less often than once a week, and without subsequent deduction or rebate on any account, the full amounts accrued at time of payment, computed at wage rates not less than those stated in the advertised specifications, regardless of any contractural relationship which may be alleged to exist between the contractor or subcontractor and such laborers and mechanics, and that the scale of wages to be paid shall be posted by the contractor in a prominent and easily accessible place at the site of the work; and the further stipulation that there may be withheld from the contractor so much of accrued payments as may be considered necessary by the contracting officer to pay to laborers and mechanics employed by the contractor or any subcontractor on the work the difference between the rates of wages required by the contract to be paid laborers and mechanics on the work and the rates of wages received by such laborers and mechanics and not refunded to the contractor, subcontractors, or their agents.

"Sec. 2. Every contract within the scope of this Act shall contain the further provision that in the event it is found by the contracting officer that any laborer or mechanic employed by the contractor or any subcontractor directly on the site of the work covered by the contract has been or is being paid a rate of wages less than the rate of wages required by the contract to be paid as aforesaid, the Government may, by written notice to the contractor, terminate his right to proceed with the work or such part of the work as to which there has been a failure to pay said required wages and to prosecute the work to completion by contract or otherwise, and the contractor and his sureties shall be liable to the Government for any excess costs occasioned the Government thereby.

"Sec. 3. (a) The Comptroller General of the United States is hereby authorized and directed to pay directly to laborers and mechanics from any accrued payments withheld under the terms of the contract any wages found to be due laborers and mechanics pursuant to this Act; and the Comptroller General of the United States is further authorized and is directed to distribute

(1)

a list to all departments of the Government giving the names of persons or firms whom he has found to have disregarded their obligations to employees and subcontractors. No contract shall be awarded to the persons or firms appearing on this list or to any firm, corporation, partnership, or association in which such persons or firms have an interest until three years have elapsed from the date of publication of the list containing the names of such persons or firms.

"(b) If the accrued payments withheld under the terms of the contract, as aforesaid, are insufficient to reimburse all the laborers and mechanics with respect to whom there has been a failure to pay the wages required pursuant to this Act, such laborers and mechanics shall have the right of a action and/or of intervention against the contractor and his sureties conferred by law upon persons furnishing labor or materials, and in such proceedings it shall be no defense that such laborers and mechanics accepted or agreed to accept less than the required rate of wages or voluntarily made refunds.

"Sec. 4. This Act shall not be construed to supersede or impair any authority otherwise granted by Federal law to provide for the establishment of specific wage rates.

"Sec. 5. This Act shall take effect thirty days after its passage, but shall not affect any contract then existing or any contract that may thereafter be entered into pursuant to invitations for bids that are outstanding at the time of the passage of this Act.

"Sec. 6. In the event of a national emergency the President is authorized to suspend the provisions of this Act.

"Sec. 7. The funds appropriated and made available by the Emergency Relief Appropriation Act of 1935 (Public Resolution Numbered 11, 74th Congress), are hereby made available for the fiscal year ending June 30, 1936, to the Department of Labor for expenses of the administration of this Act."

Approved, August 30, 1935.

AMENDMENT

[Public—No. 633—76th Congress]

[Chapter 373—3d Session]

[S. 3650]

AN ACT

To require the payment of prevailing rates of wages on Federal public works in Alaska and Hawaii.

Be it enacted by the Senate and House of Representatives of the United States of America in Congress assembled, That section 1 of the Act entitled "An Act relating to the rate of wages for laborers and mechanics employed on public buildings of the United States and the District of Columbia by contractors and subcontractors, and for other purposes," approved March 3, 1931 (46 Stat. 1494), as amended, is further amended by striking out the words "States of the Union or the District of Columbia" and inserting in lieu thereof "States of the Union, the Territory of Alaska, the Territory of Hawaii, or the District of Columbia"; and by striking out the words "or other civil subdivision of the State" and inserting in lieu thereof "or other civil subdivision of the State, or the Territory of Alaska or the Territory of Hawaii".

Sec. 2. The amendments made by this Act shall take effect on the thirtieth day after the date of enactment of this Act, but shall not affect any contract in existence on such effective date or made thereafter pursuant to invitations for bids outstanding on the date of enactment of this Act.

Approved, June 15, 1940.

[40 U. S. Code, sec. 276a–7]

The fact that any contract authorized by any Act is entered into without regard to section 5 of Title 41, or upon a cost-plus-a-fixed-fee basis or otherwise without advertising for proposals, shall not be construed to render inapplicable the provisions of sections 276a to 276a–5 of this title, if such Act would otherwise be applicable to such contract. March 23, 1941, 12 noon, ch. 26, 55 Stat. 53; Aug. 21, 1941, ch. 395, 55 Stat. 658.

AMENDMENT

[Public—No. 88-349—88th Congress]

July 2, 1964

[H.R. 6041]

AN ACT

To amend the prevailing wage section of the Davis-Bacon Act, as amended; and related sections of the Federal Airport Act, as amended; and the National Housing Act, as amended.

Be it enacted by the Senate and House of Representatives of the United States of America in Congress assembled, That section 1 of the Act of March 3, 1931, as amended (46 Stat. 1494, as amended; 40 U.S.C. 276a), is hereby amended by designating the language of the present section as subsection (a) and by adding at the end thereof the following new subsection (b): Federal construction contract laborers. Fringe benefits. 49 Stat. 1011.

"(b) As used in this Act the term 'wages', 'scale of wages', 'wage rates', 'minimum wages', and 'prevailing wages' shall include— 78 STAT. 238. 78 STAT. 239.

"(1) the basic hourly rate of pay; and

"(2) the amount of—

"(A) the rate of contribution irrevocably made by a contractor or subcontractor to a trustee or to a third person pursuant to a fund, plan, or program; and Trustee contribution.

"(B) the rate of costs to the contractor or subcontractor which may be reasonably anticipated in providing benefits to laborers and mechanics pursuant to an enforcible commitment to carry out a financially responsible plan or program which was communicated in writing to the laborers and mechanics affected, Benefit costs.

for medical or hospital care, pensions on retirement or death, compensation for injuries or illness resulting from occupational activity, or insurance to provide any of the foregoing, for unemployment benefits, life insurance, disability and sickness insurance, or accident insurance, for vacation and holiday pay, for defraying costs of apprenticeship or other similar programs, or for other bona fide fringe benefits, but only where the contractor or subcontractor is not required by other Federal, State, or local law to provide any such benefits:

Provided, That the obligation of a contractor or subcontractor to make payment in accordance with the prevailing wage determinations of the Secretary of Labor, insofar as this Act and other Acts incorporating this Act by reference are concerned may be discharged by the making of payments in cash, by the making of contributions of a type referred to in paragraph (2)(A), or by the assumption of an enforcible commitment to bear the costs of a plan or program of a type referred to in paragraph (2)(B), or any combination thereof, where the aggregate of any such payments, contributions, and costs is not less than the rate of pay described in paragraph (1) plus the amount referred to in paragraph (2). Payor obligations, method of payment.

"In determining the overtime pay to which the laborer or mechanic is entitled under any Federal law, his regular or basic hourly rate of pay (or other alternative rate upon which premium rate of overtime compensation is computed) shall be deemed to be the rate computed under paragraph (1), except that where the amount of payments, contributions, or costs incurred with respect to him exceeds the prevailing wage applicable to him under this Act, such regular or basic hourly rate of pay (or such other alternative rate) shall be arrived at by deducting from the amount of payments, contributions, or costs actually incurred with respect to him, the amount of contributions or costs of the types described in paragraph (2) actually incurred with respect to him, or the amount determined under paragraph (2) but not actually paid, whichever amount is the greater." Overtime pay computation, exclusion of benefit costs.

SEC. 2. Section 15(b) of the Federal Airport Act, as amended (60 Stat. 178, as amended; 49 U.S.C. 1114(b)), is hereby amended by inserting the words "in accordance with the Davis-Bacon Act, as amended (40 U.S.C. 276a—276a-5)" after the words "Secretary of Labor,". Airport projects. 63 Stat. 480. 49 Stat. 1011.

SEC. 3. Section 212(a) of the National Housing Act, as amended (53 Stat. 208, as amended; 12 U.S.C. 1715(c)), is hereby amended by inserting the words "in accordance with the Davis-Bacon Act, as amended (40 U.S.C. 276a—276a-5)," after the words "Secretary of Labor,". Housing projects. 53 Stat. 807; 73 Stat. 667. 12 USC 1715c.

SEC. 4. The amendments made by this Act shall take effect on the ninetieth day after the date of enactment of this Act, but shall not affect any contract in existence on such effective date or made thereafter pursuant to invitations for bids outstanding on such effective date and the rate of payments specified by section 1(b)(2) of the Act of March 3, 1931, as amended by this Act, shall, during a period of two hundred and seventy days after such effective date, become effective only in those cases and reasonable classes of cases as the Secretary of Labor, acting as rapidly as practicable to make such rates of payments fully effective, shall by rule or regulation provide. Effective date. 78 STAT. 239. 78 STAT. 240.

U.S. GOVERNMENT PRINTING OFFICE: 1968 O—314-639

Appendix C

STATUTES REQUIRING PAYMENT OF WAGES AT RATES PREDETERMINED BY THE SECRETARY OF LABOR

1. The Davis-Bacon Act (secs. 1-7, 46 Stat. 1494, as amended; Public Law 74-403, 40 U.S.C. 276a-276a-7).
2. The Federal-Aid Highway Act of 1956 (sec. 108(b), 70 Stat. 378, recodified at 72 Stat. 895; 23 U.S.C. 113(a), as amended), see particularly the amendments in the Federal-Aid Highway Act of 1968 (Public Law 90-495, 62 Stat. 815).
3. National Housing Act (sec. 212 added to c. 847, 48 Stat. 1246 by sec. 14, 53 Stat. 807; 12 U.S.C. 1715c) and repeatedly amended.
4. Federal Airport Act (sec. 15, 60 Stat. 178; 49 U.S.C. 1114(b)).
5. Housing Act of 1949 (sec. 109, 63 Stat. 419, as amended; 42 U.S.C. 1459).
6. School Survey and Construction Act of 1950 (sec. 101, 72 Stat. 551, 20 U.S.C. 636(b) (1) (E), Public Law 85-620).
7. Defense Housing and Community Facilities and Services Act of 1951 (sec. 310, 65 Stat. 307, 42 U.S.C. 15921).
8. U.S. Housing Act of 1937 (sec. 16, 50 Stat. 896, as amended; 42 U.S.C. 1416).
9. Federal Civil Defense Act of 1950 (sec. 3(c), 72 Stat. 533, 50 U.S.C. App. 2281, Public Law 85-606).
10. Health Professions Educational Assistance Act of 1963 (sec. 2(a), 77 Stat. 164; 42 U.S.C. 292d(c) (4) and 42 U.S.C. 293a(c) (5), Public Law 88-129).
11. Mental Retardation Facilities Construction Act (secs. 101, 122, 135; 77 Stat. 282, 284, 288; 42 U.S.C. 295 a(a) (2) (D), 2662(5), 2675(a) (5), Public Law 88-164).
12. Community Mental Health Centers Act (sec. 205, 77 Stat. 292; 42 U.S.C. 2685(a) (5), Public Law 88-164).
13. Higher Educational Facilities Act of 1963 (sec. 403, 77 Stat. 379; 20 U.S.C. 753, Public Law 88-204).
14. Vocational Educational Act of 1963 (sec. 7, 77 Stat. 408; 20 U.S.C. 35f, Public Law 88-210).
15. Library Services and Construction Act (sec. 7(a), 78 Stat. 13; 20 U.S.C. 355c(a) (4), Public Law 88-269).
16. Urban Mass Transportation Act of 1964 (sec. 10, 78 Stat. 307; 49 U.S.C. 1609, Public Law 88-365).
17. Economic Opportunity Act of 1964 (sec. 607, 78 Stat. 532; 42 U.S.C. 2947, Public Law 88-452).
18. Hospital Survey and Construction Act, as amended by the Hospital and Medical Facilities Amendments of 1964 (sec. 605(a) (5), 78 Stat. 453; 42 U.S.C. 291e(a) (5), Public Law 88-443).
19. Housing Act of 1964 (adds sec. 516(f) to Housing Act of 1949 by sec. 503, 78 Stat. 797; 42 U.S.C. 1486(f), Public Law 88-560).
20. Commercial Fisheries Research and Development Act of 1964 (sec. 7, 78 Stat. 199; 16 U.S.C. 779e(b), Public Law 88-309).
21. Nurse Training Act of 1964 (sec. 2, 78 Stat. 909; 42 U.S.C. 296a (b) (5), Public Law 88-581).
22. Appalachian Regional Development Act of 1965 (sec. 402, 79 Stat. 21; 40 U.S.C. App. 402, Public Law 90-103).
23. Act to provide Financial Assistance for Local Educational Agencies in areas affected by Federal activities in area affected by Federal activities (64 Stat. 1100, as amended

by sec. 2, 79 Stat. 33; 20 U.S.C. 2411, Public Law 89-10).

24. Elementary and Secondary Education Act of 1965 (sec. 308, 79 Stat. 44; 20 U.S.C. 848, Public Law 89-10).

25. Cooperative Research Act of 1966 (sec. 4(c), added by sec. 403, Public Law 89-750, 79 Stat. 46; 20 U.S.C. 332a(c)).

26. Housing Act of 1961 (sec. 707, added by sec. 907, 79 Stat. 496; 42 U.S.C. 1500e-3, Public Law 89-117).

27. Housing and Urban Development Act of 1965 (sec. 707, 79 Stat. 492; 42 U.S.C. 3107, Public Law 89-117).

28. Public Works and Economic Development Act of 1965 (sec. 712, 79 Stat. 575; 42 U.S.C. 3222, Public Law 89-136).

29. National Foundation on the Arts and Humanities Act of 1965 (sec. 5(k), 79 Stat. 846; 20 U.S.C. 954(k), Public Law 89-209).

30. Federal Water Pollution Control Act as amended by sec. 4(g) of the Water Quality Act of 1965, (79 Stat. 910; 33 U.S.C. 466e(g), Public Law 89-234).

31. Heart Disease, Cancer and Stroke Amendments of 1965 (sec. 904, as added by sec. 2, 79 Stat. 928; 42 U.S.C. 299d(d)(4), Public Law 89-239).

32. National Capital Transportation Act of 1965 (sec. 3(b)(4), 79 Stat. 644; 40 U.S.C. 682(b)(4), Public Law 89-173) Note: Repealed December 9, 1969 and labor standards incorporated in sec. 1-1431 of the District of Columbia Code.

33. Vocational Rehabilitation Act (sec. 12(b), added by sec. 3, 79 Stat. 1284; 29 U.S.C. 41a(b)(4), Public Law 89-333).

34. Medical Library Assistance Act of 1965 (sec. 2, adding sec. 393 of the Public Health Service Act, 79 Stat. 1060; 42 U.S.C. 280b-3(b)(3), Public Law 89-291).

35. Solid Waste Disposal Act (sec. 207, 79 Stat. 1000; 42 U.S.C. 3256, Public Law 89-272).

36. National Technical Institute for the Deaf Act (sec. 5(b)(5), 70 Stat. 126; 20 U.S.C. 684(b)(5), Public Law 89-36).

37. Demonstration Cities and Metropolitan Development Act of 1966 (secs. 110, 311, 503, 1003, 80 Stat. 1259, 1270, 1277, 1284; 42 U.S.C. 3310; 12 U.S.C. 1715c; 42 U.S.C. 1416, Public Law 89-745).

38. Model Secondary School for the Deaf Act (sec. 4, 80 Stat. 1028, Public Law 89-695).

39. Delaware River Basin Compact (sec. 15.1, 75 Stat. 714, Public Law 87-328) (considered a statute for purposes of the plan.)

40. Alaska Purchase Centennial (sec. 2(b), 80 Stat. 8, Public Law 89-375).

41. Highway Speed Ground Transportation Study (sec. 6(b), 79 Stat. 895, 49 U.S.C. 1636(b), Public Law 89-220).

42. Allied Health Professions Personnel Training Act of 1966 (80 Stat. 1222; 42 U.S.C. 295h(b)(2)(E), Public Law 89-751).

43. Air Quality Act of 1967 (sec. 307 added by sec. 2, 81 Stat. 506; 42 U.S.C. 1857j-3), Public Law 90-148).

44. Elementary and Secondary Education Amendments of 1967 (81 Stat. 819; 20 U.S.C. 880b-6, Public Law 90-247).

45. Vocational Rehabilitation Amendments of 1967 (81 Stat. 252, 29 U.S.C. 42a(c)(3), Public Law 90-391).

46. National Visitors Center Facilities Act of 1968 (sec. 110, 82 Stat. 45; 40 U.S.C. 808, Public Law 90-264).

47. Juvenile Delinquency Prevention and Control Act of 1968 (sec. 133, 82 Stat. 469; 42 U.S.C. 3843, Public Law 90-445).

48. New Communities Act of 1968 (sec. 410 of Public Law 90-448, 82 Stat. 516; 42 U.S.C. 3909).

49. Alcoholic and Narcotic Addict Rehabilitation Amendments of 1968 (sec. 243(d) added by sec. 301, 82 Stat. 1008; 42 U.S.C. 2688h(d), Public Law 88-164).

50. Vocational Education Amendments of 1968 (sec. 106 added by sec.

101(b), 82 Stat. 1069, 20 U.S.C. 1246, Public Law 90-576).

51. Postal Reorganization Act (39 U.S.C. 410(b)(4)(c), Public Law 91-375).

52. Developmental Disabilities Services and Facilities Construction Amendments of 1970 (84 Stat. 1316, 42 U.S.C. 2675, sec. 135(a)(5), Public Law 91-517).

53. Rail Passenger Service Act of 1970 (84 Stat. 1327, 45 U.S.C. 565, sec. 405(d), Public Law 91-518).

54. Housing and Urban Development Act of 1970 (84 Stat. 1770, sec. 707(a) and (b), Public Law 91-609, 42 U.S.C. 1500c-3).

55. Airport and Airway Development Act of 1970 (84 Stat. 219, sec. 22(b), Public Law 91-258, 41 U.S.C. 1722(b)) (this Act provides for wage determination by the Secretary of Labor but does not subject the Act to Reorganization Plan No. 14).

56. Elementary and Secondary Education Amendments (84 Stat. 121, sec. 423, Public Law 91-230, 20 U.S.C. 1231 et seq.).

57. Housing Act of 1959 (73 Stat. 681, Public Law 86-372, 12 U.S.C. 1701q(c)(3), Public Law 86-372).

58. Housing Act of 1950 (64 Stat. 78, 12 U.S.C. 1749a(f).

59. Area Redevelopment Act of 1961 (75 Stat. 61, Public Law 87-27, 42 U.S.C. 2518).

60. Mental Retardation Facilities and Community Mental Health Centers Construction Act Amendments of 1965 (79 Stat. 429, Public Law 89-105, 20 U.S.C. 618(g)).

61. Veterans Nursing Home Care Act of 1964 (78 Stat. 502, Public Law 88-450, 38 U.S.C. 5035(a)(8)).

62. Education Amendments of 1972 (86 Stat. 331, Public Law 92-318).

63. Juvenile Delinquency Prevention and Control Act of 1968, amendment (86 Stat. 532, Public Law 92-381).

Source: *Federal Register*, Vol. 37, No. 194, October 5, 1972, p. 21141.

Appendix D

State Prevailing Wage Laws

TABLE D-1.
Coverage Provisions of State Prevailing Wage Laws
1973

State	Date of First Enactment	Minimum Single Job Contract Covered	Public Work Covered (A)	Appropriate "Locality" Definition (B)	Contract Types Covered (C)
Alabama	1969	$2,000	X, demolition	County	X
Alaska	1931	2,000	X	Unspecified	X
Arizona	1912	1,000	X, demolition	a	X
Arkansas	1969	75,000	X	Unspecified	Building
California	1931	Unspecified	X, demolition carpeting	County	X
Colorado	1933	5,000	Unspecified	Unspecified	X, except highway
Connecticut	1935	Unspecified	Unspecified	Unspecified	X, except highway
Delaware	1963	2,000	X	a	X
D.C.	Davis-Bacon, itself, covers D.C.				
Florida	1933	5,000	Unspecified	Unspecified	X, except highway
Georgia	none				
Hawaii	1955	2,000	X	Entire state	X
Idaho	1911	Unspecified	Unspecified	Unspecified	X
Illinois	1931	Unspecified	X, except maintenance	County	a
Indiana	1935	Unspecified	Unspecified	b	X, except highway
Iowa	none				
Kansas	1891	Unspecified	Unspecified	County	a
Kentucky	1940	500 o	X	County	X
Louisiana	1968	25,000	X	Unspecified	X
Maine	1933	10,000	X, demolition	Unspecified	X
Maryland	1945	5,000 E	X	Unspecified	a
Massachusetts	1914	Unspecified	X, demolition, resilient flooring	Town	X
Michigan	1965	Unspecified E	X, demolition	a	X
Minnesota	Allows certain political subdivisions to set residing requirements and wage scales.				
Mississippi	none				

TABLE D-1 (Continued)

State	Date of First Enactment	Minimum Single Job Contract Covered	Public Work Covered (A)	Appropriate "Locality" Definition (B)	Contract Types Covered (C)
Missouri	1951	Unspecified	X	County	b
Montana	1931	Unspecified	X	Unspecified	X
Nebraska	Requires contractors to file statement of compliance with fair labor statement.				
Nevada	1937		X	a	X
New Hampshire	1941	500,000	X	a	X
New Jersey	1913	2,000	X	Political subdivision	X
New Mexico	1937	2,000	X, demolition	Unspecified	a
New York	1897	Unspecified	Unspecified	a	X
North Carolina	none				
North Dakota	none				
Ohio	1931	2,000	X	County	X
Oklahoma	1965	Unspecified	X	County	a
Oregon	1959	Unspecified	Unspecified	c	X
Pennsylvania	1961	25,000 E	X, except maintenance	Political subdivision	X
Rhode Island	1935	1,000	X, demolition	Unspecified	b
South Carolina	none				
South Dakota	none				
Tennessee	1953	Unspecified	X, demolition	Unspecified	b
Texas	1933	Unspecified	X	a	a
Utah	1933	Unspecified	X, except maintenance	County	a
Vermont	none				
Virginia	none				
Washington	1945	Unspecified	X	c	X
West Virginia	1933	Unspecified	X	County	X
Wisconsin	1931	25,000	X	County	X, except highways
Wyoming	1967	5,000	X	Political subdivision	X

O: $25,000 exemption for public authorities; maximum $75,000 in one year.

E: Does not apply if Davis-Bacon applies.

A: Public work covered includes construction, reconstruction, alteration, maintenance and/or repair, and painting and decorating, unless specified.

B: Appropriate locality: a=city, township, village, or other civil subdivision; b=immediate locality of work; c=largest city in county where work will be performed. Others as specified.

C: Types of contracts covered are for building, highway, drainage, sewer, levee, etc., except where noted. a=most of the above but with some specific, minor exceptions; b=building and highway construction only.

TABLE D-2.
Wage Standards Provisions of State Prevailing Wage Laws

State	Workmen Covered (A)	Prevailing Wage Criteria: Use of 1 or More USDL Standards (B)	Prevailing Wage Criteria: Collectively Bargained Rates	Prevailing Wage Criteria: D-B Rates Ascertained & Considered	Prevailing Wage Criteria: No Closely Defined Criteria (C)	Fringe Benefits: Overtime, Holidays	Fringe Benefits: Health, Welfare, Pensions
Alabama	a,d,e			X		X	X
Alaska	a,d,e,f				X	X	X
Arizona	a		X			X	
Arkansas	a			X		X	
California	g			X		X	X
Colorado	a				X		
Connecticut	a				X		X
Delaware	a				01		
D.C.	Davis-Bacon, itself, applies.						
Florida	a				X		
Georgia	none						
Hawaii	a	X					
Idaho	b				X		
Illinois	a,c				X	X	X
Indiana	—D				X		
Iowa	none						
Kansas	g	X					
Kentucky	a,e	X				X	X
Louisiana	a			X		X	X
Maine	a				02		

TABLE D-2 (Continued)

State	Workmen Covered (A)	Prevailing Wage Criteria: Use of 1 or More USDL Standards (B)	Prevailing Wage Criteria: Collectively Bargained Rates	Prevailing Wage Criteria: D-B Rates Ascertained & Considered	Prevailing Wage Criteria: No Closely Defined Criteria (C)	Fringe Benefits: Overtime, Holidays	Fringe Benefits: Health, Welfare, Pensions
Maryland	a				X	X	X
Massachusetts	a,c		X				X
Michigan	a,e		X				X
Minnesota	none						
Mississippi	none						
Missouri	c,g			X		X	X
Montana	a				X		X
Nebraska	none						
Nevada	a,c [E]				03	X	X
New Hampshire	a,c				X	X	X
New Jersey	a,e		X				X
New Mexico	a				X	X	X
New York	a	X [F]				X	X
North Carolina	none						
North Dakota	none						
Ohio	a		X			X	X
Oklahoma	a			X		X	
Oregon	a	X				X	X
Pennsylvania	a				X		X
Rhode Island	a,c				X	X	X

TABLE D-2 (Continued)

State	Workmen Covered (A)	Prevailing Wage Criteria: Use of 1 or More USDL Standards (B)	Prevailing Wage Criteria: Collectively Bargained Rates	Prevailing Wage Criteria: D-B Rates Ascertained & Considered	Prevailing Wage Criteria: No Closely Defined Criteria (C)	Fringe Benefits: Overtime, Holidays	Fringe Benefits: Health, Welfare, Pensions
South Carolina	none						
South Dakota	none						
Tennessee	a				X	X	
Texas	a				X	X	
Utah	a				X	X	
Vermont	none						
Virginia	none						
Washington	a	X					X
West Virginia	a	X					
Wisconsin	a				X	X	X
Wyoming	a,c			X			

A. Workers covered: a=laborers, mechanics, and registered apprentices; b=all manual labor; c=teamsters, usually with exceptions for suppliers; d=on-site services; 3=helpers and trainees other than registered apprentices; f=surveyors; e=all persons employed by contractors or subcontractors on public works.

B. The USDL standards are: 1. The rate paid a majority of workmen of some craft or class; 2. But if no majority exists, the rate paid at least 30 percent of workmen; 3. But if no 30 percent exists, the average rate.

C. "0" indicates specific prevailing rate criteria, as follows: 01=average of wages paid a majority of employees in county employed on work of similar type. 02=annual survey. 03=hearings held for each job.

D. Rates are set for three classes of labor: skilled, semiskilled, and unskilled.

E. Excludes apprentices.

F. Uses 40 percent instead of 30 percent.

Appendix E

UNIVERSITY of PENNSYLVANIA

PHILADELPHIA 19174

The Wharton School

INDUSTRIAL RESEARCH UNIT
VANCE HALL — THIRD FLOOR
3733 SPRUCE STREET
HERBERT R. NORTHRUP, *Director*

DAVIS-BACON SURVEY QUESTIONNAIRE

This questionnaire, prepared by the Industrial Research Unit of the University of Pennsylvania, concerns the prevailing wage requirements of the Davis-Bacon Act. It is being sent to several thousand firms representing a cross-section of the construction industry. Whether you operate union or open shop, whether you are in favor of or opposed to the Act, your response is essential to the accuracy of this survey. The Associated General Contractors and the Associated Builders and Contractors are cooperating in this study.

The questionnaire is in three parts. The first asks questions about your company, the second asks about your experience with jobs covered by Davis-Bacon, and the third about your views and attitudes toward the Act. We are interested in your views even if you have never done Davis-Bacon covered work.

It should not take you more than thirty minutes to complete the survey. When completed, please staple it so the return address is on the outside, and mail. Postage is prepaid.

If you would like a statistical compilation of the finished survey, check here ____ and we shall send you one. These statistics will become part of a major study of all aspects of the Davis-Bacon Act and its administration. If you prefer to remain anonymous, you can still get a copy of the survey results by sending a separate letter.

We shall greatly appreciate it if you return your completed questionnaire within two weeks or as soon as possible.

Thank you.

SECTION ONE
YOUR FIRM

1. Firm name ____________________
2. Address ____________________
____
3. Name and phone number of person to contact ____________________

(Omit this question if anonyimity is desired)

PART ONE
BACKGROUND

4. Approximate value of business during 1973 (or last fiscal year).

$ ____________

5. Approximate number of employees on own payroll during 1973 (or last fiscal year).

____

6. Do you operate:
___ union
___ open shop (merit shop)
___ double breasted.

7. Trades employed by company: (exclusive of subcontractors)

___ bricklayers
___ carpenters
___ cement masons
___ electricians
___ ironworkers (structural)
___ laborers
___ sheet metal workers
___ plumbers / pipefitters
___ equipment operators (various)
___ truckdrivers
____________________ (others:
____________________ specify)

8. Do you normally employ apprentices?
___ yes ___ no
If so, in what trades?
____
____

9. Do you normally employ helpers?
___ yes ___ no
If so, in what trades?
____
____

10. Other than for apprentices and helpers, do you normally pay different rates within the same craft? (example: Class A carpenter, Class B carpenter.)
___ yes ___ no

11. Give approximate percentage share of work in each of the following types:

___% heavy construction
___% highway
___% industrial and institutional
___% commercial and residential highrise
___% residential (homebuilding)
___% other: please specify
____

12. Check the type of area in which you do the majority of your work:
___ urban
___ suburban
___ rural
In what state or states do you operate most?
____
____

13. In your area, for your type of construction, in the last 3-4 years has the open shop share of construction increased?
___ yes ___ no

14. In your area, for your type of construction, how would you classify the current extent of unionization for:

general contractors____________

subcontractors____________

(Examples: mostly union, about even, mostly open shop, etc.)

PART TWO
EXPERIENCE WITH THE DAVIS-BACON ACT

15. Have you ever bid on a contract covered by the Davis-Bacon Act?
___ yes ___ no

If "no," skip to question 21.

16. About how many Davis-Bacon contracts did you bid on in the last two years?
____

17. On these bids, were the wage rate determinations greatly different in either rate or benefits from your own on private work?
___ yes ___ no

If "yes," could you give us a couple of samples from your files:

	(Include fringes)	
	own rate	DB rate
carpenter		
cement mason		
laborer		
plumbers / pipe fitters		
other ________		
________		

18. Would you say the above examples are: representative___, or extreme cases___?

Type of construction they are from: (heavy, commercial, etc.).

____

Type of area (urban, rural, etc.).

____

19. Have you <u>won</u> jobs and performed under contracts covered by Davis-Bacon rates? If "yes," please fill in the following from your files or memory.

Approximate number of bids won during past two years?______________

Approximate percent of your total $ of work this represents?______________

For the most important:

	job 1	job 2
approximate date		
type of construction		
location (county and state)		
total contract ($)		
DB labor as % of total job costs		
Estimate of contract cost total had job not been ocvered by Davis-Bacon		

20. Based on your experience with Davis-Bacon jobs, how did prevailing wage rate requirements affect:

	more	same	less
your profits			
productivity of workforce			
workforce morale			
minority employment			
general recruitment			

21. Concerning future work covered by Davis-Bacon type wage requirements, would you say your firm was:

___ anxious to obtain it to the exclusion of other work.
___ interested in obtaining it.
___ indifferent to it.
___ willing to try for it if nothing else around.
___ not interested in bidding on it.

22. If you have any specific reasons for the above, we would appreciate knowing them.

____

____

____

PART THREE
VIEWS AND ATTITUDES ON DAVIS-BACON

For each of the following statements please check according to the headings indicating degree of agreement or disagreement.

SA = Strongly agree with statement.
A = Agree with statement.
? = Do not know, or have no opinion.
D = Disagree with statement
SD = Strongly disagree with statement.

	SA	A	?	D	SD
Davis-Bacon adds stability to the industry and is desirable in the event of an economic downturn.	___	___	___	___	___
Without the Davis-Bacon Act, the construction industry would probably go heavily non-union.	___	___	___	___	___
Open shop firms make more profits when they are working on Davis-Bacon jobs.	___	___	___	___	___
The Davis-Bacon Act spreads union wage rates to the non-union sector.	___	___	___	___	___
The Davis-Bacon Act spreads urban wage rates to the non-urban areas.	___	___	___	___	___
Davis-Bacon rates are usually the same as union rates.	___	___	___	___	___
All contractors should be required to report their wages periodically to a trade association or the government so rate determinations can be more accurate.	___	___	___	___	___
The <u>average</u> rate in any given area for any given type of construction should be used as the Davis-Bacon rate.	___	___	___	___	___
The Davis-Bacon Act should be repealed.	___	___	___	___	___
Any Davis-Bacon rate lower than the union rate automatically excludes the union contractor.	___	___	___	___	___

	SA	A	?	D	SD
Minority employment possibilities are improved by the Davis-Bacon Act.					
Local contractors need protection from itinerent low-wage contractors.					
When Davis-Bacon rates are in error, it is easy to have them corrected.					
Davis-Bacon should set a rate for "construction workers."					
Davis-Bacon hinders on-the-job development of craftsmen.					

	SA	A	?	D	SD
Time required to administer Davis-Bacon provisions is a major deterrent to bidding on covered work.					
My firm would be better off if the Davis-Bacon Act were repealed.					

If you have any other specific views you would like to share with us, please write them on a plain sheet of paper and insert it in the middle of this questionnaire before folding to mail. Thank you.

Appendix F

FACSIMILE OF WAGE DETERMINATION DECISION

U.S. DEPARTMENT OF LABOR

OFFICE OF THE SECRETARY

WASHINGTON

Decision of the Secretary

This case is before the Department of Labor pursuant to a request for a wage predetermination as required by law applicable to the work described.

A study has been made of wage conditions in the locality and based on information available to the Department of Labor the wage rates and fringe payments listed are hereby determined by the Secretary of Labor as prevailing for the described classes of labor in accordance with applicable law.

This wage determination decision and any modifications thereof during the period prior to the stated expiration date shall be made a part of every contract for performance of the described work as provided by applicable law and regulations of the Secretary of Labor, and the wage rates and fringe payments contained in this decision, including modifications, shall be the minimums to be paid under any such contract by contractors and subcontractors on the work.

The contracting officer shall require that any class of laborers and mechanics which is not listed in the wage determination and which is to be employed under the contract, shall be classified or reclassified conformably to the wage determination, and a report of the action taken shall be sent by the Federal agency to the Secretary of Labor. In the event the interested parties cannot agree on the proper classification or reclassification of a particular class of laborers and mechanics to be used, the question accompanied by the recommendation of the contracting officer shall be referred to the Secretary for determination.

Before using apprentices on the job the contractor shall present to the contracting officer written evidence of registration of such employees in a program of a State apprenticeship and training agency approved and recognized by the U.S. Bureau of Apprenticeship and Training. In the absence of such a State agency, the contractor shall submit evidence of approval and registration by the U.S. Bureau of Apprenticeship and Training.

The contractor shall submit to the contracting officer written evidence of the established apprentice-journeyman ratios and wage rates in the project area, which will be the basis for establishing such ratios and rates for the project under the applicable contract provisions.

APPENDIX F (Continued)

Fringe payments include medical and hospital care, compensation for injuries or illness resulting from occupational activity, unemployment benefits, life insurance, disability and sickness insurance, accident insurance (all designated as health and welfare), pensions, vacation and holiday pay, apprenticeship or other similar programs and other bona fide fringe benefits.

By direction of the Secretary of Labor,
Alfred L. Ganna, Director
Division of Wage Determinations
Workplace Standards Administration

Department, Agency, or Bureau

WASHINGTON METROPOLITAN AREA TRANSIT AUTHORITY

Location of Project (City or Other Description)

State North. Virginia

County Arlington

Description of Work:

Construction of the Metro Rapid Rail Transit System, work includes: open cut and tunneling excavation; subway station, traction station; shop and office building construction; incidental grading, demolition, utility alteration; installation of track machinery,

Decision No.

Date of Decision

Expires

Supersedes Decision No.

APPENDIX F (Continued)

	BASIC HOURLY RATES	FRINGE BENEFITS PAYMENTS				
		H & W	Pensions	Vacation	App. Tr.	Other
Asbestos workers	$8.05	.25	.15		.015	
Boilermakers-Blacksmiths	7.65	.30	.70	.20	.01	
Bricklayers	8.35	.37	.18			
Carpenters	6.94	.20	.16		.07	
Cement Masons:						
Cement masons	6.825	.185	.20		.03	
Grinding machine	7.075	.185	.20		.03	
Electricians	7.95	.35	1% +.20		.10	
Elevator Constructors:						
Elevator constructors	7.28	.17	.185	½+a+b	.005	
Elevator constructors' helpers	5.10	.17	.185	½+a+b	.005	
Elevator constructors' helpers (prob.)	3.64	.17	.185	½+a+b	.005	
Glaziers	6.78	.46	.20			
Ironworkers:						
Structural	7.15	.35	.30		.01	
Ornamental & chain link fence	7.15	.35	.30		.01	
Reinforcing	6.70	.15	.25		.02	
Lathers	7.225	.30	.30		.025	

APPENDIX F (Continued)

	BASIC HOURLY RATES	FRINGE BENEFITS PAYMENTS				
		H & W	Pensions	Vacation	App. Tr.	Other
Lead burners	$6.00	.15		c	.01	
Line Construction						
Linemen, cable splicer, equipment op.	8.31	.15	1%		¼ %	
Truck with winch, truck pole or steel handling	6.44	.15	1%		¼ %	
Groundmen (0 to 1 year)	5.02	.15	1%		¼ %	
Groundmen (1 to 2 years)	5.93	.15	1%		¼ %	
Groundmen (over 2 years)	6.18	.15	1%		¼ %	
Marble setters	6.80	.15	.25			
Marble setters' helpers	6.10					
Millwrights	7.065	.20	.16		.07	
Painters:						
Brush, paperhangers, tapers, and spray	7.05	.41	.15		.03	
Steel, structural, sandblasters, swing stage	7.38	.41	.15		.03	
Piledrivermen	7.065	.20	.16		.07	
Plasterers	6.665	.30	.25		.06	
Plumbers	7.83	.28	.05			

APPENDIX F (Continued)

	BASIC HOURLY	FRINGE BENEFITS PAYMENTS				
	RATES	H & W	Pensions	Vacation	App. Tr.	Other
Roofers:						
Composition	$5.80	.20	.20			
Slate, tile mopmen, waterproofers, sprayers, spandrel & ironite	6.30	.20	.20			
Helpers	4.50	.20	.20			
Sheet metal workers	7.50	.31	.31		.04	
Soft floor layers	6.94	.20	.16		.07	
Sprinkler fitters	8.00	.25	.40		.05	
Steamfitters, refrigeration and air condition mechanic	7.93	.23				
Stone masons	6.80	.15	.25			
Terrazzo and mosaic workers	6.85	g	.20			
Terrazzo workers' helpers	5.95	d	.20			
Tile setters	6.85	g	.20			
Tile setters' helpers	5.95	d	.20			
Truck Drivers:						
Boom trucks	4.10	.22	e	f		
Small dump, water sprinkler, grease and oil	3.85	.22	e	f		
Flat, pick-up hauling materials, small Euclids, dump over 8 wheels	3.95	.22	e	f		

APPENDIX F (Continued)

	BASIC HOURLY RATES	FRINGE BENEFITS PAYMENTS				
		H & W	Pensions	Vacation	App. Tr.	Other
Trailers, low boys, tractor pulls	$4.15	.22	e	f		
Helpers	3.70	.22	e	f		
Carryalls, large Euclids, Euclid water sprinkler, tunnel work underground	4.25	.22	e	f		
Mechanics	4.00	.22	e	f		
Concrete mixer	3.20	.12	.15	g		
Riggers and Welders-receive rate prescribed for crafts performing operation to which welding are incidental.						

PAID HOLIDAYS:

A-New Year's Day; B-Memorial Day; C-Independence Day; D-Labor Day; E-Thanksgiving Day; F-Christmas Day.

FOOTNOTES:

a. Holidays: A through F.

b. Employer contributes 4% basic hourly rate for 5 years or more of service or 2% basic hourly rate for 6 months to 5 years of service as Vacation Pay Credit.

c. Holidays: A through F, plus Washington's Birthday and Good Friday (providing employee has worked at least 45 full days during the 120 calendar days prior to the holiday, and the regular scheduled work days immediately preceding and following the holiday).

d. Employer contributes $23.70 per man per month.

e. Employer contributes $4.00 per week when employee has worked 90 days and works 3 days in any work week.

f. Holidays: A, D, E, & F (provided the employee works the day before and the day after the holiday).

g. Employer contributes $37.92 per man per month.

APPENDIX F (Continued)

	BASIC HOURLY RATES	FRINGE BENEFITS PAYMENTS				
		H & W	Pensions	Vacation	App. Tr.	Other
Laborers:						
Carloader, choker setter, concrete crewman, corrugated metal culvert pipe layer, crusher feeder, demolition laborer, including salvaging all material, loading, cleaning up, wrecking, driller helper, dumpman, flagman, fence erector and installer, including installation and erection of fence, guard rails, median rails, reference posts, guide posts and right-or-way markers, form stripper, general laborers, railroad track laborer, rip-rap man, scale man, stake jumper, structure mover, including foundation separation, preparation, scribbing, shoring, jacking and unloading of structure, water nozzleman, timber bucker and faller, truck loader	$5.19	.25	.25		.03	
Combined air and water nozzlemen, cement handler, dope pot fireman, nonmechanical, form cleaning machine, mechanical railroad equipment, includes spiker, puller, tie cleaner, tamper, pipe wrapper, power driven wheelbarrow, operators of hand derricks, towmasters, scootcretes, buggymobiles and similar equipment, tamper or rammer operator, trestle scaffold builders over one tier high, power tool operator, gas, electric or pneumatic, sandblast or gunnite tailhose man, scaffold erector, steel or wood, vibrator operator up to 4′,						

APPENDIX F (Continued)

	BASIC HOURLY RATES	FRINGE BENEFITS PAYMENTS				
		H & W	Pensions	Vacation	App. Tr.	Other
asphalt cutter, mortar men, shorer and lagger, creosote material handler, corrosive enamel or equal, paving breaker and jackhammer operators	$5.34	.25	.25		.03	
Multi-section pipe layer, non-metallic clay and concrete pipe layer, including caulker, collarman, joiner, rigger and jacker	5.39	.25	.25		.03	
Asphalt block pneumatic cutter, asphalt roller, walking, chain-saw, with attachment, concrete saw, walking, high scalers, jackhammer (using over 6′ of steel), vibrator 4′ and over, well point installers, air trac operator	5.44	.25	.25		.03	
Asphalt screeder, big drills, cut of 4½ piston or larger, down the hole drills, 3½ piston or larger, gunnite or sandblaster nozzleman, asphalt raker, asphalt tamper, form setter, demolition torch operator	5.64	.25	.25		.03	
Powderman, master form setters	5.84	.25	.25		.03	
Brick paver (asphalt block paver, asphalt block saw man, asphalt block grinder, hastings block or similar type)	5.965	.25	.25		.03	
Miners	6.415	.25	.25		.03	

APPENDIX F (Continued)

SEWER AND WATER LINES	BASIC HOURLY RATES	FRINGE BENEFITS PAYMENTS				
		H & W	Pensions	Vacation	App. Tr.	Other
Power Equipment Operators:						
Backhoes, cableways, cranes, draglines, power shovels, tunnel shovels, tunnel mucking machines, of 1 c.y. or above	$6.14	.25	.25		.01	
Backhoes, cableways, cranes, derricks, draglines, power shovels, tunnel shovels, tunnel mucking machines up to 1 c.y. and boom cats, elevating graders, hoists, paving mixers, pile driving engines, batch plant, concrete pumps	5.89	.25	.25		.01	
Trenching machines (above 8′3″)	5.69	.25	.25		.01	
Backhoes (hydraulic, under ½ c.y.)	5.77	.25	.25		.01	
Trenching machines (up to 8′3″), boilers skeleton, well drilling machines	5.59	.25	.25		.01	
Air compressors, tunnel	5.56	.25	.25		.01	
Front end loaders (high lift)	5.54	.25	.25		.01	
Concrete mixers, power wheel scoops and scrapers, motor graders, tunnel motor men	5.44	.25	.25		.01	
Mechanics	5.42	.25	.25		.01	
Bulldozers, hydraulic tampers	5.34	.25	.25		.01	
Roller	5.24	.25	.25		.01	
Air compressors, pumps welding machines, well points	5.165	.25	.25		.01	

APPENDIX F (Continued)

	BASIC HOURLY RATES	FRINGE BENEFITS PAYMENTS				
		H & W	Pensions	Vacation	App. Tr.	Other
Apprentice Engineers						
Firemen	$4.70	.25	.25		.05	
Truck crane oilers	4.55	.25	.25		.05	
Oilers	4.50	.25	.25		.05	
Truck Drivers:						
Dump trucks	2.75	.12	c			
Dump trucks over 8 wheels	2.85	.12	c			
Flat trucks	2.85	.12	c			
Trailers	2.95	.12	c			
Fuel and oil trucks	2.75	.12	c			
Euclids	3.10	.12	c			

Footnote:

c. $4.00 per week employer contribution for all employees who have worked continuously 90 days or more and have worked 3 days in any one week.

APPENDIX F (Continued)

PAVING AND INCIDENTAL GRADING	BASIC HOURLY RATES	FRINGE BENEFITS PAYMENTS				
		H & W	Pensions	Vacation	App. Tr.	Other
Cement masons	4.35	.22	.10			
Power Equipment Operators:						
Concrete spreader operator, finishing machine, roller (rough), compressor, rubber tired loader (1½ cu. yds., or less), asphalt plant mixer	4.10	.22	.10			
Loader operator tracks (2½ cu. yds. or less), burner planer, bulldozer, mechanical welder, rubber tired loader (over 1½ cu. yds.)	4.30	.22	.10			
Asphalt spreader, hydraulic backhoe (½ cu. yd., or less), asphalt plant engineer, asphalt roller op., concrete breaker (machine)	4.35	.22	.10			
Crane operator, concrete paving op.	4.50	.22	.10			
Shovel operator	4.60	.22	.10			
Gradall operator (1½ cu. yds., or less), motor grader, loader op. tracks (over 2½ cu. yds.)	5.25	.22	.10			
G-1000 Gradall operator (over 1½ cu. yds.)	5.50	.22	.10			
Power broom, oiler	4.00	.22	.10			
Sand setter	4.35	.22	.10			
Truck Drivers:						
Truck drivers (standard)	3.85	.22	.10			
Tandem	3.97	.22	.10			
Tractor trailer (capable of moving heavy equipment)	4.35	.22	.10			

Index

Racial Policies of American Industry Series

1. *The Negro in the Automobile Industry*, by Herbert R. Northrup. 1968. $2.50
2. *The Negro in the Aerospace Industry*, by Herbert R. Northrup. 1968. $2.50
3. *The Negro in the Steel Industry*, by Richard L. Rowan. 1968. $3.50
4. *The Negro in the Hotel Industry*, by Edward C. Koziara and Karen S. Koziara. 1968. $2.50
5. *The Negro in the Petroleum Industry*, by Carl B. King and Howard W. Risher, Jr. 1969. $3.50
6. *The Negro in the Rubber Tire Industry*, by Herbert R. Northrup and Alan B. Batchelder. 1969. $3.50
7. *The Negro in the Chemical Industry*, by William Howard Quay, Jr. 1969. $3.50
8. *The Negro in the Paper Industry*, by Herbert R. Northrup. 1969. $8.50
9. *The Negro in the Banking Industry*, by Armand J. Thieblot, Jr. 1970. $5.95
10. *The Negro in the Public Utility Industries*, by Bernard E. Anderson. 1970. $5.95
11. *The Negro in the Insurance Industry*, by Linda P. Fletcher. 1970. $5.95
12. *The Negro in the Meat Industry*, by Walter A. Fogel. 1970. $4.50
13. *The Negro in the Tobacco Industry*, by Herbert R. Northrup. 1970. $4.50
14. *The Negro in the Bituminous Coal Mining Industry*, by Darold T. Barnum. 1970. $4.50
15. *The Negro in the Trucking Industry*, by Richard D. Leone. 1970. $4.50
16. *The Negro in the Railroad Industry*, by Howard W. Risher, Jr. 1971. $5.95
17. *The Negro in the Shipbuilding Industry*, by Lester Rubin. 1970. $5.95
18. *The Negro in the Urban Transit Industry*, by Philip W. Jeffress. 1970. $4.50
19. *The Negro in the Lumber Industry*, by John C. Howard. 1970. $4.50
20. *The Negro in the Textile Industry*, by Richard L. Rowan. 1970. $5.95
21. *The Negro in the Drug Manufacturing Industry*, by F. Marion Fletcher. 1970. $5.95
22. *The Negro in the Department Store Industry*, by Charles R. Perry. 1971. $5.95
23. *The Negro in the Air Transport Industry*, by Herbert R. Northrup *et al.* 1971. $5.95
24. *The Negro in the Drugstore Industry*, by F. Marion Fletcher. 1971. $5.95
25. *The Negro in the Supermarket Industry*, by Gordon F. Bloom and F. Marion Fletcher. 1972. $5.95
26. *The Negro in the Farm Equipment and Construction Machinery Industry*, by Robert Ozanne. 1972. $5.95
27. *The Negro in the Electrical Manufacturing Industry*, by Theodore V. Purcell and Daniel P. Mulvey. 1971. $5.95
28. *The Negro in the Furniture Industry*, by William E. Fulmer. 1973. $5.95
29. *The Negro in the Longshore Industry*, by Lester Rubin and William S. Swift. 1974. $5.95
30. *The Negro in the Offshore Maritime Industry*, by William S. Swift. 1974. $5.95
31. *The Negro in the Apparel Industry*, by Elaine Gale Wrong. 1974. $5.95